WITHDRAWN

RESILIENCE

Also by Jessie Close

The Warping of Al

RESILIENCE

TWO SISTERS AND A STORY OF MENTAL ILLNESS

JESSIE CLOSE
WITH
PETE EARLEY

GRAND CENTRAL
PUBLISHING

NEW YORK   BOSTON

Some of the individuals in the book have asked me to respect their anonymity due to the sensitive nature of the topics discussed. Therefore, I have modified their identities and certain details about them.

Grand Central Publishing
Hachette Book Group
1290 Avenue of the Americas
New York, NY 10104

www.HachetteBookGroup.com

Printed in the United States of America

RRD-C

First Edition: January 2015
10 9 8 7 6 5 4 3 2 1

Grand Central Publishing is a division of Hachette Book Group, Inc.
The Grand Central Publishing name and logo is a trademark of Hachette Book Group, Inc.

The publisher is not responsible for websites (or their content) that are not owned by the publisher.

Library of Congress Cataloging-in-Publication Data

Close, Jessie.
    Resilience : two sisters and a story of mental illness / Jessie Close with Pete Earley. — First Edition.
        pages cm
    ISBN 978-1-4555-4882-8 (hc) — ISBN 978-1-4555-3022-9 (large print hc) — ISBN 978-1-4789-2453-1 (audio download) — ISBN 978-1-4789-2452-4 (audio book) — ISBN 978-1-4555-4881-1 (ebook) 1. Mentally ill—Family relationships. 2. Sisters. 3. Manic-depressive illness. 4. Psychoses. 5. Close, Jessie. 6. Close, Glenn, 1947– I. Earley, Pete. II. Title.
    RC455.4.F3C56 2015
    616.89—dc23
                                                                                              2014024743

I dedicate this book to my three children, Calen, Sander, and Mattie, my mother, Moo, my father, Pop, and my siblings, Tina, Glennie, Sandy, and Tambu—and, especially, to all those who live with mental illness.

She is not an ordinary or "run-of-the-mill" human being...
—from an analysis of my handwriting
when I was seventeen

CONTENTS

AUTHOR'S NOTE

This memoir is, obviously, about my life. But my life is filled with people: family people and friends people and other people. So this memoir isn't about me alone.

Some of my memories will inevitably not jibe with other people's memories, especially those of my children. We don't operate on horizontal lines, but as a family we function on wildly divergent lines, sometimes crisscrossing, sometimes running parallel, always aware of each other.

Since becoming an advocate for mental health I have realized that the face I present to the world is not always the face that reflects me; I have learned how to hide my discomfort. I have learned to push on no matter what, if I have to, and I have learned how to step back and take care of myself when I can.

RESILIENCE

PROLOGUE

"Kill yourself! Kill yourself! Kill yourself!"

I couldn't stop the voice. It was stuck in my skull like a bad song, playing over and over and over again.

"Kill yourself! Kill yourself! Kill yourself!"

Those commands were being screamed at me by the Creature. It was pure evil. It was in my head, just behind my left ear. It was terrifying. Worse, it would not stop screaming.

"Kill yourself! Kill yourself!"

The Creature was relentless, 24-7.

I had to silence it. I had to kill the Creature, and there was only one way to do that. I would have to kill myself.

I'd already thought about different ways to commit suicide. I think most people who consider it put a lot of thought into the best way to end their lives. I knew a handgun would be the quickest, but I'd also considered getting stumbling drunk and lying down in the creek that flowed near my house in the Montana foothills. If I did this during the winter, I would freeze to death. Pills and booze were another possibility. I'd imagined myself driving my truck to Meadow Lake or Hyalite Reservoir or Sureshot Lake, armed with a bottle of muscle relaxers and a fifth of vodka. I'd sit on an inflated inner tube, paddle so far away from shore that I couldn't possibly swim back, and begin gulping down pills with swigs of booze. When I began feeling them kick in, I would slide into the cold water. In that inebriated state, it would be impossible for me to climb back on to a slippery tube or even hang on to it.

I'd drown. The Creature would finally shut up.

I'd thought about each method in intimate detail, going over each scenario repeatedly, carefully refining each step. I could see myself raising a pistol to my mouth and squeezing the trigger, leaning into a shotgun and squeezing the trigger, lowering myself into the freezing stream in the winter, or floating dead in the lake. Each time I conjured one of those images, it seemed less frightening. Even comforting. Until I'd reached the point where the idea of killing myself seemed inevitable.

"*Kill yourself! Kill yourself! Kill yourself!*"

"*SHUT UP! I'm thinking about it!*" I silently screamed back.

"*Kill yourself! Kill yourself! Kill yourself!*"

When will the Creature stop?

My thirteen-year-old daughter, Mattie, had no idea the Creature was tormenting me. Mattie was a beautiful girl with curly long blond hair and a sweet face. Would she understand why I'd killed myself? I couldn't tell her about the Creature. She wouldn't understand. I also was afraid. I didn't want to risk making the Creature even angrier.

Mattie had just walked to the main house to say good-bye to her grandparents. I was waiting outside near a two-bedroom guesthouse on their property a few miles outside Big Piney, Wyoming, a town of about six hundred people. Big Piney is a ranching community, and the number of cows, horses, and dogs is much greater than the number of humans. Mom and Dad—Bill and Bettine Close—lived on a ten-acre plot, much of it sagebrush and tiny cacti growing in sandy soil. The Wyoming Range runs north to south, the Wind River Range runs east to west, and both ranges lie far away from the treeless high desert that is Big Piney. I love these wide open spaces. There is room to breathe.

Mattie and I had come to visit my parents and my two older sisters, Tina and Glenn. Tina is an artist who lives in Jackson Hole, Wyoming. Glenn is Glenn Close, the actress, who'd flown to Wyoming for a short break after doing voice work for a Disney movie. To others, Glenn is a Hollywood icon. Glamorous. Brilliant. To me, she is simply Glennie, my big sis.

As I waited for Mattie to return, the Creature began yelling so loudly in my head that I simply couldn't take it anymore.

Everyone in the Close family knew I could be moody and unpredictable. In the previous eight years, I had bought and sold twelve houses in and around Bozeman, Montana, where Mattie and I lived. My siblings thought I was irresponsible, but they didn't say it out loud. I'd never married Mattie's father, nor had he asked me. I had burned through another love affair after him, gotten married, divorced, and then had a common-law marriage with my fifth husband. I justified the husbands by saying I could count them on just one hand. But I'd also left dozens of other lovers in my wake. All of them had eventually run from me. Some afraid. Others angry. Still others with broken hearts.

Over the years my family came to expect a recurring pattern of behavior on my part; a seemingly random acquisition of new husbands, homes, and cars.

Sometimes Mattie enjoyed it when I was filled with manic energy. I remember waking her up one morning and driving to the Target store in Bozeman. "Take whatever you want," I declared. "Let's fill up the cart!" We raced up and down the aisles, grabbing clothes from racks and stuffing dolls and other toys into a shopping cart. When I was manic, I was the fun and exciting mom! I remember watching Mattie as we filled the car that day with our purchases. Her eyes were sparkling and she was smiling and I felt really wonderful. Sometimes mania felt good, but recently it had grown so intense and so demanding that I couldn't keep up with it. The racing thoughts. The intense feeling of having to do something, anything. And worst of all now, the voice.

The Creature's voice.

Even when mania felt good, it was never worth the awful depressions that followed. Mattie never smiled during those dark periods. I would curl into a fetal position on our living room couch and be unable to even stand up—to say nothing of leaving the house. Even when we ran out of food. Literally. My bills would pile up unopened. The phone would go unanswered. I just wouldn't care, couldn't care—about anything.

"Kill yourself! Kill yourself!"

I was exhausted. It wasn't the fatigue that came after a tough physical workout at the health club that I'd joined impulsively, during a frantic self-improvement moment. Nor was it the restlessness that came after a night of tossing and turning because I couldn't go to sleep. This was more of a debilitating feeling of abiding sadness. I had hit rock bottom. I had sunk into my dark place—where the Creature reigned and where I knew I'd either have to obey his command or have him taunt me forever.

My life was a mess—and it showed. As a child, I'd had an angelic face, piercing eyes, and a mischievous smile. In my late teens I'd been approached and asked to pose for a national men's magazine. My husband at the time turned them down. But that was when my mental illness was just beginning to kick in, before I turned to booze and drugs and men to quiet my mind. Now, at age fifty, my face looked tired, my eyes seemed hollow, and I couldn't remember the last time that a carefree smile had crossed my lips. I looked like the haggard, suffering woman I had become.

What had happened to me?

I didn't have a job. I was a recovering alcoholic. My heart was breaking because my older son, Calen, whom I loved dearly, had been diagnosed with a severe mental illness, schizoaffective disorder, which had led to his being hospitalized for two long years.

I felt responsible for his suffering. After all, it was partly my blood flowing through his veins, and I suspected it was my own tainted genes that had sparked his disorder. A psychiatrist had diagnosed me with bipolar disorder, but the medications he prescribed were ineffectual. That was what was behind my swinging moods. It was behind the Creature.

"Kill yourself! Kill yourself!"

My sister Glenn was still inside the guesthouse. It was only a few steps away from me, but by the time I reached its door, I felt as if I had walked miles. I turned the knob, opened it, and stepped in.

Glennie was standing inside. She looked at my face and asked, "Are you all right?"

"I can't stop thinking about killing myself," I whispered, feeling deeply ashamed.

My big sister, six years my senior, wrapped her arms around me. I felt safe, but it didn't last. The Creature became angry. The Creature began yelling louder and louder.

"Kill yourself! Kill yourself!"

I told myself: *Hang on. Hang on. Glennie will help you. She will find a way to silence the Creature. Together we will find a way to make living worthwhile again.*

PART ONE

NOT YOUR NORMAL CHILDHOOD

I learned at a very early age that being loved was synonymous with being left: that it was a painful thing to love me, and to love.

—from my private journal

CHAPTER ONE

My story begins with an Irish setter named Paddy.

I'm starting with a dog story because canines have played and continue to play an important role in my life and the lives of all us Closes. I own four dogs. My mother, Bettine Moore Close, has three; my oldest sister, Tina, has three; and my brother, Alexander, whom everyone calls Sandy, has two. Glenn starred in the movies *101 Dalmatians* and *102 Dalmatians* as Cruella De Vil, an evil socialite who wants to slaughter puppies for their spotted fur, but Glenn is a dog lover also, with two terrier mixes. My father, William Taliaferro Close, better known as Bill or Doc—or T-Pop to us—was a dog lover all his life. When he died in January of 2009 he left two dogs, which brought my mom's count up to five. By my count, that's sixteen dogs between us—without adding the ones owned by our six children.

I know why I love dogs. They love me back. They make me feel secure. I love the silly things they do, and I love it that they love me no matter what mood I'm in. Love and security are not what I always felt growing up.

But Paddy, the Irish setter—he was responsible for bringing my parents together. Their families were actually neighbors, but the children didn't meet until they were teenagers. My mother's parents, Charles Arthur and Elizabeth Hyde Moore, owned a farm in Greenwich, Connecticut. My dad's parents, Edward Bennett and Elizabeth Taliaferro Close, lived about two miles away. My parents didn't meet until they were sixteen, because after World War I the Closes moved to France, where Edward managed the American Hospital of Paris, a facility opened in

1906, when Paris had been a magnet for American intellectuals, writers, poets, and artists.

Granny Close returned with my father and his twin brother to the United States in 1938 because it seemed inevitable that Hitler was going to invade and conquer France. The fourteen-year-old twins were sent to boarding school at St. Paul's School in Concord, New Hampshire, when they returned. My mother's only sibling, Johnny, also attended St. Paul's but was an upperclassman when the Close twins arrived. The first time my dad saw my mother was when she came to visit Johnny and he spotted her in the chapel. He glanced up at the visitors' gallery, saw Mom, and knew in his heart that she was "the most beautiful girl" he'd ever seen. But he didn't dare speak to her, and she would know nothing about his feelings until much later.

Around 1940, Granddad Close also left Paris, and Grandmother Moore decided to host a party to welcome the entire Close family back to Greenwich. She called my mom, Bettine, and Johnny into the parlor and announced that she wanted them to host a party for the Close twins.

"It would be nice if you introduced them to your teenage friends," my grandmother said, "since they don't know anyone here in Greenwich."

The idea of throwing a party for two teenage boys whom no one really knew didn't excite my mom or uncle, but Grandmother Moore didn't give them much choice. Under her watchful eye, a dinner was arranged for William Taliaferro (Billy) Close and his twin, Edward Bennett Close Jr. (Teddy). My father and his twin had been born six minutes apart on June 7, 1924—Teddy first, which is why he was the twin named after their father.

Judging from family photographs, my father was exceedingly handsome. He had strong features that reflected his English and Scottish ancestry. My mother was beautiful. She was tall and slender, with dark auburn hair and a full mouth. The party had just started when Paddy, the Irish setter, came trotting across the lawn clutching a terrified bunny in its jaws. Because Paddy was a trained hunting dog, his soft mouth allowed him to carry the rabbit without puncturing its skin or breaking any bones.

As soon as my mother and father spotted Paddy, they rushed down the steps to rescue the bunny. My father suggested the two of them carry the shaking creature to a stone wall at the end of the lawn and release it on the other side, away from Paddy.

It was during that rescue mission that my parents began talking and realized that they liked each other. As soon as my dad got back from freeing the bunny, he rushed to find Teddy.

"Miss Bettine Moore is off-limits," he declared.

The twins had a pact. If either was interested in dating a girl and was the first to announce it, the other would stay clear of her.

My dad was so enthralled with my mom that he asked her to go to a movie with him after the party ended. She agreed, and it was during that movie, when others were trying to shush them, that my father told her he was going to become a doctor.

Much later in their lives, my father would write his autobiography, *A Doctor's Life: Unique Stories*, and he would explain that he'd decided to become a doctor when he was only seven years old, while touring the American Hospital. He wrote:

The head nurse, Miss Compte, took my hand and led me on a tour... She had brown eyes and a comforting smile, and her starched white apron rustled when she walked.

My stomach was tight with anticipation as we stepped out of the elevator onto the surgical floor. Two large doors swung open and tall figures wearing white hats and long white gowns emerged, smiled at us, and walked down the immaculate corridor.

I caught the whiff of ether and clean linen. Miss Compte eased the door open just enough for me to peek through. Two gowned figures leaned over a stretcher outside one of the operating rooms... Those rooms were used by some of the surgical giants of Europe... The surgical gowns, caps, and masks were like mystical robes of high priests, and the rubber gloves suggested exploring fingers capable of delicate maneuvers. But more than anything else the sound of starched linen and the faint smell of ether stimulated my imagination.

Downstairs in my father's [hospital administration] office, I told his secretary that I would be a surgeon when I grew up, and if I wasn't smart enough to be a surgeon, I'd be a hospital administrator like my father. She thought that was cute, but I was serious. I wanted desperately to be part of that mysterious world, to share in the prestige of being called "Doctor," and to wear the proud uniform of a surgeon.

Mom was impressed. She wanted to become a nurse, but she wasn't interested in living a mundane life. Mom read at least two books per week, and she wanted to work in some exotic overseas location and have adventures like those of the heroines whose stories she devoured.

Bettine and Billy met at 5:00 a.m. the next day to go horseback riding. They paid as much attention to the swarms of mosquitoes buzzing around them as they did the moviegoers who had tried to keep them from talking. They were instantly in love. My mom still mourns the fact that she lost the little wooden ring my dad gave her when they were sixteen and became secretly engaged.

When the Japanese attacked Pearl Harbor on December 7, 1941, my parents' college plans changed. Dad told his father, "I'm leaving Harvard, marrying Bettine, and joining the Army Air Corps." My mother left Jokake School, a boarding school in Tempe, Arizona, to marry Dad before he was shipped overseas.

Bill and Bettine, both eighteen, were wed February 6, 1943. The ceremony was held at Mooreland, where my mom wore a "white faille silk gown, with a marquisette yoke, and long tulle veil fastened to a Juliet cap of silk," according to the newspaper. "She carried freesia and gardenias."

When my parents married, there was no option for a woman but to take her husband's name. The same was true of my grandparents. Grandmother Moore was a Hyde before she married Charles Arthur Moore. It's the Hydes and the Moores, both on my mother's side, where I believe the seeds that would later germinate into my own and my son's mental illnesses can be found.

CHAPTER TWO

The end of the nineteenth century was America's Gilded Age of opulence, when great family fortunes were made and mansions that rivaled European castles were built. Mrs. William B. (Caroline) Astor ruled New York's high society, and with help from a confidant she compiled the so-called Four Hundred—a secret list of who mattered and who didn't in New York society. How was that number reached? It was the maximum number of guests that could fit inside Mrs. Astor's private ballroom.

My grandfather Edward Bennett Close—Eddie—was on her list.

Originally from Yorkshire, England, the Close family had helped found Greenwich in 1640. Both my grandfather and father wore signet rings bearing the family crest and motto: *Fortis et fidelis*—strong and faithful.

By the late 1800s, Greenwich had become a sanctuary for New York's wealthy. The Rockefeller brothers had built grand estates there, joining others eager to escape sweltering summers in the city. Granddad Eddie met his first wife, Marjorie, at a dance in Greenwich when he was twenty-one years old and she was only sixteen. Four days later, he secretly proposed. Because of her age, they agreed to keep their pledge secret, especially from Marjorie's father, Charles William (C. W.) Post. It's funny that both my father and his father each became secretly engaged to sixteen-year-olds, although, in my father's case, he was sixteen also.

C. W. Post changed the American morning coffee habit in 1903, when he began selling an alternative to coffee, Postum, in Battle Creek, Michigan. Marjorie was his only child. Two years after meeting

Marjorie, Granddad formally asked for her hand. C. W. tried to prevent the marriage but eventually gave in.

Eddie Close and Marjorie were wed on December 2, 1905. Marjorie would later tell biographers that her new husband didn't want children. Even so, they had two daughters—my father's half sisters, Adelaide and Eleanor—during their twelve-year marriage. My grandfather had little to do with his daughters except for a tradition that began with them and spilled over to my father and his twin: he would take them on outings, albeit infrequently, and he called those outings "beanos." A beano would be a trip to the ice cream store or a ride in a rowboat; all beanos were great fun and remembered well.

On May 9, 1914, C. W. stuck a rifle in his mouth and squeezed the trigger, killing himself at age sixty. C. W. had been worth $33 million, which he left to be equally divided between his second wife, Leila, and Marjorie.

Marjorie felt cheated, having been told that all the family's holdings in Postum Cereal Company would be hers based on a trust signed when her parents had founded the company. Granddad Eddie went to the cereal company's headquarters and spent days digging through files until he found the original trust agreement. He returned to Greenwich triumphant, and on December 8, 1915, *The New York Times* reported that C. W.'s widow had agreed to a $6 million settlement to avoid a legal fight. Marjorie received all her father's stock and property, which was valued at $27 million—$620 million in today's dollars. Women didn't run major companies at the time. A board of directors made most decisions, and Grandad became a vice president on the board.

During World War I Grandad was sent to Europe and ended up a Major on General Pershing's staff. While he was serving in Europe, Marjorie attended a party on Long Island, where she met Manhattan stockbroker E. F. Hutton. Family legend holds that Marjorie and Hutton had an affair. When Grandad returned home in 1918 he found his wife cold and distant. Marjorie divorced my grandfather and shortly thereafter married Hutton, who helped her transform Postum into the General Foods Corporation, a move that increased her fortune to the equivalent of $3.4 billion in today's dollars.

Only a few months after the divorce, my maternal grandparents, Charles Arthur and Elizabeth Hyde Moore, planned a double date with Granddad and a young piano and voice teacher from Houston, Texas, Betsey Taliaferro. Eddie and Betsey (Granny Close) agreed, and they all traveled into New York to attend an opera.

Shortly after this date, Eddie and Betsey married. They left immediately for France, where he took charge of the American Hospital of Paris.

My sister Tina once asked Granny Close if Granddad, then deceased, had gotten a large divorce settlement from Marjorie. Granny Close had taken a last puff on her cigarette and stamped it out in her silver Scotty ash tray. She then explained that Granddad had not accepted a single penny from his first wife. In fact, without even being asked, he'd voluntarily returned all the stock that he had collected during their marriage. Granny Close quoted my grandfather as saying, "A gentleman doesn't take money from a woman when they are divorcing." Too bad for us!

Granny told us that on their honeymoon, Grandad stated he didn't want any more children. She begged and he relented, but told Granny she could only have one. Certainly not to be outdone by Marjorie, Granny was able to present Eddie with twin boys: my dad, Billy, and his brother, Ted. Twins were her revenge.

I always felt that Granny was a sad woman who thought, deep down, that her husband didn't really love her. Within the family, we believed that Grandad never got over Marjorie.

As intriguing as my Close family history may be, it is my mother's side that contains the most likely genetic link to my own mental illness.

Grandmother Moore, my grandmother, was the eldest daughter of Seymour J. Hyde and Elizabeth Worrall Hyde, members of another prominent Greenwich family. The Hydes had been farmers in New Hampshire and eventually established a highly successful dry goods manufacturing business, A. G. Hyde and Sons, famous for Heatherbloom Petticoats.

In February of 1915, Seymour J. Hyde fell from his horse and cracked his skull while riding in Greenwich. He died a few hours later, leaving behind an estate worth $2 million—about $46 million in today's dollars. His namesake son, Seymour Worrall Hyde, took charge of the family business and soon found himself caught in a scandal that was reported on February 1, 1918, on page 1 of *The New York Times* under the headline:

INSANE LIEUTENANT
KIDNAPS FOUR MEN
—
Soldiers Tell of Spending a
Night of Terror in Home
of Seymour Hyde
DETAINED AT PISTOL POINT

A *Times* reporter wrote that Seymour W. Hyde (my grandmother's brother) had taken four men hostage at gunpoint in Manhattan during what appeared to be a mental meltdown. He forced two of his hostages to undress and put on purple gowns. He then had his chauffeur transport his hostages to his father's Greenwich home, where he'd proceeded to beat one man and force him to dance until he could barely stand by threatening to shoot him. He then pulled a hot poker from the fireplace and threatened to brand another helpless hostage. During this entire episode, Hyde kept claiming to be a German spy. Two of his hostages slipped away and notified the police, who were met with pistol fire when they arrived at the Hyde property. When Hyde ran out of ammunition, the police broke inside, placed him in a straitjacket, and announced that he was clearly "insane." His mother told reporters that Hyde was simply suffering from fatigue brought on by the pressures that came from running the family business.

For a short period, Hyde was institutionalized, but he eventually returned to Greenwich, where some viewed him as completely mad. He was known to have gone riding naked on horseback through the hills, which actually sounds like a lot of fun to me...

Seymour Worrall Hyde may have been mentally ill, but he was one of the few multimillionaires to withdraw all his money from the stock market shortly before the crash of 1929. He eventually established a Hyde family trust, which still pays benefits to my mother, my siblings, and me, although through my grandmother Moore.

What all this means is that my dad, William "Billy" Close, and my mother, Bettine Moore, came into their marriage with some baggage. My dad had a father—Granddad—who had not wanted children. My mom had an uncle who had been institutionalized for a severe mental illness. Now that we know about post-traumatic stress disorder (PTSD), we can also wonder if Seymour Hyde, who fought in World War I, was afflicted with that terrible syndrome.

Given their privileged upbringing, what was really surprising about my parents was how little either of them cared about social status and money. It's possible they were that way because they grew up with social status and money. Having something as your birthright and turning it down is easier than not having it at all. We can only ignore what we have. But if anything, my dad and mom made a point of teaching us kids that social rank didn't define a person. This was particularly true of my mother. She grew up in a thirty-room home with servants. Yet she never felt that she was better than they were; they were her world.

My mother remembers a time when her parents came in very late from New York City, and the cook had waited up with a hot meal. Her father told him offhandedly, "We've already eaten." Suzanna Mannagotter, who helped in the kitchen, had heard the cook swear under his breath, "They won't be singing that tune when the revolution comes!" Mom heard the servants talk about Communists and revolution and understood the disparity between them and her family. Mom told me, when I asked her about this, that years later Suza told Grandmother Moore what the chef had said and Grandmother was horrified. She found out where he lived and apologized to him in a letter.

But rather than instilling feelings of superiority in them, that disparity caused my mother and, I believe, my father to feel a special obligation to help others less fortunate than they, true altruists.

That said, none of us can escape our childhoods. And my father, in particular, would pass a ghost from his past to all of us.

CHAPTER THREE

After she was married, my mother began following my father to a series of Texas airfields while he learned how to fly C-47 troop carriers. She'd wanted an adventure, and that's what she got.

The wives of aviation cadets were not recognized by the military, which meant that Mom was not permitted on base. The first room she rented had cockroaches skittering across the floor and no windows. Outside another, two men got into a knife fight. She followed Dad, moving from one shoddy boardinghouse to the next. That was a lot for an eighteen-year-old girl raised in genteel Greenwich.

Dad was allowed to leave the base one day a week, and my mom eagerly waited to see him, but their honeymoon didn't last long. My father would arrive at her room carrying a stack of airplane magazines and flop down on their bed to read, barely saying a word. The first time this happened, my mother ran outside and cried. As time passed, my mother would realize there was another reason for his apparent coldness.

My parents would be married nearly sixty-seven years, and they clearly loved one another. Yet my father found it almost impossible to express his emotions. But he had them, and he could be terribly sentimental. Once, when he was much, much older, he returned from a local landfill with a battered, eyeless *Sesame Street* Cookie Monster—a stuffed toy—that he'd rescued because he couldn't bear the sight of it being abandoned there. He put the Cookie Monster on a shelf in his bedroom with other favorite objects. Despite these events, he found it nearly impossible to share his innermost feelings with my mother—or any of us kids. The only time we saw him cry was when he had to put down one of his beloved dogs.

Years later, when I was an adult, my mother would tell me that she suspected Dad's inability to express his emotions was rooted in his childhood. His parents had shipped him and his twin brother off to rigid English boarding schools when they were seven years old. My mother said that when my father and his brother had been left for the first time at Summerfield, a venerable British boarding school, my father had chased after the car and leaped onto its running board, crying. The chauffeur stopped and literally peeled his little fingers from the car before driving away.

I've already mentioned that my grandfather Edward Bennett Close had not wanted children, and apparently he had little to do with either of his sons, except for the occasional beano.

I think an exchange between Mom and Dad that happened in January of 2009, shortly before Dad died, is telling. Dad was feeling ill, and late one night he turned to my mother and said, "Tell me you'll never leave me."

"Bill," Mom replied in a shocked voice, "I will never leave you! By God, we've lived together as husband and wife for sixty-six years. Why would you think I would leave you now?"

Seeing an opening, Mom asked Dad if he loved her. There had been several times during their marriage when she hadn't been certain that he had. All he would have had to say was "Yes" or "Of course!" My father had looked at her through sad eyes but couldn't utter a word. It was as if he couldn't mouth the words "I love you." He could write it in letters and, later, in his autobiography, but he couldn't speak it.

In 1944, my father completed flight training. A few months later, in June, the Allies launched the Normandy invasion. A week after D-day, Dad boarded a troopship leaving New York for France, where he immediately began flying over the front lines. Dad was smack-dab in the middle of combat, ferrying troops and supplies to the western front. One of his early missions was to supply General George S. Patton Jr. and his troops during the Battle of the Bulge, when the führer made his last-ditch effort to split the Allies' ranks. After that decisive battle, Dad became one of the first Allied pilots (he was a copilot) to fly paratroopers and supplies into Warsaw, Poland.

My dad never bragged or even spoke much about his war years. When I was young, I happened upon some pictures of skeletal bodies piled on top of each other. I asked my mom about them, and she told me to put them away. They were photos that my dad had from Poland during the war. Mom said my dad would become upset if he knew I'd seen them or asked about them.

If my father had been distant before the war, when he returned in September of 1945—four months after Germany surrendered—he was even more detached. He had been gone for fifteen months, and my mom greeted him holding a baby. It was my sister Tina, who had been conceived on the night before my father had shipped off to Europe. Tina was six months old and teething.

Mom, Dad, and Tina moved onto my grandparents' farm, Mooreland, taking up residence in Stone Cottage, a building that had been the farm's slaughterhouse before being converted into a residence. They were only a short walk away from the property's main stone house, called the Big House, where Mom's parents lived. All the buildings were clapboard with foundations of local gray fieldstone dug up and dragged on skids by horses to construction sites.

Eager to pursue his dream of becoming a surgeon, Dad applied at the College of Physicians and Surgeons at Columbia University. Unfortunately, he had gotten bad grades at Harvard, so he asked my mother's father, Charles Arthur Moore, to pull some strings.

My mom's father was quite a character. In addition to being a wealthy industrialist, Charles Moore was a noted explorer who'd participated in an 1897 expedition to the Arctic with Robert Peary. He was well known in New York, and the letter that he wrote to the president of Columbia did the trick for my father despite its tone.

My son-in-law wants to become a doctor. Personally, I have no use whatsoever for the profession. However, his determination is such that I imagine he will make a good physician.

Respectfully,
Charles A. Moore

Although my parents rarely argued in front of their children, their marriage continued to be strained. One night while my father was trying to study, my sister Tina began crying.

"Why can't you keep that brat quiet?" my father yelled.

My mother slapped him. "She's not a brat!" she declared. "She's your daughter!" It was the first and only time she struck him.

Mom had put aside her dream of becoming a nurse to rear a family. On March 19, 1947, my sister Glenn was born. She was twenty-one months younger than Tina, and they eventually became inseparable.

Despite their parents' wealth, my parents were not rich. The GI Bill paid for medical school, and my dad worked at two part-time jobs to pay their expenses. This required him to spend most nights in Manhattan, where he lived in a modest apartment. At night he worked at a blood bank, and between classes he collected women's urine from a retirement home for a professor who was studying postmenopausal gonadotropins— hormones that stimulate the gonads. Dad earned five dollars for each five-gallon jug of pee that he brought back to campus. The elderly donors called him the Cider Man because they didn't feel comfortable saying "urine" when he knocked on their doors for their specimen bottles.

On June 28, 1949, my mother gave birth to a son whom they named Duncan, but he died ten days later because of a defective heart. They buried him next to my grandfather Edward Bennett Close at Christ Church in Greenwich. Duncan's death permanently cracked my mother's heart into many pieces. She never got over losing him. To this day she feels his loss. A year and a half later, on November 18, 1950, Mom gave birth to Alexander Drummond Close, my big brother.

Seven months later, in June of 1951, my father graduated from medical school and began his residency at Roosevelt Hospital in Manhattan. He was thrilled, as he wrote later in his autobiography:

> I experienced the urgent drama of a dropping blood pressure and speeding pulse as a patient's life hovered on the brink of extinction. I heard the surgeon snap orders against a background of hissing, pulsating equipment as he enlarged the wound to expose and clamp

an errant bleeder. I felt relieved as the pressure stabilized and the operation could resume... "Someday," I said to myself, "someday it will be my turn to operate." I loved the operating room... I spent many hours sitting with patients at night. I heard, in their whispers and sleepless sighs, the hollow sounds of pain and fear of the unknown void beyond. When death claimed one of them, I redoubled my efforts to learn more and work harder. Death was defeat and my aim was victory.

Dad moved into the hospital staff's living quarters, where he put a photo of my mom next to his bed, but he only came home every other weekend. Most of those times, he was so exhausted that he only had time to eat and sleep before returning to Manhattan.

Roosevelt Hospital drew patients from poor and often dangerous neighborhoods. At least twice a night, ambulances with wailing sirens would arrive with a patient in urgent need of care. My father sewed together wounds of passengers injured in a dramatic subway-car collision and patched up gunshot and knife wounds. When there wasn't an emergency, he walked the hospital floors, chatting with patients, investigating the most difficult cases.

It's a funny thing about my father: while he found it difficult to express his emotions to those closest to him, he had a warm, reassuring bedside manner. He listened closely to his patients, genuinely cared about their well-being, and had an air of confidence that made them feel safe.

I arrived in our family on July 17, 1953, while my father was still climbing the intern-resident-physician-surgeon ladder. Mine was the only birth that my dad attended. Mom later told me that Dad was funny when it came to childbirth. He had no trouble doing surgery, but he had been known to faint during childbirth and couldn't stomach seeing mothers in pain and screaming. Somehow, though, he made it through my birth without passing out.

Within hours after I was born, a nurse entered my mother's hospital room, glanced at me, shrugged, and declared: "Well, you gotta take what you get!" Nice! I was a skinny infant but am told that I had a loud voice and rarely slept.

Tina was eight, Glenn was six, and Sandy was three. A family photograph shows Tina and Glenn, wearing cotton blouses and cuffed pants, sitting on their ponies in the front yard of Stone Cottage. In another family snapshot, Tina is sitting on a wooden cart while Glenn is on all fours in front of it, wearing a harness. Years later, when she was famous, Glenn would cause everyone in our family to burst out laughing when she revealed on *The Tonight Show* that she'd wanted to be a horse until she was eight.

We had a pony at the farm named Brownie, who came from an amusement park. He was only one of our family's menagerie. By the time I turned two, my parents had bought another pony from a neighbor. They also owned three collies and four little dogs. Most had been rescued by Dad from the hospital's labs because he didn't want them used in classroom experiments.

Because his little dogs were mutts, Dad called them the Flea Pack. One weekend morning my father was taking a much-needed break. He'd borrowed a horse from my grandparents and was riding through the Greenwich countryside with the Flea Pack when they encountered a hunting party. The men were all dressed in their red-and-black riding gear and were mounted on stunning horses surrounded by carefully bred hounds.

The Flea Pack attacked, and a horrified master of the hunt called out to my father: "Sir, call off your dogs!"

Looking down at the fighting mutts, my dad said: "There's not a damn thing I can do about this!"

The fox hunters were not impressed, but my father didn't care. He much preferred riding with his scrappy mutts than being part of an exclusive hunting club.

My parents quickly outgrew Stone Cottage on the Moores' farm, so they moved to the larger Close property, which was called Hermitage Farm, on John Street. Granny Close sold the farm, except her small house, to my parents at a cut-rate price, thinking they would live there forever. I wish we had.

The memories I have of my first five years on Hermitage Farm, refreshed by family stories and snapshots, are all wonderful ones. My brother, Sandy, and I would lie on top of the stone wall that encircled the farm. The rocks were warm from the sun, and we'd use our fingers to squish the tiny red mites that crawled through the crevices. The green lawn seemed endless. A barn that smelled of the perfectly wonderful scents of hay and horses held our ponies. I loved walking to the lake below the fields, holding the hand of whatever family member was willing to take me there. Granny Close kept an aluminum canoe on the lake-shore, and I remember being taken out onto the water—we would paddle around the tiny island that jutted up in the lake, a safe nesting place for migrating geese.

The main farmhouse had steep wooden stairs that led to a screened-in porch. My memories are of the kitchen, where I sat in a high chair eating from a brightly colored divided plate; of our collie, Ben, who was shaved one summer for some forgotten reason and who hid in the bushes from embarrassment; of a little outdoor slide that made me squeal when I zipped down it; and of a pedal car tiny enough for me to drive. I had my own tricycle, which I would ride around the circular driveway, singing and yelling.

I remember once my parents gave a dinner party and I stole a cold stick of butter from the kitchen. Then I found refuge under the dining room table. From my vantage point, I saw pairs of shoes pointed toward me from under a formal white tablecloth that reached down near the floor. I was perfectly content with my butter in my makeshift tent.

I was stubborn, even as a small child, I'm told. When my mom ordered me to go upstairs to my bedroom, I glared at her and then walked up the stairs *backwards* in defiance. Me? Ha! I already was planting the seeds for being the family troublemaker.

My earliest childhood memory of my sister Glenn comes to me as a scene. We were in the upstairs room that she shared with Tina, and she was teaching me my letters. Glenn drew each letter of the alphabet on a blackboard. I remember being fascinated by the dot on the top of the letter *i*, and I kept copying that letter because I wanted to dot the *i* over and over again. There is no other letter in our alphabet that has a dot over it, except for small *j* of course. Perhaps I was already drawn to the unusual.

In the fall of 1953, my mother was asked to speak during a memorial service at the Greenwich public library for local soldiers who'd died fighting in World War II. The library was dedicating a plaque in their honor. Mom's brother, John Campbell Moore, and a cousin had died overseas. Mom had known most of the boys whose names were inscribed on the memorial because they had been her brother's classmates at the Edgewood School in Greenwich and then at St. Paul's. She told me that twelve soldiers were killed from his class. My uncle Johnny died on November 26, 1943, while riding on the British troopship *Rohna*, which had been hit by a glide bomb, a new weapon the Germans had developed. The ship had been overloaded with troops and quickly sunk in the Mediterranean Sea north of Algeria.

His death devastated my grandparents. Grandfather Moore never recovered from the shock of his only son's death. He'd been hard on Johnny because my grandfather had been a tough businessman and adventure seeker, and he had wanted his son to grow up to be like him. Instead, Johnny had been a poet and gentle soul. I was told my grandfather died five years later, haunted by regrets.

In an emotional speech at the library, my mother eulogized Johnny and his classmates. Afterward she was approached by two women who asked if they could call on her and my dad privately in their Greenwich home.

When Mom asked them why, the women said they were on a mission—a dramatic one—to radically change the world. Mom invited them over. She was completely unaware of how that chance meeting was about to change her life and all our lives forever.

CHAPTER FOUR

The two mysterious women arrived at our doorstep carrying a pamphlet entitled "What Are You Living For?"

> Only the very selfish or the very blind person is content to leave the world as it is today. Most of us would like to change the world. The trouble is, too many of us want to do it our way.

Those words had been penned by American evangelist Frank Nathan Daniel Buchman, a charismatic preacher and founder of a "world-changing through life-changing" international movement called Moral Re-Armament, or simply MRA. Buchman launched MRA in London on May 28, 1938, when the winds of war were gathering over Europe. Great Britain was arming itself, and Buchman struck a popular chord when he declared before a rousing crowd of three thousand gathered in a theater that nations not only needed to arm themselves with military weapons to defeat Germany but also needed to "re-arm morally."

Buchman's rearmament sermon was reprinted in a book entitled *Moral Rearmament: The Battle for Peace*, which sold more than a half million copies. By 1940, Buchman's message had attracted followers in the United States, and when Americans entered the war, the ranks of MRA swelled.

Harry Truman praised the organization's war efforts, and after the war ended, Buchman turned his sights on creating world peace. Flush with cash, MRA bought a hotel in Caux, Switzerland, that had housed 1,600 Jews rescued by the Kasztner train. Their lives had been spared after a ransom of gold, diamonds, and cash had been paid to Nazi death camp supervisor Adolf Eichmann.

Buchman's devotees revitalized Mountain House Hotel in Caux, Switzerland, above Montreux and the lake of Geneva. It served as the inspiration for the Hollywood animated classic, *Snow White and the Seven Dwarfs,* turning it into a showplace.

Eager to recruit followers in the United States, MRA began holding summer conferences on Mackinac Island, Michigan, where Buchman's disciples preached that world peace and moral integrity came from adhering to MRA's "Four Absolute Standards"—Absolute Honesty, Absolute Purity, Absolute Unselfishness, and Absolute Love. "Changing the world starts with seeking change in oneself," the Reverend Buchman declared.

My parents proved easy targets. Still fragile from the death of her father and infant son, Mom was also still mourning her brother Johnny's death and wanted to prevent future wars. "People are still fighting and dying in the world," she told her two MRA guests during their visit. "That's got to stop!"

My father would later confess in his autobiography that he'd been drawn to MRA because it offered him a way "to straighten out a few personal 'sins'" that he'd committed during the war and "immediately jump into a world arena."

While Dad was enjoying his residency, he wasn't looking forward to paying his dues as "a junior physician attending in the varicose-vein clinic." That drudgery seemed boring, especially when "compared to the prospect of a 'world mission' that would change people and entire nations!"

There was yet another reason why my twenty-nine-year-old parents were seduced by MRA. My father would write frankly about it later.

At that time our marriage was under considerable stress. I was preoccupied with surgery; Tine [my father's nickname for my mom] was at home taking care of four small children. My work at the hospital was exciting and sometimes dramatic; her days were routine and repetitive. She craved adult conversation; I longed for sleep. My visits home were rare and short. Tine felt that if we both faced our natures squarely, and were honest with each other, our marriage might be saved...

The first that we kids learned about MRA was when an MRA nanny moved into our house. Mom and Dad were leaving for an MRA brainwashing camp, although I'm certain the Reverend Buchman hadn't called it that.

When they returned, my father announced that he was resigning from his surgical residency six months early. Granny Close was furious with him. During the coming years, MRA nannies took care of us while Mom and Dad made MRA pilgrimages to the Philippines, Burma, Japan, India, and other parts of the world.

Four years after their introduction to MRA, my parents sold Hermitage Farm and donated most of their money to the movement. If Granny Close had been disappointed before, she was absolutely livid then.

Mom and Dad moved us to Dellwood, an estate in Mount Kisco, New York, that had been donated to MRA by Mrs. John Henry Hammond, a descendant of the wealthy Vanderbilt and Sloane families. Like any proselytizing group, MRA was targeting America's wealthy and disenchanted widows. They also targeted celebrity families and young idealists who wanted to change the world. In addition to my parents, their recruiters got Grandmother Moore to give them a sizable contribution, but Granny Close refused to have anything to do with "those people."

Because my family had made major donations, we were allowed to live in Dellwood Cottage, one of the nicest houses in the compound. My parents once again hit the road, and we saw them—mostly Mom—only when they returned periodically to look in on us. I was only five, but this is when I first began hurting myself. I would rub a spot on my left hand between the thumb and finger until it became raw, and began to bleed and scab over. Then I would pick at the scab. My parents, nannies, and siblings all noticed, but no one said anything. I think they thought it was just a passing stage, but it would become a lifelong habit that I would return to over and over again whenever I came under great stress.

My best friend at Dellwood was a girl named Betsey whose parents didn't have much money, so they lived in a tiny house far from the main building. One day while walking there to see her, I discovered a hole in one of the large stones that was part of the property-line fence. I stuck my finger in the hole, and it soon became a habit whenever I was going to or coming from Betsey's house.

Many years later Glenn and I would return to Dellwood on a trip to investigate our pasts. A land developer had purchased Dellwood and flattened the entire compound. All the beautiful buildings—the farm with its barns and sheds, the pool and playground, everything that I remembered from my past—was gone. Glenn was driving, and I asked her to stop when I saw the stone wall near where Betsey's old house had been. I leaped from our car and ran to the wall. The stone with the hole in it was still there; I realized that my memories of that place had been reduced to a hole in a stone.

It's difficult for me today to look back at my parents in 1958 without wondering: *What the hell were you thinking, joining a religious cult?*

But I stop myself, because that's unfair. My mother had lost her only brother, a baby, and her beloved father. Dad had seen unspeakable atrocities. Both were haunted by the war and wanted to make a difference. The Reverend Buchman's call to "morally re-arm the world" touched them.

You must remember that this was also before the 1970s, when non-traditional religious groups, such as the Children of God, Reverend Sun Myung Moon's Unification Church, and the Hare Krishnas began appearing on our streets. It was before 1978, when the Reverend Jim Jones committed suicide along with 909 of his religious followers in Jonestown, Guyana, prompting magazine cover stories about "brainwashing" by "religious cults."

I try to keep an open mind about others' religious beliefs, but to me MRA was a cult, plain and simple.

In 1959, our family attended a summer conference at Mackinac Island in Michigan, where MRA had a huge center. The Great Hall, where everyone gathered, was made entirely out of logs. As a five-year-old, I would stare up at the tall ceiling of logs and wonder what kept them from crashing down. An enormous dining room and conference rooms fed off the Great Hall. Everyone was given a job, even me. The children set tables, cleared dirty dishes, filled water glasses, and served coffee. I learned the proper way to set a table.

Just as we had been in Dellwood, that summer we were lodged in a lakefront house called Bonnie Doone. Sandy became an expert at skipping stones, but I had trouble making them bounce against the small waves.

Most of my memories of Mackinac Island are fond ones that bring back a smile. Sandy and I had become buddies who plotted against Glenn and Tina. All of us would walk into town and buy the fudge the "townies" made. I remember the taste of maple with walnuts, although I liked vanilla and chocolate fudge, too. There are no cars allowed on Mackinac, except for a police car and fire truck. Everyone else walked or rode in horse-drawn buggies or rented bicycles. You could ride to any beach. Picnics were all the rage among MRA families. Peanut-butter sandwiches were warmed by the sun; the grape or strawberry jelly would soak into the top piece of the white bread.

My MRA nanny, who was named Meta, got married that summer on the island. She asked me to be part of the wedding party, and I decided, during the ceremony, to try to stand on my head. My panties showed, which didn't please either my parents or the other stern-faced MRA adults.

Sandy and I roomed together in Mackinac. I felt safe going to bed, knowing my brother was there with me. I remember being scared of my dad. I'd had a nanny nearly since birth, and I don't remember Dad having much to do with me.

My best memory of that summer was when Dad gave me a new tricycle with multicolored plastic streamers flowing from its handlebars. My worst memory was also of my father.

One night my dad overheard Sandy and me talking. Someone said something about going poo-poo or pee-pee. Dad burst into our room, and when he saw that we were sitting next to each other on the same bed, he snatched Sandy up and slammed him onto the other bed. Our conversation had been completely innocent, but Dad began yelling at us for "dirty talk." Not satisfied, he grabbed our hands and dragged us into the bathroom, where he crammed a brick of soap into our little mouths, all the while haranguing us about not talking "dirty." Sandy still remembers that it was Ivory soap. I remember pieces of soap stuck to my teeth and how that tasted later. The only things that encounter taught us were to whisper and to be afraid of my dad. The next day Sandy and I were put in separate bedrooms, a wall between us; a wall of righteousness.

Sometime thereafter, a thunderstorm hit the island. Terrified, I pulled the covers over my head, but I could still hear the thunder and see the lightning through my light summer sheets. I wasn't supposed to get out of bed, but I couldn't bear being alone. I tried to remember everything Meta had told me about thunder. She claimed it was God moving his furniture—or did she say it was his angels? I'd also been told the sound was made by clouds crashing into each other, but that seemed unlikely. No one had ever told me what caused lightning.

Storms on Mackinac Island can be especially intense, and when another bolt of lightning and a thunderclap burst outside my window, I dug myself deeper and deeper into the mattress, trying to disappear. I reached one arm out from under the covers and raised my hand above my head until I could feel the wall. Making a fist, I struck the wall three times hard, waited, then hit it again.

Sandy was in the room next to mine. Was he awake? Was he as scared as I was? Was that possible? My brother was brave.

After what seemed like forever, I heard a tap back, so I hit the wall again, and he responded. I tapped again.

Knowing Sandy was next door made me feel less afraid, but I still wished that he was in the bed next to mine. I felt totally alone.

Finally, I fell asleep.

VIGNETTE NUMBER ONE
by Glenn Close

It's strange how memory can distill something down to a single image and yet somehow that single image retains its power to invoke all the other senses. I realize now that my memory of my little sister, Jessie, when she was a child is a collection of images around which other sensations move in and out of my consciousness. Maybe that's because, compared to most other families, our family has a shocking lack of pictures, especially throughout Jessie's childhood and beyond. For the most part, at a certain point the pictures just stop. Hers is the only baby-picture book that remains painfully incomplete. Of course, Jessie was the fourth child, and our mother's days were full of tending to three other kids, a herd of various pets, and a husband who came home from interning at Roosevelt Hospital in New York City only on weekends, if then. I treasure any pictures of us that were taken as we were growing up because they shine a light onto memories full of shadows. Without their validity and light—solid evidence surrounded by a solid frame—all is vague and mutable. So I will attempt to reconstruct a few memories of Jessie from images in my mind's eye that I have carried with me all these years.

Jessie must have been about eighteen months old—a pale baby with patches of wispy blond hair and big blue eyes. I notice the blue veins in her temples. Mom is trying to feed her. For some reason this image is set in a tiny back room of Stone Cottage, our family's first home. The walls of the room are painted a dark green, as it is our father's study when he is home. There are shelves stocked with strange-looking medical instruments, including clamps and long, skinny metal tweezers. Could that be true? I don't remember a desk. Had that room been turned into Jessie's room?

Jess was always an extremely picky eater. Mom would spend hours trying every baby-seducing trick she could think of in an effort to get her to open her mouth. There is a little rhyme she would use in an attempt to throw Jessie off guard:

Knock, knock! (Mom gently knocks on Jessie's forehead)
 Peep in! (Mom pushes up Jessie's eyebrow)
 Lift the latch! (Mom gently pinches the end of Jessie's nose)
 Walk in! (Jessie's cue to open her mouth)
 Chin-choppa! Chin-choppa! Chin-choppa! (Mom moves Jessie's chin up and down as if she were chewing)

Every now and then, the enthusiastic coaxing and funny faces would make Jessie laugh, and Mom had to be quick on the draw to get in a spoonful. Sometimes nothing worked, and Mom, exhausted, would have to declare a truce, defeated by the stubborn little person in the high chair. When she got older, Jessie went through a plain-spaghetti phase; later, red licorice seemed to be her sole sustenance. She was always a skinny little thing. She still isn't that thrilled by food and has never had the desire to cook. When she does, it is usually with less than felicitous results.

Our lives changed after we moved from Stone Cottage to Hermitage Farm, on John Street in Greenwich. Our parents bought the farm from Granny Close after Granddad Close died. Granny herself moved into a tiny cottage next door, over a high stone wall. Our parents were getting more and more involved with Moral Re-Armament, so they weren't around a lot. Meanwhile, Granny was determined that we get a religious education. Most Sundays we would straggle behind her up the blue-stone path into the local Episcopal church, dreading Reverend Bailey's boring sermons. The church was called St. Barnabas, so we called our Sunday travail the Barnabas and Bailey Circus. There are no images of our mother and father in that scene. Without them it was as if the center of our universe had fallen away and we were solitary planets with no gravitational pull to keep us from spinning away into separate orbits.

We eventually moved into a house on an estate called Dellwood, in northern Westchester. Dellwood had been donated to MRA by one of Vanderbilt's granddaughters and was used as an MRA center. In my memory Jessie is often nowhere to be seen. What was it about those sad days that my mind refuses to retain? Tina was twelve. I was ten. Sandy was eight, and Jessie was almost five. We weren't abused. We always had clean clothes and good food and a solid roof over our heads.

I have always felt very solicitous of Jessie. She touched and amused me. She was funny and deeply original and had a wonderfully expressive face. I loved her quirky outlook on life. I used to tease her, knowing that her reactions would be dramatic and funny. Looking back, it seems horribly cruel, but at the time it was just big-sister razzing. Once, we were washing dishes after dinner in the kitchen at Dellwood. There was a window behind the sink. Night had turned the window black. Jessie was drying dishes at my side, my happy helper. Suddenly I stiffened and stared into the darkness outside, widening my eyes and pretending to hyperventilate. Jessie froze. I moaned and then built up to a shout: "Oh, no…oh, no…oh, *no-o-o!*" Jessie started screaming and stamping her little feet, looking like she was running in place, whipped into hysteria in a split second.

Another time, I put a sheet over my head and slowly peered around the door into Jessie's bathroom, where her nanny, Meta, was giving her a bath. Jessie was standing up in about three inches of water as the tub filled up. When she saw the ghostly sheet, she started screaming and stomping her feet. Water splashed all over the walls, not to mention all over Meta. I got yelled at, and Jessie eventually calmed down enough for a bedtime story. Needless to say, she was too young to think it was funny.

My most powerful image from that time in our lives: we are in the upstairs hall at Dellwood. I think it is daytime, but there is not much light in the hall. I am about eleven years old, so Jess must have been about five. She is standing in front of me in a summer dress. She has two long, blond, skinny braids that reach to below her waist. She is not looking at me, and yet even though I can't see into her eyes I can tell that she is upset. With her right thumb and forefinger, she is violently rubbing the soft skin between her left thumb and forefinger. She has worried it for so long that it is red and crusty. Sometimes it bleeds. I can feel her distress. I pull her hands apart to try to make her stop. She pauses for a moment, looks up at me, and then starts rubbing again. I don't understand why she keeps doing something that must cause her pain.

In my mind the scene has no conclusion. It is simply the two of us wordlessly facing each other in a somber hallway. I am intently focused on what my little sister is doing, not understanding *why* she is doing it and not being able to stop her. I know that outside there was a garden and a lawn gently sloping down to a shaded, grassy path leading into shimmering hay fields. Maybe our collie, Ben Nevis, was trotting up from those fields at that very minute. Downstairs and out the front door of the house, across the driveway and up a set of stone steps, were a swimming pool and a set of swings. I'm not sure if there was a sandbox, but there was cool sand under the swings. Through the open, shaded windows in the bedrooms that opened into the hallway, we would have been able to hear the metallic, sawing sounds of cicadas in the high heat of the summer day. But all I see in my memory is a silently distraught little girl, my sister, standing alone in front of me, mutely intent on making herself bleed.

CHAPTER FIVE

When I turned seven, our family left the United States and moved to the renovated hotel now called Mountain House in Caux, Switzerland, which MRA had converted into its international headquarters and training center. A photograph of my sisters, brother, and me shows Tina as a slim teenager, a freckle-faced Glenn smiling, Sandy looking very much like a disgruntled adolescent, and me with very long braids; after almost two years in Caux, those appearances would change dramatically.

Although Mountain House has a fairy tale look to it, I found it to be a cold and formidable place. If my memory serves me correctly, I was on the seventh floor, in room 721. It was connected to room 720 by a door, and Mom or whoever was taking care of me stayed there. My siblings were scattered throughout the four-hundred-plus-room hotel. Tina held the record for switching accommodations, moving to thirty-two different rooms during our stay.

I remember the Reverend Buchman lived on the fourth floor, and everyone was told—especially children—to walk quietly and never run on that floor! There were no dogs at Caux and almost nothing fun for me to do. Tina and Sandy got into trouble a lot, although Tina was better at not getting caught. Sandy and his Nigerian friend, Azecaru, recruited me once to throw rocks down onto the little cog railway that came up the mountain from Montreux every day. When the train stopped, we ran, screaming, across the grounds into Mountain House. Thankfully, we weren't caught. MRA didn't believe in sparing the rod, although in MRA the "rod" took the form of a lecture.

In Caux, we were all told we needed to "have guidance." Adults were supposed to have guidance as soon as they woke up each morning. Those most on the ball would be expected to attend the 7:30 a.m. set up and plan for the big 11:00 a.m. meeting. It was held in a massive room that had a grand domed ceiling. Everyone who wasn't on some work shift was expected to attend, and each meeting began with a chorus singing snappy MRA songs loaded with message. For a child, it was all incredibly boring. And uncomfortable. It was difficult to sit still for that long when you were small. We had to wear dresses; as a result my bare thighs would stick to the metal folding chair and my underpants would bunch up. I would put my head back as far as it would go onto the back of the chair and pretend to be sliding down the slope of the domed ceiling high above me. I would create a whole world up there, above our heads. I have kept my habit of looking up at ceilings and imagining how a room would flow if it were upside down.

We were told to call the Reverend Buchman Uncle Frank: his second in command, Peter Howard, was Uncle Peter. I was convinced, at seven years old, that Uncle Frank was God and Uncle Peter was Jesus.

During the morning meetings, Uncle Frank would sit in an elaborate wooden armchair, always with his cane, on a raised podium covered by Persian rugs. His wire-rimmed glasses connected his huge ears to his long, pointed nose. I tried not to look, but the end of Uncle Frank's nose, besides usually having a drip poised to drop, resembled a tiny butt, and that was a "dirty thought," which we weren't supposed to have and which I certainly didn't want to have to confess. Every night after saying my bedtime prayers, the woman with me would ask if I had had any dirty thoughts that day. Once, not being able to think of any, I told her I'd been wondering what Uncle Frank looked like without any clothes on. I got into big trouble! I was told that I was bad and that I had a "dirty mind." Guilt was how we were punished, and it worked well.

Under the strict thumb of the Reverend Buchman, MRA leaders dictated what was and wasn't permissible behavior—not just for us children but for our parents, too. Any independent thinking was seriously "off the ball" and went against God's will. MRA's mantra was "When man listens, God speaks"—and, as in all cults, only the leaders had the ability to discern when God was speaking.

My father later wrote:

When I squeezed my past, including my activities as the squadron morale-and-booze officer during the war, through MRA's moral wringers, I was pronounced ready to serve...Freed from guilt and energized by self-righteousness, we sacrificed our personal ambitions and sexual drives to a noble cause...We committed our lives to God, to MRA, and to living by the Four Absolute Standards.

My parents' decision to dedicate their lives to the Four Absolute Standards meant that we had to follow them, too. Adults who were "freed from guilt" put guilt into their children as a matter of course and as a method of control.

What I remember most about living in Caux is being isolated and lonely. I hardly saw my siblings. I missed Hermitage Farm and would have preferred living in Dellwood. At least my siblings and I would have been together.

With my parents gone, the job of rearing me fell mostly to Meta. Each morning when I got up, I took out the notebook she had given me and tried to think about God and what he wanted me to write. I had been told to focus on my sins and carefully record all of them so I could share them with everyone at the 11:00 a.m. meeting. I really couldn't think of any sins—I was only seven—so I wrote down what I had heard another girl say the day before, and then I got dressed.

Each of us had chores to do. Mine was helping clear the tables in the hotel's dining room. The plastic trays were heavy, so I had to be careful when I carried empty glasses and dirty plates so I wouldn't drop them.

After chores, I walked to our MRA school, which was about a ten-minute walk from the hotel, inside a two-story house called Chalet de la Forêt. It was where all the younger children attended school, which was taught by MRA teachers. There were about fifteen of us—sometimes more when new families arrived at the hotel. Although I didn't see Tina and Glenn, I knew both of them were day girls at St. George's School outside Lausanne. I wasn't sure where Sandy was being taught.

The teachers taught us to sing and on special occasions asked us to dress in our national costumes. Because I was from the United States, my national costume was my everyday clothes. I was jealous of the girls from Holland and Germany, who got to wear fancy dresses, while the boys wore lederhosen. Jealousy was a sin, so I didn't tell anyone, but I craved the other girls' outfits.

The Reverend Frank Buchman was in his eighties in 1960 and nearly blind, but he liked to be onstage and wanted us children to sing whenever a big group came to visit. On our birthdays, we would receive a present from him—it was always a handkerchief embroidered with either a Swiss chalet or a Swiss man blowing one of those long horns—and our teachers would help us write Uncle Frank a thank you note or send him a drawing that we'd made.

I wrote him a thank you note that was later reprinted in a book published by MRA.

> Dear Uncle Frank
>> Thank you very much for the handkerchief.
>> There are lots of cows around the chalet where we are.
>> Two roosters are always calling to each other.
>> Every day we go for long walks.
>> In the morning the cowbells and the roosters wake me up. I hope you have
> gotten more strength because that is wot I have been praying for.
>> Sincerely,
>> Jessie Close

I would wonder years later how I could spell *handkerchief* correctly but misspell *what*. I decided all of us learned the word *handkerchief* rather early, because that is what the Reverend Buchman gave everyone on their birthdays.

Glenn would later tell me that she met Uncle Frank in the "inner sanctum," where he lived. He told her that a drawing she'd given him was "priceless." As soon as she was escorted from his room, Glenn began crying. She thought "priceless" meant that her drawing wasn't worth anything.

Each of us would grow up with different memories of the two years that we spent in Caux. As an adult, Sandy would recall bitterly how he had been taken into a room with other preteen boys by an MRA leader who demanded to know how many times they masturbated every day and then pressed them for details about what excited them—all under the guise of helping them overcome their sins. Tina would remember how she was put to work in the hotel's main kitchen. It was exhausting, but she was a hard worker and would be moved up the ranks. Eventually she would become a server in the Reverend Buchman's private dining room, but she would only last a week there before she would get caught flirting with one of the boy servers and sent back to the kitchen as punishment.

One of my most terrifying memories is of the black iron fence that edged the MRA compound. An MRA leader warned me to stay inside the fence, otherwise a "Communist" would grab me. I wasn't certain what a Communist was, but I sure didn't want to risk getting kidnapped by one.

In addition to my thank you note to Uncle Frank, the commemorative book that MRA published printed black-and-white photos of other children and me. In it, my hair is cut in a functional pageboy. I am wearing a bulky coat. I look lost. The book's authors explained in the text that "this was a period when separating children from their parents in [service of] what was perceived as the greater good was sanctioned... [because the parents] were needed elsewhere, doing work which would create a safer and more peaceful world for their children."

That sounds so noble when you read it, but it wasn't really. Even today, Tina's eyes fill with tears and her voice chokes with emotion when she recalls living in Caux. She felt completely abandoned by our parents. We all did.

If any of us complained as children about being separated from our parents, MRA grown-ups would make us feel guilty by telling us that we were selfish. How dare we put our own desires above the good that our parents were doing? I remember writing a letter to Jesus thanking him for taking my parents away from me to do good in the world. Many years later, a therapist asked me if I understood how unnatural that thank you letter was. Parents were supposed to protect, not leave. I was in my thirties at the time and really hadn't thought of my parents' leaving as being unnatural.

Because I rarely saw either of my parents, I didn't know what their great mission was. I would learn about it later, largely from reading my father's autobiography. It's strange reading about your father's life during a period when you were little and wanted to be part of it but were left behind.

In April of 1960, my father was one of five men and one woman selected by MRA to become missionaries in what then was known as the Belgian Congo. My dad wasn't chosen because he was a medical doctor. They wanted him because he spoke French, which was the country's official language. My mother was not assigned by MRA to go with him.

"I guess I'll take my black bag along," my father told her when he was packing to leave Caux. "You never know; it might come in handy."

"How long do you think you'll be gone?" she asked him.

My father would later write:

I looked at her, but turned away. I wanted to take her in my arms and hug her, but that was "impure" in MRA, so I stood there, an empty, hollow feeling mixing with fear of the unknown.

My father wrote that MRA expected him and the others to be in the Belgian Congo six weeks. My mom started crying when he told her that he'd be away that long. Instead of comforting her, my father recited a passage of scripture.

Jesus said, "I tell you this: there is no one who has given up home, or wife, brothers, parents, or children, for the sake of the Kingdom of God, who will not be repaid many times over in this age, and in the age to come, have eternal life."

MRA expected sacrifices from him and my mom as well as us kids. It was all part of some grand scheme.

My father kept a journal about his mission trip. He and the others arrived in Leopoldville, the Congolese capital, a few days before the

Belgian government relinquished control of the country to its own people. The Belgians had governed the country with a brutal hand for more than seven decades, and the Congolese people hated them and other whites with good reason.

Patrice Lumumba was elected prime minister, and three days after he took control from the Belgians, his troops mutinied against the white Belgian officers who were still in charge of the military. Riots and looting broke out. Whites were warned to stay off the streets. Most Europeans began fleeing the capital. My father and the newly arrived MRA missionaries were told to get out while they could, but all the roads to the airport had been seized by Lumumba's men. Whites were being beaten and murdered in broad daylight.

The other MRA missionaries hid in an apartment, but my father grabbed his medical bag and slipped out under the cover of darkness. Hiding behind trees and ducking down alleys, he dodged the soldiers patrolling the streets and made his way to the Hôpital des Congolais, four blocks away.

The hospital was overrun by wounded patients and was in complete disarray. My father introduced himself to the Congolese emergency room doctors and immediately began helping out. All the other white surgeons had fled. My father moved from one emergency to the next, pausing only long enough to use the bathroom. When he became so exhausted that he couldn't physically continue performing surgeries, he slipped out a side door. He realized that he could not possibly rest at the hospital, so he found his way back to the MRA apartment for a sandwich and some much-needed sleep.

A few hours later, he risked his life again by returning to the hospital, only to be caught by guards outside who threatened to beat him. Fortunately, hospital nurses recognized Dad and intervened.

My father performed more than three hundred surgeries during the next eighty days, according to his logbook. He removed bullets, amputated fingers and legs, performed skin grafts, and dealt with non-war-related medical issues, such as tuberculosis of the spine, penile cancer, and sickle-cell anemia. He even repaired a soldier's harelip.

At one point during the unrest, Prime Minister Lumumba asked the Soviet Union for help in stabilizing his country. The United States responded by secretly starting a civil war in the Congo and throwing its support behind Colonel Joseph Mobutu and his troops.

The number of wounded escalated, and one afternoon my father asked to be driven to the gate outside Mobutu's fortified military encampment. When Mobutu's car emerged, my father stepped into the middle of the road, blocking Mobutu. Guards confronted him with their guns drawn. The only thing that saved him from being shot was that he was white and wearing his doctor's coat. And it helped that he was fluent in French.

Mobutu lowered his limousine window, and my father said, "I'm a surgeon at the Hôpital des Congolais, and I wondered if you could do something about the violence in town so we can catch up at the hospital."

Apparently his request stunned Mobutu, who paused, stared at him a moment, then said, "Yes, I think I can," before his driver moved on.

A few days later, my father noticed that the number of patients streaming into the hospital had begun to decrease—although he was never sure why.

Four weeks after that dangerous encounter, Mobutu sent a car to the hospital, and soldiers told my father that the colonel wanted to see him.

Many Congolese were still resentful of whites, and my father wasn't certain why he was being summoned. He was escorted into Mobutu's paramilitary camp, to a grand house where Mobutu lived. Inside, a concerned Mobutu was standing next to his great-aunt, who was gagging. Mobutu said they'd been eating fish when a bone had gotten lodged in her throat. My father could see the tip of it peeking over the crest of her tongue, so he grabbed it with a clamp and pulled it out. My father was sent back to the hospital.

A few days later, Mobutu sent his soldiers again. This time the colonel asked my father to visit and examine another aunt who was living in the capital. She was dying, and there wasn't anything my father could do to save her. He wasn't certain how Mobutu might react, but my father told him bluntly that there was no hope for the elderly woman. Mobutu said he had not dispatched my father to treat her but rather as an act of presence to comfort her and her family. That gesture was a sign of respect and also of Mobutu's power.

Thanks largely to the CIA, Mobutu toppled Lumumba, who was arrested, beaten in public, forced to eat copies of his own speeches, and then made to disappear. Rumors circulated that he had escaped from his captors. The truth was that Lumumba had been murdered.

Because my father's missionary trip had turned into a several-month-long adventure, my mother flew to Africa to visit him. One morning my parents discovered that thieves had broken into their apartment while they had been sleeping and had made off with my father's medical bag, my mother's camera, a radio, and my mother's purse. The thieves had left behind two large stones on the floor next to my parents' beds. The police said the stones were there to smash my parents' heads if they had woken up.

My father's work at the hospital angered his MRA colleagues, who had come out of hiding by then and were doing missionary work, primarily teaching Buchman's Four Absolute Standards to the Congolese. They needed my father as a translator, but he was busy operating. Senior officials in Caux ordered my father to stop going to the hospital and to start evangelizing.

That order came too late. Being at the hospital had reminded my father of his first love, and spending time around people who were not MRA devotees had helped him snap out of the MRA spell. He announced that he was not going to stop working as a doctor. His rebellion infuriated MRA leaders, but it turned out that there was nothing much they could do. By this time, Colonel Mobutu was running the country, and he asked my father to serve as his personal physician and take charge of the Congolese army medical corps, which oversaw the army's medical operations. My father realized he would have to live in Africa for as long as Mobutu wanted him there.

"I don't know anything about military medicine," he told Mobutu.

"Don't worry. If you have any difficulties, just apply article fifteen," Mobutu told him.

A Congolese officer told my father later that article 15 didn't exist, that it meant "*débrouillez-vous*—work it out any way you can."

When my father told MRA that he was not returning to Caux, my mother decided it was time for us children to leave Switzerland, too. Mom booked passage on the RMS *Queen Mary*, and in August of 1962, Tina, Glenn, Sandy, and I left for the United States, where we were going to live with Grandmother Moore. I was happy to be reunited and happier yet to be leaving MRA's headquarters, although none of us was completely free of MRA—not yet.

CHAPTER SIX

A knock on our classroom door caused everyone to look away from our elementary school desks. Hollywood actor Vic Morrow poked his head into our classroom and barked: "Private Close! You're needed at the front!"

Obediently, I sprang from my desk and marched forward while my teacher and schoolmates watched with open mouths. At eight years old, I was off to join King Company's Second Platoon—a fictional World War II squad whose exploits were chronicled each week in the popular 1960s television series *Combat!*

This was my daydream. I was obsessed with the black-and-white drama, and I often dreamed about how fantastic it would be to have Vic Morrow or Rick Jason suddenly arrive at the Parkway School in Greenwich to tell me that I was needed—on the front!

My brother, Sandy, and I were given an air-powered pistol that looked somewhat like a Browning automatic. It shot BBs, pellets, and little darts that had green and red hairs. I loved that gun. During the summer of 1963, my sisters, brother, and mother could find me patrolling the grounds of Grandmother Moore's estate, armed with the air pistol, a kitchen timer that served as my radio, and rawhide dog chews that served as my rations, along with banana-flavored Turkish Taffy. My dog, Rocket, had an army-green colored leash, and he was my constant, beloved companion. Even then, my favorite way to play was to be alone with my dog. Hunting imaginary Nazis kept me entertained.

Rocky was a Shetland sheepdog, and he would bark and run beside me across the terrain, occasionally stopping to wag his tail and wait when I fell to my knees, barely escaping machine-gun fire only I could hear.

At night, we even snuck out my bedroom window to patrol and spy on the few neighbors near my grandmother's house. Most of Grandmother Moore's estate had been sold off after Grandpa died, but I was a welcome guest on the land that used to be ours.

I wanted an army uniform more than anything that summer, and I asked Mom to take me to the toy store on Greenwich Avenue, where I'd seen uniforms in the window. After days of pestering, she finally agreed, but I made her promise that she wouldn't tell the sales clerk that the uniform was for me. We would say it was for a boy who happened to be my size.

I immediately picked one that was just what the men on *Combat!* wore, and I was excited when we made our way to the register. That's when Mom betrayed me.

"It's for my daughter," she announced.

I was so embarrassed I wanted to melt into the floor, but I had my uniform.

When I wasn't patrolling the grounds on Nazi hunts, I was in my bedroom, writing or drawing. I completed my first book—a story about a family and its pets—before my ninth birthday. I illustrated it, too, and thought myself very clever, as each character's face was shaped differently.

Mom had a wing added to Grandmother Moore's house for us, and I had my own room with strawberry-patterned wallpaper and an off-white carpet. My bedroom furniture was painted a happy light green to go with the leaves in the wallpaper, and the whole room was Rocket's and my domain. After living in a hotel and borrowed MRA houses, I was glad to have my own sanctuary. At some point after moving in, I stopped rubbing the "worry spot" between my thumb and forefinger that I had irritated in Caux—no doubt because this was the first time had I felt an actual sense of family, even though my father wasn't with us.

The two and a half years that I spent with Grandmother Moore, Mom, and my siblings are golden in my memory. To me, they represent my only childhood. It was a time when I got to ride my hand-me-down pony, Nubbins, and actually spend time with my sisters and Sandy, who had become strangers to me in Switzerland. The summer when I turned ten was special, too, because my Mom was home with us. This was a great treat. Mom, Rocky, and I would pile into her blue station wagon and drive to Nielsen's ice cream store at the top of Greenwich Avenue. I always chose raspberry sherbet and allowed Rocky to lick one side of the cone while I licked the other. Mom didn't mind. Then we'd head down to Indian Harbor and watch the water and boats.

Round Hill Road intersected Mooreland Road, and that was where I waited for the school bus in the fall, winter, and spring. Each morning, Rocky would trot along with me and stay until the bus carted me off. He would be waiting when I returned. Together we would have made a wonderful Norman Rockwell painting.

Although my parents had irritated the MRA hierarchy, my sisters were still deeply caught in it. Tina gave testimonials at MRA conferences. Glenn sang and performed in MRA's Sing-Out '65. Mercifully, Sandy and I were spared. Because my dad was not much a part of our lives, Sandy's father figure became Alec Duncan, a Scotsman who worked for my grandparents for more than thirty years on their estate. We kids called him Ikey, and he became such a substitute father figure to Sandy that my brother began referring to Ikey as his real dad.

Suza, or Suzanna Mannagotter, was my rock during those years at Round Hill. She ruled her domain: the kitchen, her little dining room, and an apartment upstairs. Suza was an elderly German woman who kept her red hair until the day she died at age one hundred. She wore cotton dresses and little white socks and always had the same kind of shoes: leather, with laces. When Suza spoke to me she would grab my wrist and wouldn't let go until she finished saying what she wanted to say. She did the same with everyone. She always had a snack ready for me when I got home from school which was a glass of very cold whole milk and a piece of pound cake or cookies. She taught me about taking care of animals. She always said, "Acht, Miss Yessie," in her German accent, "you must feed your animals before you eat. They cannot get it for themselves." She made friends with my canary and two little turtles. And of course, she loved Rocky. She knew I wasn't allowed to watch *Combat!* but turned a blind eye to me sneaking up to her apartment to watch the forbidden show. Whenever I could, I would arrange a situation that would get me sent out of the big dining room to the kitchen. I remember once, when I had a spoonful of apple sauce and was threatening to flip it; my mom told me that if I did I would be sent to the kitchen. I did. I much preferred eating in Suza's dining room and she liked the company.

I was terribly shy; I frequently felt awkward and much preferred the company of Rocket and my imaginary pals to others my age. I was younger than most of my friends by a year because the schooling at the MRA school in Switzerland had been so rigorous that I was allowed to skip third grade upon our return. I do remember talking to my siblings about our futures. Tina said she was going to be an artist, Glenn an actress, Sandy a truck driver, and I would be an author. I remember Glennie's belly laughs when I told her that if I cut myself, monkey hair would pop out. I wonder if I was already feeling uncomfortable in my skin.

Sadly, our time together proved brief. When the school year started, Tina and Glenn left for Rosemary Hall, the boarding school that our mother and her mother had attended. Sandy was sent to the Harvey School in Katonah, New York. I was left behind, and that sense of family that I had discovered was soon replaced with a new feeling. For the first time, I began to sense that I was a "problem child." I was the reason why my mom couldn't be with my father in Africa.

By 1965, it had become clear that my father had no intention of leaving the Congo—which, after the Belgians left, had changed its name from the Belgian Congo to the Democratic Republic of the Congo. President Mobutu had issued him a certificate he proudly displayed above his desk. It declared that William Close was the president's personal medical adviser and authorized him to wear the uniform of the Congolese army as a lieutenant colonel.

I knew Mom missed Dad and wanted to be with him, so I asked her one day why we all didn't move to Africa together. I would forever regret that question, as it quickly led to the end of a period in my life that I still dream about.

We didn't all move to the Congo. Only Tina and I went with Mom. Sandy remained in boarding school, and Glennie stayed in the States to continue working with MRA's Up with People, a new show being performed by MRA's youth.

I was inconsolable when it was time to say good-bye to Rocky. I had been given a beautiful Arabian gelding the summer before by our neighbor, and when I went to say good-bye to him he pressed his forehead into my chest. I breathed in his scent and felt his velvet muzzle and cried some more. And Nubbins, who was as naughty as a Shetland pony could be—I would miss him, too.

After the interminable flight to the Congo, we moved into the Hotel Memling in the nation's capital, Kinshasa—formerly Leopoldville. The hotel had been built in 1937 and named after a fifteenth-century painter, Hans Memling. From our windows we could see the Congo River drifting by, and at night the darkness was pierced by a large beam of light coming across the river from Brazzaville. It was the capital of the Communist-controlled Republic of the Congo, and the two different sides shined spotlights at each other across the river at night.

Moving from Grandmother Moore's spacious house, with its sweeping lawns, to one of Africa's biggest, most congested cities came as a complete culture shock for me. Outside our hotel, traffic snarled, impatient drivers honked, and hundreds of bicycles darted between the cars. The smell of garbage and sweat permeated the air, and I learned very quickly what it felt like to be a minority; it scared me at first.

The first night we were at the Hotel Memling we chose an outdoor café for dinner, and I heard something that sounded like it was coming from under the table. It was a man with no legs who traveled on a low wooden cart with wheels, pushing himself with his calloused hands. I screamed. Mom gave him a few coins.

Safely inside the hotel, there was absolutely nothing to do. Tina and I played endless games of double solitaire, and then I would retreat to my room and cry. I missed my animals. My heart was broken.

We finally moved into a house in the paracommando camp where President Mobutu lived. He wanted his "docteur" close by. There were still a lot of violent uprisings happening across the country, although we were isolated from them. Dad turned the house's master bedroom into a clinic where he set up a lab to test blood and feces. Sometimes I would get to help him. Working in his lab gave me a chance to be near my dad. Patients would bring stool specimens wrapped in leaves and secured with thin vine. I would put on the nose clips that I used for swimming and open the package. Dad showed me how to make a slide and what to look for through a microscope. There was always a long line of people waiting outside the clinic, and everyone was always staring at me. I hated that!

My parents enrolled me in the Catholic Sacré Coeur school, where I was the only white student. They wanted me to learn French fluently and thought that by throwing me into a French-speaking environment I would learn quickly. I told my parents that if they didn't take me out of that school I would run away. Just as I thought things couldn't get any worse, of course they did. My beloved Rocket was struck by a car and killed while walking on the same road where he used to follow me to the school bus. Granny Close wrote that blood had been coming from his mouth. I never forgave her for putting that image in my mind.

I was so distraught that my parents enrolled me in TASOK, the American School of Kinshasa, where most of the students were mission-ary kids, but I was still unhappy. I just didn't fit in.

Although Tina and I now lived with our parents, my father remained as aloof as he always had been, a fact he later candidly admitted in his autobiography.

My work at the hospital and with the president . . . allowed little time with the family. I was more comfortable dealing with professional responsibilities than with the needs at home. Did I feel guilty about my family? Sometimes, but the weight and imperatives of my other responsibilities were effective guilt suppressors . . . Anyway, with little understanding of children or their problems, I felt useless as a father.

I hate to admit it, but I was afraid of him. He would yell at me for minor infractions, so I stayed out of his way and learned not to ask him anything. I'd use Mom to pitch questions; she knew his moods and the set of his jaw better than I did. Many days he was gone, traveling in a small plane that he piloted to villages to inspect clinics and treat patients. Those days were easier than when he was home.

Not long after we arrived in Africa, I developed what my father diag-nosed as a chronic sinus condition. I had constant headaches, and my sinuses were a mess. Africa became a bit more tolerable after my brother, Sandy, arrived. At age thirteen, I met my first boyfriend at school, and we kissed. We kept it a secret. His father worked for the CIA, although everyone thought he was a shipping company executive. Because of my father's close proximity to Mobutu, everyone suspected Dad of being a CIA operative, too. He always denied that, but I guess he would, so I'll never know. A neighbor gave me a pet monkey with a blue face. I also acquired a chameleon, an owl, and a dog, Trooper.

Still, I wanted to go home. I remember one dreadful afternoon when I rode with my mom to the post office near the center of town. I wasn't feeling well, so I stayed behind in the van when she went inside. Besides, I hated being stared at because we were white.

It was hot under the noon sun, so I slipped into the front seat. Our van's windows were open, but there was no breeze to dry my whitish blond wisps of hair, which were glued to my forehead, held tightly there by stale sweat.

"Mam'selle! Mam'selle!" a young voice called.

A teenage boy, his teeth sparkling brightly in a wide grin, appeared outside the driver's-side window.

"Oui?" I replied softly.

"Papier, mam'selle?" he asked, hoisting up a stack of newspapers for me to see.

"Non, merci," I replied.

I noticed that his shirt, a rag, really, was unbuttoned and draped over his scrawny shoulders. His black skin was covered with dust, giving him a gray, cadaverous appearance. I glanced at his thin chest and looked downward at his bulging navel and the V of his exposed abdomen. His khaki shorts were ripped and fastened below his hips with a piece of twine. His shoeless feet were white with calluses and scars.

"Mam'selle, papier?" he repeated.

Before I could reply, he dropped below the window, out of sight, but resurfaced, the newspapers no longer in his hands.

"Mam'selle," he said, smiling as he brazenly opened our van's door.

"Non!" I shrieked, reaching too late for the handle.

He stepped into the opening and grabbed my right hand. "Papier, mam'selle?" he asked.

"Non! Je n'ai pas d'argent!" I declared. I tried to pull my hand out of his.

He dug his long, dirty fingernails, like fishhooks, into my skin, preventing me from pulling away.

"S'il vous plait," I yelled. "Leave me alone!"

He freed my hand, which I immediately clenched into a fist because my palm stung. I thought I was rid of him, but he reached up and grabbed my left breast with his right hand.

"No!" I shouted, stunned. I tried to knock away his hand, but he knocked mine away instead and squeezed my breast hard again while lowering his left hand to my skirt. He tried to work it under the material, but I clenched my thighs together as tightly as I could and prevented him.

With a frantic shove, I pushed his hand off my breast and scooted backward on the van's seat, kicking at him, causing him to back away. Lunging forward, I grabbed the van's door, slamming it shut, and then darted into the backseat, taking refuge on the floor.

I opened my palm. Four crescents from his fingernails appeared, each bleeding.

The teenager circled the van, calling out, "Mam'selle!" Pressing his face against the glass, he peered into the backseat, staring at me. "Mam'selle, vien."

I looked away.

As quickly as the teen had appeared, he vanished.

"Jess?" my mom called as she opened the driver's-side door.

"Look what a boy did to my hand," I said, offering up my palm.

She took my hand into hers and inspected the cuts. "How awful! What happened?"

I began to cry. "I couldn't lock the doors. I don't know how to lock the doors in this lousy van!"

I jerked my hand from her and closed it again.

"I'm sorry," Mom said. "I didn't know."

I curled up on the backseat and pressed my hot and tear-stained cheek against its vinyl. Closing my eyes, I listened to my mom start the van and back it out of the parking space. I thought about Grandmother Moore's yellow house in Greenwich, with its green lawns and stone walls that ran down into the field behind it. There were lilacs in the yard and freshly mowed grass.

With all my heart I wanted to go home.

CHAPTER SEVEN

I was soon on a flight back to the States with my very frustrated mother. After two and a half years in Africa I was being sent to live with my mother's relatives in Connecticut. My parents were hoping that my health would improve, but I suspected that my trip home was also about my attitude. I had made it clear that I didn't like Africa, and my parents had probably grown tired of my unhappiness.

Mom enrolled me in the Kathleen Laycock Country Day School for girls, about twenty miles north of Greenwich in a community called Westport. I was sent to live with the family of Mom's second cousins. Kathleen Laycock was built on the former estate of R. T. Vanderbilt and boasted an enrollment of 250 girls of all ages along with thirty teachers.

Having been born into MRA's cocoon of the Four Absolute Standards, I found myself at age fourteen living in a world just as foreign as the one I'd seen in Africa. Women wore makeup, adults smoked and swore, and my surrogate parents drank cocktails every night before dinner.

Years later, when we were adults, my siblings and I would decide that all of us should have spent time with a deprogrammer after we left Caux and before we were reintroduced to normal society. You don't spend the first ten years of your life under the direction of strict MRA nannies while your parents are off doing God's work without undergoing culture shock when you see how other families operate.

I didn't get along well at my new home or in my new school. I spent a lot of time in the school infirmary. The nurse couldn't find anything physically wrong with me; I just felt lousy and lifeless. I wasn't doing well academically, either. It wasn't because the schoolwork was difficult; I simply didn't care or apply myself. I think part of my problem, besides being a teenager, was that I'd been berated in Caux by my MRA teachers for being, as one wrote in my report card, "too competitive." The teacher chastised me for not being an "obedient girl." Within MRA, a good girl didn't compete with boys. That teacher's lecture was reinforced by MRA nannies and unintentionally by my own mother, who, I felt, had surrendered her own aspirations to assist my father and his work in Africa—to the point of abandoning us as children.

Living with my relatives soon became untenable, and my mother boarded another flight back to the States to deal with what was becoming known as "the Jessie problem." I could almost hear my parents asking themselves, "What do we do with her now?"

Their solution was to move me back to Grandmother Moore's house. I would finish the rest of the school year being chauffeured to classes and cared for by an MRA nanny, an older woman whose nickname was Tweedie. Before returning to Africa, Mom warned me that Tweedie had epilepsy and that if I caused her too much trouble, she might have a seizure and die.

In addition to my grandmother and me, there was Tweedie and Suza living in this big house. I moved back into the wing that my mom had added for a family of six. At night I would lie in my bed, listening to every creak and strange noise, painfully aware that I was isolated and alone. I wondered what my sisters and brother were doing. I felt unwanted by my parents. Every morning I would step out of my room and run as fast as I could, screaming, down the long green hall to the main house, where everyone else stayed. Monsters were after me, but if I screamed I would be all right.

Now that I was back home, I was reunited with Valentina Quinn, the youngest child of the Academy Award–winning actor Anthony Quinn and his first wife, Katherine DeMille, daughter of the legendary Cecil B. DeMille. I called my friend Valli. Her parents had been recruited by MRA, but unlike my mom and dad, Anthony Quinn had rebelled at becoming an MRA convert. His refusal had caused strains in his marriage, especially when Katherine had gone to be indoctrinated in Caux without him. That's where I'd met Valli for the first time. We had gotten into trouble in Caux for pushing flowerpots off a windowsill—it was fun to see and hear them crash on the cement several floors below. Our MRA nannies had separated us and sent us to a so-called Four Table, which meant we each had to eat at a table with three adults, who grilled us about why we had broken the MRA's Four Absolute Standards by being naughty. Ugh...

Valli's mother moved her family back to California from Caux, and then everyone went to Italy, where Anthony was filming the 1961 movie *Barabbas*. During shooting, Anthony Quinn had a highly publicized affair with an Italian seamstress, whom he impregnated. Valli's mom brought the kids back to the States, where she filed for divorce and eventually moved east.

I had a lot in common with Valli. Her two older sisters were off traveling with Up with People, the MRA singing group that toured college campuses and military bases. My sister Glenn was one of the group's singer-songwriters. Valli also had a deeply troubled relationship with her famous father. The truth was that both of us were raising ourselves.

Occasionally I would have some contact with Glenn or my other siblings. I think all of them realized that I was drifting on my own. Sandy wrote a letter to our parents telling them that I needed to be with them, no matter how loudly I screamed the opposite. I didn't know about it until years later. His pleas fell on deaf ears.

Without a strong parental figure to guide me, I began testing adult waters with my friends. Susie, a classmate from school, and I raided her parents' liquor cabinet one night when her parents were out. There was another girl with us, and she got so drunk that she blacked out. We thought she might be dead, so we panicked and called Susie's parents, who hurried home and telephoned the girl's father. The girl's mother blamed Susie and me and claimed that in addition to drinking, the two of us were smoking pot. At that point, I didn't even know what marijuana was, but that would soon change.

I think alcohol affected me differently from the way it affected most young girls. It not only made me feel less inhibited and eased my painful shyness, it affected my brain. My thoughts seemed to slow down. I didn't feel as if I had a jackrabbit jumping through my head.

I began smoking Tareyton cigarettes, too. Its commercials featured a smoker with a black eye who boasted, "Us Tareyton smokers would rather fight than switch." It seemed so adult, and that slogan appealed to my rebellious streak. Smoking also seemed to soothe my brain.

Susie and I were both boy-crazy, and I quickly realized that boys were interested in me, too. I had long, naturally blond hair, and my boobs had become so enormous that my brother, Sandy, embarrassed me once when I'd been in Africa by asking how I managed to stand straight up without tipping over. I was five feet four inches tall, weighed 110 pounds, and when I bought my first bikini, I had to purchase a size 6 bottom for my hips and a size 8 for my breasts.

Susie was cute, too, with fiery red hair. I soon fell desperately in love with a townie from Westport named Greg. Susie and I would pile into a car with Greg and one of his friends and head to a local drive-in theater, where we would drink beer and make out for hours.

It was 1967, the so-called Summer of Love, and Susie and I thought of ourselves as rebels. We decided to see who could lose her virginity first. I won.

Greg and I had sex almost immediately after we'd met. I turned fifteen that summer. We used a contraceptive. Just the same, a part of me hoped I'd get pregnant. If I had a baby, I'd have someone who would love me for who I was. I would have my own family.

When the school year ended in the spring of 1968, my parents wanted me to spend the summer in Africa. I dug in my heels, because I didn't want to leave Susie or Greg. A compromise was reached. Susie would come to the Congo with me for half the summer, and I would spend the rest of the summer with her family. The first thing Susie and I packed were our newly purchased Beatles records.

Susie wasn't used to living in a paracommando camp that white girls couldn't leave without an escort. After four weeks living with me, Susie confided that she'd never met parents as "stiff" and "appallingly uptight"— her words—as mine were. She said my father was self-engrossed and oddly disconnected from the rest of us. My parents, meanwhile, didn't like Susie at all. They thought she was a bad influence on me. Her comments were the first to show me how others saw my parents and my family. We were different.

To me, my dad was totally preoccupied with his African adventure and my mother naturally supported him. She took a special interest in Tambu Kisoki, a teenager who was hired to help around our house, and began teaching him English. He was such a pleasant and enthusiastic student that my parents decided to informally adopt him and help pay for his continued education in the United States. Legally, he was not a Close, but emotionally he was quickly accepted.

Tambu and I were moving in opposite directions. I was becoming more removed from my family at a time when he joined it.

Susie and I lost contact in the fall, when we enrolled in different schools. Mom sent me to her alma mater, Rosemary Hall, where the teachers quickly discovered that I was not like the earlier Moore and Close family girls. I was told I had to repeat the ninth grade, which was humiliating and made me feel even more insecure and rebellious. Mom also decided that I should board at Rosemary Hall rather than live with my grandmother. Wanting to fit in, I developed a reputation for being the girl who would try anything. One night, someone suggested that we put our dorm mother's cat down the laundry chute. "I'll do it!" I volunteered.

In a short span, I'd started drinking, smoking cigarettes, having sex, and establishing a reputation as a rebel. I'd come a long way from being the reclusive tomboy wearing an army uniform and hunting imaginary Nazis with Rocket.

When the school year ended in the spring of 1969, my parents were told that I would not be welcomed back at Rosemary Hall for my sopho-more year because of my grades and antics. Once again, Mom boarded a flight from the Congo, returning to the States to deal with the problem child.

Mom and Dad were not happy. Not only had I embarrassed myself by failing at Rosemary Hall, Mom also discovered that I had had sex. I was clearly out of control.

Having run out of ideas about how to control me from Africa, my parents decided to get me out of Greenwich before I did further damage. They legally surrendered their parental rights. I was being turned over to my oldest sister, Tina, who was now living in Pacific Palisades, outside Los Angeles.

Much like mine, Tina's life had been scarred by MRA and restricted by my parents. She'd wanted to attend art school after graduating from Rosemary Hall and had been accepted at Parsons School of Design, but my father had dismissed a career in art as being impractical. He'd urged her to become a nurse. Uncertain what to do, Tina had returned to the Congo, doing odd jobs that our dad had arranged while she was living with them. Out of the blue, she had received a letter from Diarmid Campbell, a Scotsman thirteen years her senior who was in MRA. His sister had met Tina and had assured Diarmid that Tina would make a good wife. Diarmid's proposal was a way for her to escape from Kinshasa and begin her own family, so Tina agreed to marry him and move to California.

I was used to being away from my parents, but giving Tina legal rights to me was something I didn't understand. Anger toward them burned inside me, but on the other hand I looked forward to living without their interference and rules. As far as I was concerned I was still on my own; Tina didn't have a clue.

I moved into my twenty-four-year-old sister's two-bedroom bungalow and immediately began pestering her about getting my driver's license. A few weeks after I settled in, Valli showed up on our doorstep. Her mother had grown weary of what she called "Greenwich snobbery and isolation" and had decided to move back to Los Angeles, too. She'd sent Valli ahead so that she could enroll at Palisades High School, which was two blocks away. Valli's mom planned to follow and buy a house as soon as she sold their home in Greenwich.

Once again, Valli and I were bringing up ourselves.

Valli and I dutifully enrolled for classes that fall, but neither of us was interested in high school. We began skipping classes; instead we would go to the beach, get high on pot, and meet boys. We would get up each morning, put on bikinis, and walk down Temescal Canyon Road to the ocean.

Driving is close to breathing in Southern California. I wanted my license so that I could be independent of my now-pregnant sister and her husband. Tina hired a private driving instructor, who arrived in a yellow sports car with a stick shift, which I had requested; I wanted to know how to drive anything and everything. For someone twice my age, he was cute. During our third or fourth lesson, he asked me if I could get him some weed. The next time he showed up, we drove to his office and got high. He tried to put his arms around me, but I pushed him away and we went on with our lesson stoned. Welcome to California in the late 1960s and early 1970s.

There was a window in my new bedroom that I crawled out of a lot after Tina and Diarmid went to bed. The driveway at their one-story bungalow sloped down to the street, so I would release the brake of the boxy Datsun that my parents had bought for me long-distance and let the car glide down to the street with its driver's-side door open. Once there, I would crank the engine. Tina and Diarmid never heard me driving away.

Even though I was only attending classes at school periodically, the times when I did go were torture to me. I hated the noise, the confusion, and the thousands of kids crowded in the halls. The school demanded that I take driver's ed, even though I already had my license. The instructor gave us numbers from his seating chart. He called on me one day without using my name, only my number. Filled with teen outrage, I slammed my books on my desk, stood up, and started for the door. I never went back. I felt so small, so insignificant; a person of no value. Being a number was just too much.

Not long after that I overheard Tina talking on the phone to my mother. Tina had put a blanket over her head to muffle what she was saying, but it wasn't difficult for me to figure it out. Tina was worried that a truant officer was going to knock on her door. Here we go again, I thought. The problem child was acting up. Only this time it was Tina who was frustrated by my antics.

It turned out that Tina's worries were unfounded. No one at school missed me.

VIGNETTE NUMBER TWO
by Glenn Close

For years we were a fractured family, widely dispersed and infrequently in touch. The farthest apart we ever were—and for the longest time—was nearly 6,400 miles, the distance between Greenwich and the Democratic Republic of Congo—then Zaire—where my parents lived for sixteen years. Each of my three siblings lived with them at various times, but I never did, although I did have a couple of long visits. For five years, right out of high school, I was with a singing group called Up with People, organized by MRA in order to reach a younger generation. After five years of living out of a suitcase, I finally rebelled and applied to the College of William and Mary. From college, I went straight to New York City and began my career. For years after our parents moved back to the States, when I addressed a letter to them, I would have to stop myself from automatically writing "B. P. [Boîte Postale] 1197, Kinshasa, Zaire."

The connection to our parents was tenuous at best. Love was fading ink on thin blue stationery. My siblings and I were living out our individual lives, mostly away from any kind of family life. I always counted myself lucky that I knew what I wanted to do. The burning desire to be an actress gave my life purpose and direction.

From that unhappy, fractured time, there is one image that is seared into my heart. Jessie was living at the house in Greenwich with Suza, our grandmother's beloved cook. Jess's shadow was Rocket, her fabulous Shetland sheepdog. She must have been living there because it was from there that I received a call. Who from? Suza? Or maybe it was

Tweedie, a retired nurse who had worked with our father in the Congo. Anyway, I was on the road with Up with People, singing my little brainwashed heart out, trying to save the world, when I received a call saying that Jessie was not in a good way and I should come home. Our parents were far away, in Zaire. So I asked for a meeting with the Up with People leaders and got permission to go home to see what was going on.

The painful image in my mind is of Jessie, sobbing uncontrollably in my arms. We are clasped together on her bed in her room with the strawberry wallpaper. She is terrified because she has lost her virginity and is totally alone with the grief and guilt. I remember that she was fifteen. I stroke her hair and hold her until the jagged sobs subside. We talked. I don't know what was said. I was a twenty-year-old virgin, and I had absolutely no knowledge of sex. I had kissed maybe three boys in my life. And I was caught in Up with People, spouting platitude after platitude with impressive sincerity and belief. So that's what I probably did in my pitiful ignorance, holding Jessie in my arms. I must have been somewhat comforting, because I was family and I had come home for her sake. Did we talk about birth control? Did I suggest she see a gynecologist? I hope I did. We certainly clung to each other, because that is my strongest image. And I'm sure that loyal and loving Rocket, Jessie's dog, was right there with us on the bed.

The appalling thing was that I didn't stay long. I didn't call back the leaders and say I needed to stay with my sister, that she needed me more than they did, which was the truth. And I had no tools to recognize another truth for the both of us—the truth that I needed Jessie as much as she needed me. I left and went back on the road, sworn to secrecy by my distraught little sister.

Then I learned a terrible lesson. When one has basically substituted a group with a mission for one's family, the leaders of that group become substitute parents—dictating the group-family's culture—sometimes subversively seducing, other times outwardly exhorting everyone to please their leaders, obey the rules, and be completely committed to the mission. One is always thinking of ways to get in their good favor so one will be seen as a leader in her own right and a valued member of that bogus family. In my desperation to please, when I returned to the group, I went straight to the wife of the leader and, as if I were applying for some kind of service badge, told her about Jessie—told her everything, so she would think I was the brave one, the caring one. I broke my promise. Speaking of Jessie's shame somehow shone a brighter light on my goodness, on what had become my appallingly skewed sense of morality. It was a despicable betrayal, and as I write this, my heart is palpitating with mortification and remorse. Afterward, I was sickened by what I'd done and deeply ashamed. It was the beginning of my desperate need to escape from the clutches of the group and start a real life. However, the image of my little sister, again alone, weeping, with no family around to ease her pain—that is seared into my brain forever.

CHAPTER EIGHT

Valli dropped out of school and began taking acting lessons. We rebelled against everyone and everything. One night while we were speeding down Santa Monica Boulevard, I reached over and grabbed the steering wheel of Valli's car, causing us to swerve across several lanes of oncoming traffic. Valli freaked out.

"Don't ever do that again!" she screamed. "You could have killed us!"

I didn't care. I was pushing the limits.

The two of us drove to Sunset Boulevard looking for pot. Two cute teenage girls wearing tank tops and shorty-shorts hitting the Strip was like two flies nose-diving into a spiderweb. A pimp hustled over to us as soon as we parked at the curb.

"What you two fine ladies looking to get tonight?" he asked.

"We're trying to score some weed," I declared.

Breaking into a grin, he said, "Follow me."

We fell behind him like children dancing after the Pied Piper. When we reached the seedy building where he lived, Valli slipped into his apartment, but I hesitated at the doorway, keeping our exit options open.

"Ain't you coming in?" he asked.

I shook my head, indicating no.

He frowned, then disappeared into a bedroom. When he emerged, he was holding a shoe box full of brightly colored pills and Baggies of grass.

"Let's party," he said. "Come on in."

"We gotta go," I said, suddenly afraid.

We bought some weed then bolted for the car, both of us convinced that we were lucky to escape unharmed yet proud that we'd pulled off our little caper.

One day Valli stood on the sidewalk outside Tina's house and called up to me: she wanted to introduce me to a boy. As soon as I saw Brad Sobel, I knew he was trouble. Brad was a dead ringer for Charles Manson, whose photo was in all the papers. In August of 1969, Manson's followers had committed the Tate and LaBianca murders. Brad had stringy dark brown hair and a scraggly beard. But the real clincher was his Rasputin eyes—yellow-brown, like those of a predator. Like Manson's, they seemed to look right through you.

Valli had a crush on Brad, but as soon as he saw me, he lost all interest in her. She was a knockout, with her Hollywood father's brown Mexican skin and black hair. But I was a California girl with long blond hair that hung well below my waist. A legitimate modeling agency had begun to recruit me.

By this time, I understood that my looks gave me an advantage. I was learning how to flirt with and manipulate boys. A couple of beers or a joint could turn me into both a flirt and the life of the party. Yet underneath that confident facade, I was still a frightened and lonely girl who felt abandoned and unworthy of love.

Somehow Brad sensed that. He was quick to tell me exactly what I wanted—and needed—to hear. I'd never met anyone like him. He was everything my parents hated and everything MRA preached against—and that added to his appeal. A cocky rebel, Brad flaunted his antiauthority, antiestablishment, counterculture attitude.

Not long after we met, Brad and I were walking down a street when he spotted an elderly woman out for an afternoon stroll.

Running up to her, Brad screamed, "You're going to die soon! You're going to die 'cause you're old!"

After letting out a frightening laugh, he calmly turned away from the terrified woman and walked back over to me.

Brad turned me onto Seconal, also known as reds, and amphetamines, which we called cross whites or speed. I was willing to try anything, and Brad used me as his private guinea pig. The speed got us high. The reds brought us down. Brad liked getting high while having sex.

Valli didn't come around as much after Brad and I hooked up. I didn't realize she was angry because I had stolen her boyfriend. It probably wouldn't have mattered. Although Brad was only a year older than I was, he soon was dominating my life. He talked me out of signing with the modeling agency that wanted me. No one but Brad was going to have me.

Brad had been adopted as a baby by a doctor and his wife and had grown up in an affluent home. He'd been an impossible child to control. Many years later I would look up the word *psychopath* and decide that it described Brad perfectly. But at age sixteen, I mistook his need to control me for love.

When Tina had her baby, my mom came from Africa to see her first grandchild. With Brad's help, I had built a damning case against Mom and Dad.

To snub my mother, I decided to stay at Brad's house once during her long-awaited visit.

She telephoned me there. "Jessie, you need to come home. It's getting late."

My heart was pounding, but I'd watched and heard how Brad treated his parents, and I channeled his attitude.

"I'm not coming home," I declared.

"What?" Her irritation instantly became anger. "You're only sixteen, and you're not spending the night with that boy."

If I hadn't met Brad, I wouldn't have had the gall to disobey her, but I did.

"I hate you!" I replied, years of resentment sweeping up inside me. "If loving me means you have to come see me, then don't love me anymore!"

My mother was silent and then said, "Okay, if that's how you feel."

I slammed down the receiver, and Brad gave me a smug look. I was empty inside; I wanted my mother to love me, but not like this. It seemed she was never there. I put on a triumphant face for Brad, but inside I was ashamed and felt guilty about what I said to Mom.

I received a monthly stipend from a trust fund set up by Grandmother Moore. I'd been getting it ever since my parents had cut me loose. When I mentioned it to Brad, he decided my allowance would be enough to allow the two of us to move in together.

During the summer of 1970, my parents sent word from Africa that they wanted me to visit them there. I wouldn't go, I told them, unless I could bring Brad along. Mom and Dad reluctantly agreed, so Brad got a passport and we boarded a flight to Kinshasa.

Mom tried to find something about Brad that she liked, but there was nothing about him that my father found redeeming. I relished their disappointment. I was rubbing their faces in my new independence. Hey, you rejected me. Now I reject you. It was childish, but it felt good.

Before flying to Africa, I'd told Brad about a scary experience that I'd had going through customs. It happened in Paris, where agents had removed everything from my luggage, even taking my tampons apart, searching for drugs. Because of that story, we hadn't risked bringing any drugs with us. I thought maybe we could find something in my father's clinic, but he'd moved it out of their master bedroom into a locked building a short drive away. We waited until my parents left us alone, then we ransacked the house. Brad found Dad's bush kit, which he used when flying into the field, and discovered several morphine syrettes. He stole them all. I was scared, but Brad assured me that morphine would make me feel wonderful, so I let him shoot me up with a syringe in my thigh. I didn't know it, but a morphine overdose can cause asphyxiation, and when I began having trouble breathing, I felt as if my heart were slowing and it was going to stop. I began counting my heartbeats, convinced that if I stopped counting, I would die. It was horrible. The next morning I told Brad that I wasn't going to ever take morphine again. He just laughed.

After that, we got a driver who worked at the American embassy to score us weed. He arrived in an embassy car, American flag fluttering, and delivered it to us. He gave us so much that we made it into cigars, wrapping it in blue airmail paper. My parents didn't recognize the smell or that we were high. They were so clueless.

A few days after we'd settled in, I told Mom that Brad and I were going to use my trust fund to live together when we returned to Los Angeles.

"No: absolutely not!" she announced.

I knew my mother well enough to recognize the set of her jaw, the thinning of her lips. There was no arguing with her. She told my father, and they decided it would be better if Brad and I got married—immediately—in Africa rather than face the embarrassment of the two of us living together in sin and my possibly getting pregnant. That's how some people thought in 1970.

Perhaps this was also an answer to the eternal question of what to do with Jessie.

I thought they might be bluffing, trying reverse psychology. If that was their strategy, it backfired.

"Okay," I told them. "We'll get married."

Brad liked the idea, probably more because of my trust fund than because of me.

I was turning seventeen on July 17, so it was decided I would get married ten days after that. Because of my father's lofty position and his friendship with President Mobutu, my wedding was quickly becoming an event. One of Mobutu's top generals, General Bumba, volunteered to give "the daughter of Dr. Close" a wedding reception like none that had ever been seen before. Before I knew what was happening, I was shown a guest list of several hundred strangers.

I started to panic. This was happening too fast. Moving in with Brad had seemed like a good idea. It would get me out of Tina's house and on my own. Marrying him was entirely different. Didn't these people realize I was still a teenager?!

There was something else about marrying Brad that frightened me. He liked sex, which was fine, but he liked it wherever and whenever he wanted it, which was daily. What I wanted, or whether I was even interested, didn't matter. If I complained, he seemed to want it even more and would force himself on me anyway. One night in the living room in the Congo, Brad forced himself on me. I was so scared that my parents would walk in that I had to grit my teeth. I simply waited for him to finish.

As my wedding day approached, I began having third and fourth thoughts. I wasn't certain how I was going to get out of this mess, but I wanted out. The answer, I decided, was to swallow a bottle of muscle relaxers I found in my parents' bathroom cupboard.

I took them in my bedroom and waited. I began feeling weird and started thinking about Greenwich and Rocky and my horses and how all those things that I loved were gone and how my life was in the toilet. But then I thought of my mother's face and I got scared. I didn't want her to find me dead, so I forced myself up and off the bed and made my way to her bedroom.

"I just swallowed a bottle of pills," I told her.

She jumped into action, driving me to Dad's clinic, where he pumped my stomach, an especially painful procedure. He didn't seem angry but was clearly concerned, even loving. When he finished, he put me in a private room to recover, and when a Belgian nurse came to check on me, I began sobbing.

"I have something to tell you," I blubbered. "But please don't tell my parents."

She promised, so I blurted out: "I don't want to get married. I don't want to marry Brad. I'm scared of him."

The nurse and everyone else in the president's camp knew about my wedding. After she left, I felt better. Surely she would do exactly what I'd made her promise not to do—tell my parents. They would force me to call off the wedding. I would be saved.

My dad came in to see me a few minutes later and decided it was okay for me to go home. Mom was waiting outside. When we got home, they escorted me into their bedroom so we could talk without Brad listening. Ah, I thought. The nurse told them. I started to relax.

"Were you really trying to kill yourself?" Dad asked in a skeptical tone.

I demurred. "I don't know."

"Then why did you swallow those pills?" Mom asked.

I looked at them and realized that the nurse hadn't tipped them off. They didn't know that I was scared of Brad and didn't want to get married. It was time for me to speak up. They were giving me my opportunity. All I had to do was tell them the truth.

My brother and I had joked about how MRA's Four Absolute Standards had the opposite effect on the children who were raised with them: Absolute Honesty became Absolute Dishonesty, so that we could stay out of trouble; Absolute Purity became Absolute Perversion for the sake of fun and rebellion; Absolute Unselfishness became Absolute Selfishness, as we watched our own backs; and Absolute Love became Absolute

Obsession. I truly wanted to be loved, but I didn't know how to be loved and mistook obsession for devotion.

I looked into my parents' faces and felt torn. I didn't want to disappoint them. I didn't want them to have another of their "What do we do with Jessie?" discussions. But I didn't want to marry Brad. What would happen if I turned Brad away? Would rejecting him mean I was admitting that my rebellious behavior had been wrong? Despite my defiant attitude, I wanted my parents' acceptance. I wanted their love. I wanted to be wanted by them. I wanted to please them.

There was also a practical question that I had to answer. If I didn't marry Brad, what would happen to me? I didn't want to live with them in Africa. I didn't want to live with Tina any longer, either. Where would I go?

"Everything is okay," I said. "I just got confused. I want to marry Brad. Everything will be fine after we marry."

They looked relieved. Watching them, I felt as if I could read their thoughts: *This is just another example of Jessie being melodramatic, of our youngest daughter calling attention to herself.*

They smiled. I smiled back. But I knew I had just made one of the worst decisions of my life.

PART TWO

HUSBANDS AND OTHERS

The first time I dropped acid, everything changed. I felt that I had lost my innocence. I felt I had entered a new stage in my life and that my childhood was over.

—from my private journal

CHAPTER NINE

Brad and I returned from Africa married, and we set up housekeeping in a two-story apartment building at 11550 Nebraska Avenue in Los Angeles, which resembled a brown stucco 1960s-era motel. One of the first decorations that we put on our walls was a poster of a defiant Angela Davis wearing her hair in a huge Afro. We were radicals, hippies, and revolutionaries, and Angela symbolized our contempt for mainstream society and its holdover 1950s values.

Davis was accused of buying guns for three black convicts who took a judge and others hostage in a courtroom. That same year, 1970, was also when Ohio National Guardsmen fatally shot four unarmed Kent State University students who were demonstrating against the Cambodian campaign during the Vietnam War. The Chicago Seven were on trial in Chicago, and yippie Jerry Rubin shocked America when he lit a joint and tried to pass it to David Frost on national television, seconds before a gaggle of yippies planted in the audience stormed onto the stage yelling expletives.

During a demonstration in Griffith Park, I screamed into a police officer's face: "Fuck the pigs!" He pulled his nightstick, and I took off running.

Although the zeitgeist that had rocked the 1960s—with Woodstock, free love, communes, antiwork attitudes, and psychedelic drugs—was starting to wane, Brad and I were still eagerly waiting for a revolution. It became clear to us that music was the best way to usher in this new Age of Aquarius.

Our tiny apartment became a hangout for other free thinkers, partly because Brad and I were generous with our pot. We smoked weed every day, sometimes dropped acid on Wednesdays (Wednesday being my favorite day), and tried any and all drugs we could get our hands on, all the while tuning in to rock and roll.

It was our love of music and our intent to change society that led us to decide to launch our own radio station. Brad began reading wiring schematics for radio equipment and began a hunt for cast-off electronics, which were plentiful in those days, thanks to military surplus being shipped back from Vietnam.

Two teenagers taking to the airways with an illegal radio broadcast seemed like an improbable dream, which is what made it so damn exciting.

Neither of us was employed. My trust fund paid me five hundred dollars per month. We were biting the hand that was feeding us, and we celebrated the irony of it. Brad began turning our salvaged parts into a broadcasting station in our bedroom. He built a recording booth in our walk-in closet. We moved our bed into the eating area next to the kitchen. Late one night, we climbed the roof of our building and plunked down a Vietnam War–surplus transmitter and antenna, hanging the wires down the outside wall of our building and into our apartment.

Our renegade radio station hit the air the first week of November, 1970, broadcasting through a fifty-watt transmitter that could be heard from Pacific Palisades to the Los Angeles International Airport.

We named it KPOT.

On a Monday night three days later, there was a knock on our door. About twenty of us were in our apartment, and when I opened the door, two uniformed police officers and two men in suits were in the hall. Oh, God, I thought. It's a drug bust.

"You're operating an illegal radio station, and we're here to shut it down," one of the suits declared. He and his partner said they were from the Federal Communications Commission.

The two FCC men pushed past me into the apartment, going directly into our makeshift studio.

"KPOT," one of the cops said with a smirk. "How'd you come up with that handle?"

"The knobs on a mixer board are called potentiometers," I replied indignantly. "That's why."

He didn't buy it, and I managed to keep a straight face.

"Did you know you could go to jail for a year and be fined ten thousand dollars for operating an illegal station?" one of the FCC men asked.

I felt like laughing but didn't. We were broadcasting the *1812 Overture*—one of the most popular Fourth of July independence songs—when the FCC pulled our station's plug. So much for free speech in the USA, I thought.

One of the cops said our neighbors had complained because our broadcasts were interfering with their television and radio reception. We had made it clear to our neighbors that if they experienced difficulty with their TVs or radios we would provide them with a filter. Obviously, we hadn't heard from all of them.

"Who built this?" an FCC man asked.

"I did," Brad replied.

"C'mon—where'd you get this?"

"I built it from scratch," Brad replied.

"How old are you?"

"Nineteen."

"There's no way a kid could have built this," the man stated.

After jotting down information about Brad and me, our unwelcome guests left. Thankfully, the police didn't comment about the smell of marijuana. We were told that it would be up to the FCC commissioner to decide if formal criminal charges would be filed. If so, Brad and I would be arrested, handcuffed, and taken in for booking and arraignment.

I was scared, but Brad wore the closing down of KPOT as a badge of hippie honor.

Our FCC raid caught the eye of a *Los Angeles Times* reporter. She arrived at our apartment the next morning to interview us. KPOT made page 1 under the headline FCC RAIDS CLOSET RADIO STATION. The newspaper photo accompanying the story showed Brad and me in our cramped recording booth. Brad had shoulder-length brown hair and a full beard, turning him from Charles Manson into a Jesus wannabe. Poised behind him in the photo was his flower-child bride—me—with long flowing blond hair that dropped well down my back. I was wearing a peasant blouse and no makeup. Power to the people!

"Everyone was so upset when the police showed up," Brad was quoted as saying in the article. "We were all crying."

I explained to the reporter that everyone worked at the radio station for free. We were doing it because we loved rock and roll and believed it was our right to play whatever music we wanted. Brad and I were financing the station and living off my family trust fund because neither of us believed in working for money. "We had the money to live; we just wanted to do something for the people," I was quoted as saying. "We never planned to go commercial."

"Just because we didn't have a license didn't mean we weren't responsible," Brad added. A local commercial station had donated an emergency broadcast monitor to us, which was one of the requirements for operating a licensed station. "We wanted to make it as legal as we could."

Brad explained in the news article that he had investigated applying for an FCC license, but "they told me I needed all this money, much more than we had." Those fees were simply another example of how mainstream society kept young people from airing their voices.

"We were totally open," Brad told the reporter. "We didn't try to hide anything. We even gave the station's phone number and address over the air."

The Times's story turned KPOT into a cause célèbre. Rock-and-roll radio stations across the country called us for interviews. Radio Caroline, the pirate radio station that operated on a tanker ship off the coast of England to circumvent the BBC's monopoly, rallied with us. Petitions calling for the FCC to not punish us were circulated during a concert at the Hollywood Bowl. The FCC commissioner took note of all the publicity and decided to not prosecute. We got away with the warning that if we were ever again involved with an illegal station we would get jail time and a fine.

Seizing the moment, Brad contacted the owners of Theta Cable, a fledgling company launched in part by the Hughes Aircraft Company. Cable television was just starting in Los Angeles, and Brad pitched the idea of adding a cable radio station into the mix of television stations that Theta was offering customers.

Three weeks after KPOT was shut down, Theta announced that it had decided to give us a one-year experimental contract as one of the nation's first cable radio stations. Because we would only be heard by Theta's four thousand subscribers and not on the public airways, we weren't required to get an FCC license. We made up new call letters, CABL, and were 108 on the FM dial.

The *Los Angeles Times* announced KPOT's return. A Theta Cable spokesman said, "Theta is interested in helping minority races and the youth movement, and this CABL 108 station is trying to do something of interest with community youth."

What that story didn't say was that Theta was not paying us. Basically, I was picking up the costs. We didn't care. I mailed a business proposal that outlined how we planned to launch our new radio station to Grandmother Moore, and she responded with a ten-thousand-dollar donation.

On January 1, 1971, we began broadcasting twenty-four hours per day, using taped music from midnight until 9:00 a.m. Obviously, our new station needed DJs, and I was determined that at least one of them would be a woman. One morning while I was returning to the station from an errand, I noticed a music store. I ducked inside and struck up a conversation with an attractive young girl working behind the counter.

"I'm Jessie Sobel," I announced. "My husband and I run CABL 108."

"The renegade station," the girl enthusiastically replied.

"Yep, that's us."

The clerk turned out to be the owner of the store, Cindy Paulos. Her husband was a bass guitar player in an LA band, and, like me, she had an income of her own, only she was from Beverly Hills. She'd married right out of high school and opened the store because she loved music.

"How would you like to be a disc jockey?" I asked after a few minutes.

"I'd love it."

As quickly as that, we had our first female DJ. During the coming year, Cindy came in every day, even though she wasn't paid. I got along with everyone. Brad didn't. Cindy thought he was egotistical and a male chauvinist.

The panache of a renegade station with its young staff and anything-goes attitude appealed to emerging rock stars. Our station became the cool place to introduce your music in LA. I remember answering the phone and talking to George Carlin. He liked to phone in with song requests. Rock star Frank Zappa came by for an on-air interview. I engineered a show for Flo & Eddie. Memphis soul singer Ann Peebles and folk singer Hoyt Axton were guests. When Hoyt came in, he put down one of the longest, thickest lines of cocaine that I'd ever seen for us to enjoy. He'd written "The Pusher," a song about the difference between frequent marijuana use and heroin. "The Pusher" was performed by Steppenwolf on the band's first album and later was on the *Easy Rider* movie sound track. Axton told me his lyric "God damn the pusher man" was so controversial that officials in North Carolina insisted that Steppenwolf substitute the words "gosh darn" when the band played there. I really liked Hoyt but knew he was struggling with addiction. Everyone was trying to find a place where you could smoke pot and use drugs to expand your mind without having them overtake your life—and that included Brad and me.

To us, our little apartment became the epicenter of LA's rock-and-roll scene. We didn't have to buy weed or pills anymore. Record company promoters dropped by weekly and made certain our apartment was well supplied with pot and cocaine.

Executives for Theta Cable asked me to speak to their sales force about how to best pitch our station to potential subscribers. I arrived at the meeting wearing shorty-shorts and a tiny halter top that showed off my eighteen-year-old breasts. After I finished my speech, an older gentleman took me aside and said, "You did a good job of explaining your station, but you might want to dress differently, more conservatively, next time." He said my appearance had been so distracting that the salesmen weren't listening to what I said.

When RCA Records invited us to speak at a seminar, I wore skin-tight pants made of fake snakeskin and a bright velour blouse, but I still didn't put on a bra. I was against wearing them.

I was having a blast working at our radio station. I developed a knack for identifying hits. I could listen to the first five beats and tell you what the song was, who the artist was, and what label it was released on, and when. When a new single came in I could tell right away if it was going to make it onto the *Billboard* Hot 100. Everyone was having fun. Our apartment was always swarming with people. I also owned two dogs I'd gotten from the animal shelter, one named Poo and the other Bowie, but the real shocker when guests came in to be interviewed was my pet rabbit. I named him Rarebit of Mischief.

My rabbit did his business in a litter box on the apartment's balcony, but I never cleaned it and it was disgusting. Rarebit chewed the bottoms off our sliding-door curtains until they were two inches too short. He grazed on the linoleum around the toilet in the bathroom, and he chewed up chunks of our gold shag rug. I'd also bought a pet mouse and got a surprise when she had a litter. One of them fell out of the cage. Instead of putting him back, I decided to let him roam free, and he ended up nesting in our stove, which I never used. We survived on burgers and fries from Jack in the Box and a nearby A&W drive-in. We went there so much that the teenagers used to give us free fries for my dogs.

I gave the mouse who nested in our stove the name HM, an abbreviation for House Mouse, and I remember laughing whenever we would have a guest come in for an on-air interview and House Mouse would walk into the studio, stand up on his hind legs, and look at the guest. He was tan with a little white patch on his chest, so he didn't look like a wild mouse. The guests would be enthralled by his boldness.

Our apartment and menagerie were all part of who we were as hippie radio operators. Glenn came to see me once, and she laughingly told me there was nowhere in my entire apartment where she could sit because everything was covered with pet hair.

Glenn had finally broken away from Up with People and MRA and was attending the College of William and Mary in Virginia. I didn't give a damn about going back to school. Why should I? I was married and too busy managing our station.

We'd been broadcasting for more than a year when Crystal Sound Recording Studios offered me a job as an assistant engineer. Crystal Sound was built by Andrew Berliner, who started out by building a studio in his apartment—just as Brad and I had done with KPOT. Their studio had outgrown the apartment and become a well-respected operation. Carole King's first album, *Writer*, was recorded there in 1970, as was James Taylor's *Mud Slide Slim and the Blue Horizon* the following year.

Going to work at Crystal Sound was a tremendous opportunity, and I was excited, but when I told Brad, he freaked out.

"No wife of mine is going to work as an assistant engineer," he announced. He didn't like the idea of me working late at night with musicians. He wanted me in our apartment, where he could keep an eye on me. He also didn't want me working for anyone but himself.

"I like engineer work," I complained.

Brad and I had been married long enough for us to have had several arguments. But this one was different. He got physical. "You aren't going to work there!" he shouted, grabbing my shoulders and shaking me. "You'll do what I tell you to do. You're my wife."

I will never forget the furious look in his eyes. Brad had gotten physically abusive with me before, but only during sex in our bedroom. I was pretty naive at the time. I didn't know that a husband could rape his wife. It wasn't a common thought during the 1970s.

I was about to learn that his grabbing and shaking me was a prelude of what was to come.

CHAPTER TEN

"Where ARE you?" he whined.

"I'm just here," she said as she stepped to her left to flush the toilet and exit their bathroom.

"I woke up and didn't know where you were," he complained.

She entered their dark bedroom, her eyes on the floor, her arms folded across her breasts.

"I hate waking up without you next to me," he said.

She glanced at him, the bulb from above the bathroom sink lending the bedroom a small glimmer of light. He sat up in bed, his thin chest sunken to the contour of his spine, his neck hidden by a scraggly beard. She wished she wasn't naked; her skin crawled at the sight of him.

"Come here," he commanded, looking up at her, a small pout pushing out his lower lip. His small, round stomach bulged against the covers.

"I got up to pee . . ." she mumbled.

She crawled under the covers and lay on her stomach, as close to the edge of the mattress and as far from him as possible. She kept her face turned to the wall away from him.

"I'll make you feel better," he said. "Come here."

He reached out, putting his moist palm on the small of her back. She shrank from the touch, her skin turning to gooseflesh, her nipples hardening, not from excitement but from fear.

"Come here," he said again. She felt him move closer to her, felt his beard on her shoulder. Slipping an arm around her waist, he rolled her over onto her back. His beard covered her mouth—she could taste the stench of beer and cigarettes. His hand slid to her belly and down, between her legs.

"Relax," he whispered into her ear.

"I'm not really awake," she told him and grasped the covers with the hand that wasn't trapped next to his side.

"But your nipples are hard," he said and took one in his teeth. "Touch me," he ordered, his tone urgent.

She let go of the covers and found him, biting her lip so she wouldn't scream. He pushed his fingers into her, painfully. She tried to will her body to respond to him and lessen the punishment, but couldn't. She clenched her jaws tight when he shoved himself inside her.

"See?" he said. "You ALWAYS want me, DON'T YOU?"

In pain, she nodded, her cheek rubbing against his ear.

"I can't hear you," he said, stabbing into her hard, before pulling back for another thrust. He grabbed a handful of her hair, pulled her head back, and raised himself to look into her eyes, his chest hurting her breasts.

"You ALWAYS want me, don't you?" he demanded, his yellow-brown eyes boring into hers.

"Yes," she whispered, squeezing her eyes shut. She was lying, but knew what was required—and what she needed to do. She lifted herself against his pounding, knowing he'd finish sooner that way.

"Yes," she said, feigning, feeling him move faster. "YES!"

A series of grunts escaped from his throat, and he collapsed, his body pressing her into the mattress, making it difficult for her to breathe. Her eyes remained closed.

She heard her dog in the living room bark and thought she heard footsteps outside their apartment window. She opened her eyes to glance at the window to the right of their bed. She heard footsteps again—she was sure of it; they were behind the apartment building. Someone was walking in the alley.

She lay still, her small body suffering under her husband's, and pretended she was making the footsteps . . . pretended she was the one escaping.

I didn't want Brad reading what I'd written in my journal. I doubted he realized how disgusted I felt whenever he had sex with me. We didn't make love. In my mind, it was rape. I wrote about it in my journals to release the frustration and anger swelling up in me. We had been married three years by 1970, and whatever love there was—if there ever had been any—had died.

We could no longer live and broadcast our cable station from our tiny apartment, so Brad and I moved into a unit upstairs and had a home without volunteer DJs, singers, record salesmen, and assorted other hangers-on traipsing through. We were alone again. And that was the horrible part: we were alone again.

The only bright spot for me was when the postman arrived one day with a filthy kitten who, he explained, had been used as a baseball in a game of catch by some teenagers outside our building. He was delivering him to me because he knew I loved animals. When I put the kitten on our rug the sun was shining behind him and his orange fur lit up, suspending him in light. I decided to name him Ziggy Stardust and fed him baby food, cottage cheese, and gave him, of course, a much-needed bath. Ziggy soon grew into a plump, long-haired orange cat who liked to sleep on our dinner plates in an open cupboard. Thankfully, House Mouse stayed downstairs in the studio.

I knew Brad was having sex with other women because he didn't try to hide it; he used our downstairs station headquarters for his trysts. A year earlier, Nena and George O'Neill had published a national bestseller called *Open Marriage*, which had sold more than 1.5 million copies. It promoted the idea that adulterous sex without jealousy was possible—and desirable. It was the talk of our nation in that time of experimentation.

Brad began showing me magazine photos of women having sex with each other. They turned him on. He started talking about a threesome. The more I resisted, the more determined he became. We were in our new bedroom one night when he grabbed me by the back of my head, twisting his hand in my hair, and forced me to look at graphic photos of lesbians.

"Look at them!" he screamed. "Look at them!"

"I don't want to," I said, closing my eyes.

"Look!" he yelled. "Open your eyes and look!" He twisted my hair more tightly in his fist and pushed my face against the page, bending my neck until it hurt.

I was embarrassed by what I saw. Sex with a man was one thing, but I couldn't imagine having sex with another woman. The thought terrified me.

Not long after that encounter, I was painting a mural on our new apartment's living room wall with another teenager who liked hanging around the studio and was a friend of mine. I'll call her Alice. She was sweet, innocent, and cute. We decided to drop acid, and when we were high Brad suggested that Alice and I strip down and paint in the nude. Before I realized it, the two of us were naked, holding paintbrushes, giggling, and laughing. Brad sat back and watched.

A few nights later, Brad fed me downers, and when Alice arrived he maneuvered both of us into our bedroom. He got what he wanted. I was shocked at how gentle and tender Alice was when we embraced. My only sexual experiences had been my rather clumsy first sexual outing, when I'd lost my virginity to Greg at age fifteen, followed by my rushed marriage to Brad.

In the coming weeks, Alice visited our bed several times, and I began to wonder if I was a lesbian because I enjoyed being with her more than I enjoyed being with my husband.

At about this same time, I walked out of our bedroom one afternoon naked and found Brad and one of his friends in our living room. Eyeing me closely, his friend announced, "Now, that's the most beautiful thing I've ever seen!"

Brad replied, "She's my wife. You're not sleeping with her."

I realized that Brad considered me to be his personal property. What I said or thought didn't matter. If I had any doubts about this, what happened next proved it.

Another young woman named Grace became a regular at our station, and Brad wanted desperately to screw her. She wasn't interested. Brad began scheming. He soon became obsessed with her.

"I want you to seduce Grace's husband," he announced one night.

"What are you talking about?" I replied.

"Go over to their apartment and have sex with him," he said. "You can do that, and when Grace finds out, she'll sleep with me."

Brad was now trying to pimp me out. I felt degraded. I also felt helpless. Brad had become physically abusive. It had started with a slap about two years earlier and had escalated quickly. My husband would become enraged, grab me by my long hair, and knock me to the floor, where he would punch and kick me. One night he beat me and then poured his beer over me; he might as well have been urinating on me for the shame I felt. During another argument, I went for a butcher knife; he stayed away, but it just made him angrier.

The next time we got into an argument, we were standing outside our apartment, and he began slapping me. I fell down, so he began pulling me by my hair along the concrete. A man saw us, and I screamed, "Call the police!" The man paused, looked at Brad, and then kept on walking. That was how it was.

After that beating, I decided to tell Brad's parents about their son. I waited until he was asleep, then began walking to Brentwood, where they lived. I chose to walk because I didn't want to risk starting our car and waking him. I'd gone about two miles on the three-mile journey when I decided to lie down on a stranger's lawn for a few minutes to catch my breath. I looked up at a tall palm tree. The scent of the flowers and the cool grass reminded me of Grandmother Moore's lawn in Greenwich. I began to cry, but soon gathered myself and pushed on. Why was my life so difficult?

I woke up Brad's parents, and when we were all seated in their living room, I blurted out that Brad was physically abusive. I asked for help. I didn't know what to do.

"You just need to be patient with him," his mother said.

My father-in-law stayed silent.

I could tell from the tone of Brad's mother's voice that she felt abuse was something women were simply expected to endure. Cindy, the DJ whom I'd hired, had told me that she was living in an abusive marriage. It's just how some men are, I was told.

I walked home feeling completely overwhelmed.

The term "domestic violence" hadn't yet become part of society's vernacular. A year earlier, in 1972, the Ninety-Second Congress had approved the Equal Rights Amendment, but before it could become law, it had to be ratified by thirty-eight states, and Phyllis Schlafly was leading a highly publicized fight against its passage. Women were still second-class citizens when I turned twenty, in July of 1973, and I was clearly one of them.

Brad had taken control of me mentally, too. He'd undercut what little confidence I had and slowly stripped me of my dignity. I was afraid to challenge him, to argue with him, or disobey him. I didn't think anyone would want me if he abandoned me. I felt like my own parents hadn't wanted me. I felt ashamed, and I certainly didn't want Glenn or any of my other siblings to know that our marriage was a sham. Once again I felt trapped. Where would I go? I had worked hard to make our radio station successful, and I didn't want to turn my back on that. My animals and the station were the only good things that I could claim in my life.

After several days of unrelenting pressure from Brad, I drove to Grace's apartment when I knew she was at the station with Brad. Her husband answered and proved easy prey. He was older, and I was struck by how gentle he was when we had sex. I also realized that I was not a lesbian; maybe I was bisexual. I could enjoy making love to a man, even an older stranger. It was Brad who repulsed me.

Brad was waiting like a dog on a stoop when I returned to our apartment. I thought he would feel triumphant, but he was furious. He'd told Grace that I was seducing her husband, but rather than expressing a desire to get even, she had gotten upset with Brad and fled the station.

"Did you do it?" he snarled.

He asked me for details, and when he realized that I had actually enjoyed myself, we got into a bitter argument. I vowed to never let Brad do that to me again.

And then things got even worse.

I woke up feeling sick. The next morning, it happened again. A doctor confirmed I was pregnant. The same mothering feelings that I'd had when I was fifteen and had fantasized about having a baby swept over me. I would have someone I could take care of and who would love me. I wouldn't need Brad.

I told Brad, and he called his parents. None of them was happy. Neither of us had a paying job. We smoked pot every day, and I was taking more and more pills to make my marriage to Brad tolerable. Brad's parents said they didn't think I should have the baby. We were too young and irresponsible. Besides, it might be born with a defect because of all the illegal drugs that I was consuming.

Brad agreed. He didn't want a baby. Our priority had to remain the radio station. He had plans to expand and eventually make it profitable. What had happened, I silently wondered, to all his bluster about not giving a damn about money?

Brad's father was a medical doctor, and he spoke to a physician friend of his who was a gynecologist. Abortions were still illegal, but the gynecologist agreed to give me a D & C—a dilation and curettage—which all of us knew would accomplish the same goal. Brad's father drove me to the office to make certain I went through with it. I cried after it was over. Brad assumed it was because the D & C was painful. But it was the loss of the baby I had been speaking to in secret—the child whose tiny presence in my body had given me hope for myself and my future—that made me cry.

Every time I thought I'd hit rock bottom, I fell down deeper.

I'd not seen Valli Quinn for months when she stopped by our apartment one night. She was still studying acting, but she confided in me that she had been hospitalized for depression. She talked about her famous father, who had left her mother for his new wife, sired three more children, and recently had fathered another child outside his marriage. What was it with men and infidelity? Valli was estranged from her dad. I understood. Although my dad would write long letters from Africa, the opening was always "Dear Kids," and his notes were filled with news about what *he* was doing. He didn't have a clue about what my life was like. He signed his letters "Love, Dad," but I considered him a stranger.

Valli began stopping by more and more, and one night when she showed up, I was stoned in the living room. I watched as Brad led her into our bedroom. Valli had always found him attractive, and Brad would screw any woman who was breathing. I didn't care.

Valli disappeared from my life after that. She vanished. We would not become reacquainted until three decades later, and when we talked about that night, she apologized. Going to bed with Brad had made her feel cheap, she said. What she had no way of knowing was that I felt cheap with him too; dirty and worthless is how I felt with him.

Our emotions have a way of blindsiding us no matter how hard we might try to keep them tamped down. One morning, after Brad had humiliated me again by having sex in our bedroom with yet another woman, I found myself standing in our apartment kitchen feeling as if time were slowing down.

Brad was broadcasting from our studio downstairs. Our monitor was on upstairs. He had just started playing the Rolling Stones' new song "Angie" when I decided to kill myself.

"Angie" had been written mostly by Keith Richards, and it hit the *Billboard* Hot 100 list in 1973. It was about a dying romance, which is probably why it seemed so poignant to me. Much later Richards would reveal that Angie had not been a woman at all. It had been a pseudonym for his addiction to heroin.

Listening to it that morning, I began to cry. I dropped down onto the tile floor, raised my knees up against my chest, and began rocking back and forth. Ziggy Stardust pushed against me, purring loudly. I clung to my cat like a lost child, crying so hard that Poo, my dog, came over and nuzzled me, clearly worried. I had to escape from—what? Brad? No. More than Brad. Reality. My life.

When "Angie" finished, I heard Brad's voice return to the radio. I climbed to my feet and took out a large plastic bag of cross whites. I scooped up a handful and stuffed them into my mouth. I kept swallowing until the entire bag was empty. I'd downed at least fifty pills—more than enough to do the trick, or so I thought.

With the plastic bag still in my hand, I walked downstairs to the studio, where Brad was on the air. I wanted him to know what I had done and that he was the reason why. I wanted him to know my death was his fault.

He did a double take. "What did you do?"

With tears wetting my cheeks, I replied, "I've taken them. All of them. I can't stand living like this anymore; I want to die."

A look of disgust mixed with fear washed over his face as he flipped the switches to put our station on autopilot.

"You stupid bitch," he snapped, coming toward me. "I can't take you to the hospital. They'll call the cops. You'll be arrested and sent to a loony bin. Which is where you belong! As your husband, I could have you committed!"

He shoved me into a nearby chair.

"Stay here and don't do anything stupid," he said.

Cross whites dissolve quickly, and I was beginning to feel pain in my head as they hit my brain. Suddenly I felt intense physical pain, and I got scared. I was actually going to die.

Brad came back in with a neighbor who was an RN. She took one look at me and hurried into the kitchen, emerging with a chalky, thick concoction in a glass.

"Drink this!" she ordered.

I drank, and by the time I made it to the toilet, I was heaving up the pills. She forced me to drink another glass of whatever it was. There was nothing left in my stomach, but I still kept retching. My body was covered with sweat, my throat burned from vomit, and my head felt as though it would burst open. The nurse took my blood pressure every few minutes at first, then once every half hour. She stayed all night with me.

That night I made myself two promises. I would never attempt suicide again by taking drugs, and the next time I tried it, I wasn't going to tell anyone.

I looked a mess. My hair was falling out because of the diet of uppers and downers that I was taking daily and my poor nutrition. The only food I ate, when I ate, was junk food. I was emaciated, barely weighing a hundred pounds, and my eyes were withdrawing into my skull. There were scabs on my head, and I kept myself so stoned that days were beginning to blend together in an endless, meaningless blur.

Glenn telephoned to check in on me. I hadn't told her about any of my problems—my suicide attempt, the abortion, Brad's physical abuse, our failed marriage, or my growing dependence on drugs. I'd not told her because I didn't want to be the problem child anymore. What was the point? What could she do to help me? She was finishing her final year at college, where she was acting in plays and would be elected to the Phi Beta Kappa honor society upon graduation.

Our lives were opposites. I was trapped in an abusive marriage, wanting to kill myself. I was afraid to leave Brad because he'd told me numerous times that if I tried, he would track me down and kill me. I believed him. During our call, Glenn sensed something was wrong, and after she hung up she called my mom and they agreed to fly to Los Angeles to check on me.

When I answered the door, they both gasped. I was in such miserable condition—mentally and physically—that they decided I needed to leave with them immediately. Mom said she was taking me to Wyoming. After spending nearly sixteen years in Africa, my parents had bought a ranch in western Wyoming. Sublette County was the least populated county in the least populated state in the union. They had chosen a remote area where, as my dad later put it, the two of them could "get off the world for a while."

I didn't argue. I needed to be rescued. It was the only way I could free myself from Brad. Glenn began packing clothes while my mom went to tell Brad that I was leaving.

"Jessie is leaving you. She's coming home with me," Mom announced.

He was angry and began arguing. My mother held her ground. She had lived, often alone, in a paracommando camp surrounded by violent soldiers. My twenty-one-year-old husband didn't intimidate her.

In words that seemed to be spit from his mouth, Brad replied, "You Close women are all cunts!"

"Bradley," my mom said, "don't you ever, *ever* talk to me that way again."

Brad ducked past her to the place where Glenn and I were standing. "Don't you dare go," he warned me.

I wondered if he would become violent by grabbing me or striking Glenn or even my mother. I saw the fury in his eyes. It was a look of pure contempt.

"I'm leaving," I said.

Brad had to have the final say.

"Go ahead," he said with a smirk. "The only reason I married you is because of your money."

CHAPTER ELEVEN

It's about a two-hour drive from Jackson Hole to blink-and-you'll-miss-it Big Piney, Wyoming, aptly nicknamed the Icebox of the Nation. Winter winds have been known to whip endlessly across the high desert plateau, causing temperatures to dip to some of the coldest found in the Lower 48 and creating a moonscape of white when the ground gets blanketed by snow.

My dad's desire to "get off the world for a while" came after he'd become disillusioned with his friend President Mobutu. Starting in 1971, the president began forcing his country to return to its native roots. All Western-style clothing was banned, and the president demanded that his people rid themselves of their European, "colonial" names. He changed his own name from Joseph-Désiré Mobutu to Mobutu Sese Seko Koko Ngbendu Wa Za Banga. My parents had been living comfortably in Africa in Mimosa, a compound built exclusively for medical personnel. The community, built next to the river, boasted thirty houses for thirty doctors. My father had helped transform the city hospital into a two-thousand-bed medical center, and he still loved seeing patients. However, the president had begun collecting wives, and to pay for their expensive tastes he'd started looting the national treasury. Torture, corruption, nepotism, and extravagance would soon become the hallmarks of his dictatorship. It had been a good time for my parents to leave.

Ever since they were young, Mom and Dad had dreamed of retiring to Wyoming. Shortly after they returned to the United States, they flew to Jackson Hole and hooked up with a real-estate agent. When they saw the ranch in Big Piney, they fell in love with it.

The main lodge and outbuildings were located on 640 acres, nine thousand feet above sea level, tucked in between mountains with names such as Old Baldy, Bare Mountain, and Triple Peak. For them, it was perfect. The fact that in winter the ranch was not habitable didn't bother them. The Mickelson family sold the ranch to Mom and Dad and also offered them their "honeymoon cabin" on their ranch to use during the winters while they built on ten acres near them. This gave my parents a mountain getaway and a "city" home located on the outskirts of Big Piney.

I arrived at their mountain lodge in 1974, after Glenn and Mom rescued me from Brad and took me away from my beloved radio station and Los Angeles. Dad met us at the Jackson Hole airport in an old yellow pickup truck. I couldn't stop staring at the mountains. I had never seen anything like them. I chose to ride in the back of the truck so I could better take in my new surroundings as Dad drove along the Snake River, weaving between peaks and through valleys. The sun seemed brighter here than in LA. The air was cool to the tongue. I had never seen such seemingly untouched beauty.

When our truck finally made it up a rock-covered road into my parents' new home, a sense of relief washed over me. In this remote spot, I would be safe from Brad and far outside his grasp.

My parents' new home was an old dude ranch. The lodge was made of thick logs cut from the nearby timber. Next to the lodge, four cabins were placed one after the other, strung together by a boardwalk, with one other cabin behind them. The lodge contained a large kitchen, pantry, and walk-in freezer, a dining room, and a massive living room. The lodge's porch was enormous, and off the porch, on a lawn, was an outdoor barbecue grill, picnic tables with benches, and a hammock. I was assigned to one of the cabins, each of which had two bedrooms and two baths.

As soon as I got settled in, the phone rang. It was Brad. My hand began shaking as I held the phone up to my ear. He was whining and explained that he wanted to talk to me one last time before he killed himself.

I was scared, and after I hung up, I went into the living room and began pounding my head against the wall, screaming and screaming. Everyone came running. I was pulled away from the wall and forced to lie down on a couch. I was hysterical. Dad gave strict orders to anyone visiting us to hang up on Brad if he called again. He did, but Dad got the phone this time. Brad declared to my father that he was coming to Wyoming to get me. My father replied: "If you take one step into Wyoming, I'll have the FBI and local police arrest you."

Exactly what Brad would be arrested for was never clearly stated, but my father sounded so convincing that Brad backed down. Meanwhile, I was touched that my father cared enough about me to threaten Brad. For the first time in a long while, I felt protected.

Years later I would discover that Brad had no intention of killing himself. He'd called me from a cheap hotel room, where he was with a woman. With me gone, our radio station had no funds. Brad would have to shut it down and find a paying job. That's why he had sounded so desperate.

I had no intention of staying with my parents forever, but I needed time to lick my wounds and recover both mentally and physically. The discussion about what I should do next wasn't long in coming. No sooner had I unpacked than I began feeling the same old anxiety that I'd always felt around my parents. "What are we going to do about Jessie now?"

At first I planned to return to California, maybe to San Francisco, where I could use my contacts to get a job in the music business. My parents didn't like that idea because they feared I would fall back in with the same drug-using crowd. Dad suggested I find work as a secretary. Mom wanted me to return to school to earn my high school diploma. I realized how little they knew about what I had been doing with our cable radio station—CABL 108. Brad and I had been underground celebrities: we were known at the Troubadour and were sought out by magazines and counterculture types who wanted to launch their own stations. Coming from LA, I was a bit of a radio snob and thought the stations in Wyoming were awful.

I felt like an alien in Wyoming in other ways. On August 8, 1974, I sat glued to the seat in our van, refusing to leave the radio while my parents were having a picnic. The banks of the creek near them were dotted with cow pies, and that was all I could smell and I hated it. I was waiting to hear President Richard Nixon announce his resignation. I was thrilled that he was being forced out, and I knew my friends in LA would be celebrating, but it didn't appear that anyone in Big Piney even cared that he had been such a crook.

I soon realized that not much had changed between my parents and me—especially between me and my father. Conversations were awkward, except when both of us had a few drinks to lubricate our tongues. The booze helped me relax, and I enjoyed listening to him talk about his adventures in Africa. One night, I asked him why he and Mom had let me marry Brad when they knew beforehand that I had taken a drug overdose.

"Jess," my father said, "you are very convincing when you want to be. We believed you wanted to get married."

Was I really that convincing? I wondered. Or was that an excuse?

I filed for divorce from Brad. Still hoping for a free ride, he demanded alimony from me, but a judge—thankfully—denied it. I turned twenty-one years old on the verge of being a divorced woman. My parents gave me an etching of a mouse as my birthday present, and, in an immature and ungrateful way, I didn't hide my disappointment. To please me, they decided to give me an old Volkswagen bus they had at the lodge.

It was time for me to move on, so we decided that I would drive my van to Tucson, Arizona, where Grandmother Moore was by then spending all her time. I packed my VW bus and headed south with Ziggy Stardust the cat and Poo the dog, still a flower child at heart, driving her hippiemobile.

I'd spent most of my early teen years with Grandmother Moore, so I felt welcome there, enough to enroll in Pima Community College, even though I'd not finished high school. I liked my classes and was determined to do well, but old habits are hard to change, especially when you're twenty-one, recently divorced, and out on your own. Shortly after I arrived I abandoned my grandmother's guesthouse and moved into a tiny house on East Glenn Street. This house was built for a midget. The sinks and showerhead were very low, and I'm not tall but I had to bend my knees to take a shower. Still, I liked it. I was on my own for the first time in my life.

At a popular watering hole called the Cushing Street Bar, I found a new gang to hang with. The bar had opened a year earlier in a historic building that had two-foot-thick adobe walls, an antique cut-glass chandelier hanging over its bar, and an art nouveau statue of Cleopatra as its trademark. My new crowd not only drank heavily but also smoked weed and got high. I'd already tried cocaine in LA, and now it was sweeping across the nation.

I loved the energy that snorting coke gave me. Sleep was irrelevant. I would stay up until 4:00 a.m. or later and spend my time writing, listening to music, and drawing. I felt liberated in Tucson and soon was racing from one man to the next, going on so many dates that I'd get them confused. One man called me, and, thinking it was someone else, I began to complain about what a dull and boring date I'd been on the night before.

"This is the dull and boring man," he snapped and hung up.

I was so mortified that I slipped into a depression and didn't leave my bed all day. I did, however, get gussied up for another night out—again—even though I was shouting to myself to stay home.

My tiny brick house was connected by a carport to another house that was the mirror image of mine. Two college-age boys lived in it, and one night I stripped naked, put on a blue silk kimono, and went next door to borrow a cup of sugar. I knew these boys had been ogling me, and I wanted to torture them. I let the opening of my kimono slip a bit, but not so they could see everything, and talked to them for a while. I was proud of my legs, and the kimono was very short; by the time I left they were practically panting.

I'd discovered that sex gave me power, and I enjoyed both sex and power. As soon as I got a man to fall in love with me, however, I lost interest and dumped him. I had no idea why I was doing this. I wondered if my promiscuousness was aimed at my father and feelings of male rejection. Was I punishing these men because of him?

One of my favorite lovers was a man who was a bum. He actually lived on the streets. After a night of lovemaking at my house, I awoke to discover that he'd stolen my truck. Another lover was an African American. When my landlord saw us together, he threatened to throw me out because I was "cohabitating" with a black man. That only made me more determined to do whatever I wanted. One night I brought a businessman home with me from a bar. We had sex, and after he was dressed he pulled a hundred-dollar bill out of his wallet and put it on my bureau. I was outraged and handed it back to him. But when he left I thought, *Gee, that could be an easy way to make money!*

There were times when I would wake up in the morning and think, *Okay, Jessie, this has to stop. You are not going out tonight.* But when darkness came, I would start applying makeup and picking out an outfit. It was as if I were having an out-of-body experience, because I could actually see myself putting on lipstick in front of my bathroom mirror—as if I were floating above the scene, totally helpless to prevent the train wreck below. I seemed powerless to stop this woman I was watching from going out, from sleeping with men, from doing drugs.

At one point, I was dating a coke dealer whose best friend was another coke dealer, and he was dating a girl, Leslie, who was the close friend of a Tucson doctor. This doctor had the hots for both of us and came over to Leslie's house one night promising to shoot us up with a drug that, he claimed, was even better than cocaine. In return he wanted a threesome. Leslie and I plopped down on her couch while he opened his medicine bag.

"I'm going to inject you with morphine," he announced. "It's going to make you feel as if you'd gone to heaven."

I panicked because Brad had given me morphine in Africa and it had nearly killed me, but the doctor was convincing and I decided this was different because he was a medical professional. I closed my eyes when the needle hit my skin, and within seconds I could feel the morphine racing through my blood, causing me to relax. Leslie was soon high, too, and we began to kiss. When the doctor tried to join us we told him no. We went into Leslie's bedroom together, leaving him frustrated and alone. We thought his agony was funny.

Leslie and I spoke every day after that, and I began to wonder, again, whether I was bisexual. Then an odd thing happened. Leslie got jealous. She didn't want me sleeping with men. We had a nasty argument, and during it I suddenly flashed back to Brad. It didn't matter if I was in love with a man or a woman—either could become possessive and controlling. Having lived through one abusive relationship, I wasn't going to let Leslie take control of my life. I ended our relationship. On the drive home from her place, a jackrabbit bolted in front of my car and I hit it, leaving its smashed body on the road. I suddenly felt tremendously guilty and actually wished I were dead. I was having major mood swings, although I didn't have the vocabulary to describe it. I was going from being giddy and sexy to feeling depressed and suicidal. I assumed it was the drugs and booze.

The coke dealer I was dating asked for a favor. He and several others in our crowd had bought a "brick" of cocaine—about a pound—from a dealer in Mexico. My boyfriend had found a buyer, but they needed a mule to transport the brick. It sounded exciting and easy. I'd never sold drugs, but I didn't want to disappoint him.

I soon found myself driving across Tucson with a brick of cocaine on the seat next to me. The exchange was going down at a friend's house. I arrived early and hid the coke under a cowboy hat that I spotted near the front door. My boyfriend and his pals arrived, and a few minutes later some strangers pulled up.

"You got the money?" my boyfriend asked.

One of the two buyers opened a briefcase, and I could see that it contained stacks of hundred-dollar bills. *This is just like the movies*, I thought.

"Where's the cocaine?" a buyer asked.

"She's got it," my boyfriend replied. I was the only woman in the room with five men.

Suddenly, the two strangers drew pistols and yelled, "FBI! Everyone down on the floor! Now!"

All of us fell on our bellies.

Oh, my God! I thought. *I'm going to go to prison and will have to send a telegram to Mom and Dad telling them what I've done.* My entire body began shaking, and I began to cry. One of the gunmen noticed how frightened I was and apparently felt sorry for me.

"It's okay," he said, "We aren't really FBI agents. We're just ripping you off. Now, where's the cocaine?"

My boyfriend, who was lying next to me, whispered, "Don't tell them!"

"What?" I asked.

"I'll handle this," he whispered.

He was a Vietnam vet, and I realized that he was planning to leap from the floor and attack the two armed men. He was going to get us killed.

Before he could, I screamed: "It's under the white cowboy hat by the door!"

My boyfriend shot me a furious look as the gunmen snatched the cocaine.

"Let's take the blonde with us," one of them said.

I let out an ear-piercing scream followed by another. I couldn't stop screaming.

"Okay, okay, never mind!" a gunman yelled. "Just shut up."

Both of them bolted from the house with their briefcase of cash and our coke. My boyfriend and his buddies grabbed their guns and ran after them. I ran from the house, too, but in the opposite direction.

When I got to my house, I packed an overnight bag and drove to my grandmother's house. It was time for me to get out of Tucson.

I had relatives on the Close family side who lived in Washington, DC, and when I called they offered to take me. As soon as I could, I left Tucson and didn't look back.

What had happened in Tucson—the endless string of men, the drugs, the dope selling? Why was I acting so wild?

Sometimes, only when you look back in life can you understand your past actions. This is true for me. I was still more than thirty years away from being correctly diagnosed by a psychiatrist as having bipolar disorder. Only decades later would I learn that severe mental illness had been a driving force in my life since my teens, often causing havoc, although I was completely unaware of its influence.

Although no one really knows exactly what causes our brains to go haywire, the National Institute of Mental Health, our government's leading research institution for the investigation of mental disorders, has declared that serious mental illnesses such as mine are biologically based and passed along genetically. Bipolar disorder is a mood disorder, which means it can cause you to go from feeling elated to feeling worthless within minutes. Another common serious mental illness, schizophrenia, is a thought disorder that can cause you to hear voices or see things that are not there. It is not uncommon for both conditions to surface in women in their late teens and early twenties, a time when girls are often experimenting with sex, drinking, and drugs.

Of course, I didn't know any of this when I was in Tucson. Nor did I know that two common symptoms of bipolar disorder in young women are risky behavior and hypersexuality. Dr. Kay Redfield Jamison, a clinical psychologist at Johns Hopkins University School of Medicine in Baltimore and one of our nation's foremost experts on bipolar disorder—an illness that she has—has shown through research that women with bipolar disorder often are promiscuous. Fifty-seven percent of young women diagnosed with bipolar disorder become hypersexual during periods of mania. Typically during mania, a person has rapid thoughts, stays up all night, takes foolish risks, and pushes the limits—all things that I was doing in Tucson between 1974 and 1975.

I was just damn lucky that my drug use, hypersexuality, and risky behavior didn't end up with my getting a sexually transmitted disease or being arrested, imprisoned, or killed. When I was finally diagnosed, I would understand why I felt as if I were hovering above my own body at times, watching myself, helpless to intervene. I'm not trying to excuse my actions. I've been frank about them. I am trying to put them into context, however. And in Tucson, my untreated illness was driving the train, and I was clearly a passenger on that crazy ride.

I fled Tucson with an impressive college transcript in hand, despite my extracurricular activities. I'd gotten all As and was still determined to finish college. My first choice was New York University, partly because Glenn was living in Manhattan. I landed at my relatives' house in Washington, DC, but immediately boarded a train for New York to visit Glenn.

She was appearing in small roles on Broadway. If I could get into NYU, the two of us could room together, I thought, although I knew my sister's life was focused on her career, not on men, drinking, and drugs. That was a good thing, I decided. She could help me get my partying under control. So I relaxed with Glenn for a few days while waiting to be accepted at NYU. I tagged along, eating and drinking at the Joe Allen restaurant with her theater buddies. It was exciting to listen to her chat about the plays she was auditioning for. She was determined to make it, and I admired her single-minded direction.

NYU rejected me, and I didn't take it well. I fell to my knees and sobbed. My dreams of New York living with Glenn were dashed. Instead I began applying to schools in Washington, DC, and resigned myself to living with relatives, at least until I could get back on my feet.

What none of us realized was that I was not alone. My mental illness was still hiding deep within me—undetected—and it had no intention of sparing me.

VIGNETTE NUMBER THREE
by Glenn Close

Mom and I have arrived in Los Angeles to rescue Jessie from her abusive husband, Brad. I remember the broad slabs of sand-colored sidewalk and the perfectly manicured grass between the sidewalk and the curb—Los Angeles grass, strangely tough and spiky, watered by ubiquitous sprinklers, sucking up the dwindling aquifer. I remember the apartment building, with its reddish, pebbly facade, resting on cement pillars and softened by an undulating landscape of manicured scrub and palm trees. It's not fancy, but it looks downright grown-up for my little sister.

Upstairs in Jessie and Brad's apartment it is another story. At first look, the apartment seemed to be a place occupied by a couple with things on their mind other than housekeeping. The living space wasn't big, but it seemed comfortable enough. I see white walls and not much furniture. I think this was the only time I saw one of Jessie's apartments. She had been married to Brad for a while, but I had never seen where they lived. I had no concept of what their life together was like. I knew that in one apartment, visitors had been encouraged to add their personal graffiti to a wall. I knew that they had started a pirate radio station in a closet and had been busted by the FCC. But I think this was another apartment. It was the first time I'd been in a living space that my little sister shared with a guy.

When Mom and I arrived, tense and not knowing what to expect, we must have been shown around a bit, because I remember Jessie telling us about the mouse that lived in the stove and how she had to pound on the top before she lit a burner so the mouse wouldn't get cooked.

She always loved mice, as did I. She had a brown mouse when she was little named Elsa Baxter. She loved Beatrix Potter, especially her stories about mice. What better excuse to not learn how to cook! The mouse had his rights.

I can still remember being aware of the fact that Mom and I were there together and were actively extricating Jessie from a bad situation. It wasn't an action on behalf of any group, condoned by committee. It was for one of us, a family member, who needed help. Jessie had been left to fend for herself much too early. Even though the scene was unhappy and fraught, Mom being there was hugely significant and made me happy.

Brad was skinny, with long, dark, dirty-looking hair, wearing baggy jeans and a faded T-shirt. When he realized that Jessie was serious about leaving him and that Mom and I were serious about taking her away, he started getting more and more agitated and verbally abusive. We tried to ignore him, because there was no use reasoning with him, and anyway the case was closed. As Jessie hastily threw some things into a bag, Mom and I tried to keep Brad at bay. He was saying terrible things, but there didn't seem to be any danger of his getting physical. He ended up propping himself against the doorjamb, gathering himself for another aggressive verbal assault.

The image that is frozen in my memory is of our mother standing squarely on her feet, as if ready to take a punch. She is facing Brad, who suddenly lunges forward and screams, right into Mom's face, "All you Close women are *fucking cunts!*"

Now my image of Mom unfreezes. She pulls herself up to her full five-foot-nine-inch height—making her taller than Brad—plants herself directly in front of him, and, like a lioness defending her cub, says in a voice that makes my hair stand on end, *"Don't you EVER say that to me again or you will REGRET IT!"* Brad was practically blown backwards and looked as if he'd been slapped, stunned into silence by her raw ferocity. He abruptly left the room and never reappeared. To this day I can still feel how astounded I was by Mom—stunned and then positively elated. I believe she would have taken blows for Jessie. She was saving her, protecting her, breaking Brad's hold over her. It was incredible.

Somehow she had found a voice I had never heard before and had used it to defend her child, and that voice seemed to rebalance the world.

Mom and I got Jessie safely back to Wyoming and up into the foothills of the Wyoming Range, which edges the southwestern side of the Green River Valley. In 1974, Mom and Pop had bought what had been a rustic dude ranch, and it had become a haven for our family. It ended up being an impractical place to live year-round because the elevation meant that it was snowed in until June, but at the time I'm writing about it was summer, and the ranch was the first private family-owned gathering place we'd had in more than thirty years.

That night Brad called Jessie and told her that he was going to kill himself if she didn't come back. He was like a virtuoso, playing Jessie like a violin until she started screaming. She screamed so loudly and for so long that a friend who was staying in one of the adjacent guest cottages came sprinting over in his boxers, thinking she was being attacked by a bear. It was incredibly upsetting to see Jessie so distraught, caught up in such a destructive relationship. We calmed her down as best we could. I was happy that she was out of Los Angeles and living in a place with vast, stunning vistas and cool, clean air.

One day all of us went on a picnic-hike up into the mountains behind the ranch. We quickly discovered that Jessie wasn't able to walk any appreciable distance without getting completely exhausted, so the going was slow. I'm sure the elevation didn't help. Pop loved to fly-fish, so we made our way to a beautiful mountain stream and found a perfect place to spend the day. With Pop happily fishing, Mom, Tina, Jessie, and I thought it would be fun to wander downstream to a place where we could strip naked and take a dip—back-to-nature girls. We found a picturesque little pool and stripped down together—a first for all of us. We had visions of lolling in the water under the hot, high-summer sun, but when we stuck our toes into the swiftly running stream all three of us gasped and screamed in unison. The water was glacial, unimaginably cold! It was impossible to even put a toe in it for more than a second. We suddenly realized that of course there was still snow in the mountains, so we'd just stuck our toes into melted ice. It was hilarious and made us feel like ridiculous tenderfoots. So much for our dream of being carefree mountain nymphs!

Alarmed at Jessie's pallid skin and lack of energy, Pop had her blood tested at the clinic in town and discovered that she was malnourished and dangerously anemic. She confessed that she had only eaten at Jack in the Box for the previous year. She looked scrawny and unwashed and had let all her body hair grow. In a family where wearing suede was considered revolutionary, hairy legs and underarms were blatant signs of outright rebellion. But she was back with family for now, and we were concerned for her.

Thinking back, I realize that even though Jessie had tried to kill herself twice, and even though she seemed to have no control over her sexuality and had gotten herself into an abusive relationship and was doing drugs to cope, in spite of all that, none of us *ever* thought that she might be suffering from a mental disorder. The possibility simply wasn't in our consciousness and was never part of any conversation. From our perspective, she was living on the edge, unfocused and out of control. She had made all the wrong choices. She was basically uneducated, having walked out of high school in tenth grade and never gone back. Her impending divorce would be a recurring behavioral pattern in the years to come. In our ignorance, the family consensus was that she either had to get an education or get a job.

Little did I know at the time how the events of that summer would change my life. I had just graduated from college and had suffered through several series of national theater auditions. I hadn't been offered anything. The phone service up in the mountains was nonexistent, so on a grocery run into Big Piney one day I called Grandmother Moore's house, where I was based at the time, to see if I'd gotten any messages. Suza, the cook, said that someone from the New Phoenix Repertory Company in New York had called for me. The message was a week old! I returned the call and was told that they wanted me to come in to audition for their fall season of three plays to be produced on Broadway. I flew back to New York a few days later, auditioned, got the job, and began my professional career.

I left Jessie that summer in Wyoming hoping that she would come to some kind of understanding with Mom and Pop, hoping that she would be able to make a viable plan for the next stage in her life. Little did I know how infrequently we would see each other in the years to come. We didn't have a tradition of close contact as a family. People didn't call each other as much back then. Cell phones and the Internet didn't exist. So it was easy to go for weeks, even months, without making contact. Jessie became a peripheral figure in my life. I vaguely knew what she was doing and rarely saw her. It was two more years until Mom and Pop moved back from Africa for good. They settled in Big Piney, and Pop revived and ran the Marbleton–Big Piney Clinic. Our lives veered away from each other. Now it seems inconceivable that I was so cut off from my siblings, but that is the way it was. They all eventually gravitated to Wyoming or Montana, initially to be nearer to our parents, but I was rooted in New York theater and soon had the beginnings of a movie career. Family was not on my mind.

CHAPTER TWELVE

Mount Vernon College for Women in Washington, DC, had just been accredited as a four-year college and was trying to expand, so it accepted me as a student despite my on-again, off-again attempts to complete my education.

Although I had planned on living with my relatives when I'd fled Tucson, I used my trust money to rent a one-bedroom apartment in an old building across from the Washington National Cathedral in northwest DC. I enjoyed visiting the giant church. Sometimes I would wander around in its catacombs in jeans and a sweater, causing churchgoers to look at me strangely—or at least I thought they were looking at me strangely. My apartment was a ground-floor unit with bars on the windows. There was a garden out back, but there were too many trees to let in the light, so there were no flowers and only a few blades of grass. The apartment was cell-like, so I bought a calico kitten to keep me company, but she insisted on climbing my body with her needlelike claws, always ending up on my head, which made it difficult to study. I took her back. I felt very alone.

An English teacher at Mount Vernon was impressed with my writing and told me that a friend of hers, a reporter named Kandy Stroud, needed an assistant. I drove to Georgetown to meet her.

Kandy was one of a handful of young, attractive female reporters making names for themselves in the 1970s in journalism circles. A profile she'd written of former secretary of state Henry Kissinger was typical of the New Journalism sweeping the country—a style known for the personal remarks that reporters would often include in their stories.

"What are you trying to do? Seduce me?" Kandy quoted Kissinger as saying when they met for an interview. "You know I like these hot pants very much," he reportedly added, referring to the skintight shorts that Kandy was wearing. She then delivered her trademark knife into Kissinger's back by writing, "One cannot help wonder if the movie stars [whom Kissinger dated] mind that the ankle socks of Washington's greatest swinger are falling down, that his wiry chestnut hair, which flashes golden in the intense white sunlight, is too close-cropped to run their fingers through or that at least 10 of his 178 pounds protrude over his thin black belt, somehow shortening his 5 feet 9 inches."

Kandy was writing a book about Jimmy Carter's 1976 presidential campaign, and she hired me as a typist and researcher. One afternoon she sent me to cover a speech that Rosalynn Carter was giving in a hotel ballroom swarming with reporters, all dutifully scribbling down Rosalynn's every word. I started taking notes, and then the absurdity of the scene hit me.

"This is kind of stupid," I whispered to a reporter next to me. "I mean, one of us should just write this down and give it to everyone else. It would save a lot of time."

The reporter glanced up from her notes long enough to glare at me. "This is how we make our livings," she said.

Kandy was pleased with my reluctant note-taking, but I was beginning to question whether being a reporter was something I'd want to do. Not long after that, Kandy asked me to join her at the 1976 Democratic convention, being held that July in New York's Madison Square Garden. I jumped at the chance. The Democratic and Republican conventions had always seemed riveting on television, especially when Chicago mayor Richard J. Daley unleashed his police on demonstrators at the 1968 Democratic convention.

Kandy got us credentials that enabled me to sit in an area reserved for the media and to interview delegates at ten-minute intervals on the convention floor while she stuck close to Carter and his entourage. My enthusiasm quickly waned. Everyone knew Carter already had locked up more than enough delegates to capture the nomination, so there wasn't much real news happening.

By day two, Kandy was beginning to get annoyed with my cynical comments and note-taking. Most of what I was seeing was meaningless fluff orchestrated for television. I didn't like crowds, so I avoided actually going on the convention floor. When a band struck up "Dixie," I groaned.

I also felt uncomfortable in the press box because the male reporters working around me were incredibly sexist. A well-known ABC political reporter grabbed the back of my knit dress, causing the clinging material to pull snug around my figure. Laughing, he made a comment about my breasts. The women reporters were just as obnoxious. Helen Thomas, the legendary UPI reporter and White House correspondent, noticed that I was taking notes about what she was saying one afternoon. Without warning, she grabbed my writing tablet and hissed, "Don't you *ever* write anything about us!"

I needed a break from the droning convention speeches, so I slipped away to visit Glenn, who was having dinner at a friend's apartment. Glenn had just finished appearing in *Rex*, a Broadway musical about the life of King Henry VIII, with songs by Richard Rodgers. It had opened and closed in less than two months, after only forty-nine shows. Months earlier, Glenn had invited me to a rehearsal, and Rodgers had asked me what I thought of the show.

"It's coming along," I replied truthfully.

Glenn had been mortified.

Reviewers had loved Glenn's portrayal of Princess Mary Tudor, which marked her first musical role on Broadway.

When I arrived at the apartment where Glenn was having dinner, I noticed a little Baggie of cocaine with a mirror and razor next to it in the living room. I certainly knew the coke wasn't Glenn's, because she never did drugs. As soon as she and her friend went into the kitchen to fix dinner, I took a snort. Actually, I took several, and before I knew it, all the coke had gone up my nose. I licked the mirror clean of any white dust. Still not satisfied, I helped myself to a bottle of tequila that was innocently sitting there. I was in such a rush that I didn't bother to pour it. I simply began chugging.

Glenn was angry when she returned and saw me. Our host wasn't too thrilled, either. I was asked to leave.

Still not wanting to be at the convention, I hailed a cab and had the driver take me to a party that *Rolling Stone* magazine was throwing. It was mobbed, and admittance was by invitation only, but I pushed my way to the door and flashed my press credentials. The beefy guard there wasn't impressed.

"That don't work here. You got to have an invitation!" he snarled.

Just then I spotted Jimmy Messina, of rock group Buffalo Springfield and Loggins and Messina fame.

"Jimmy," I screamed. I knew him from our cable radio station days.

"Let her in!" he hollered.

The bouncer stepped aside, and within seconds I was smoking a joint. I noticed a correspondent from *60 Minutes* smoking, too. When I woke up the next morning, I couldn't get on my feet, so I simply groaned and rolled back over.

Kandy had arranged for me to interview Lillian, Rosalynn, and Amy Carter that morning. We were supposed to ride in a horse-drawn carriage from the convention to Central Park and back, and my job was to ask the three generations of Carter women about their impressions of Manhattan. I was specifically told to not ask anything political or controversial. Pabulum.

I wouldn't be able to interview anyone in my condition, I realized, especially a possible future First Lady, her elderly mother-in-law, and her young daughter while riding in a horse-drawn buggy during a muggy summer Manhattan morning. The very thought made me vomit, literally; I just made it to the bathroom. I fell back in bed and went to sleep.

Kandy fired me that same day. I caught a train back to our nation's capital. My journalism career hadn't lasted long.

Anyone else would have been thrilled to interview the Carters and been excited about covering a convention. What was wrong with me? Glenn had called me completely irresponsible.

Back in my dank apartment, I tried to focus on classwork but found myself easily distracted. One night, I felt someone staring at me. I was sitting at my desk, reading in my apartment, when I felt a pair of eyes boring into my skin. I needed to turn my head to see who was there. But I was afraid to look, afraid of what I might see, so I stared harder at the textbook in front of me and tried to ignore that intense feeling of being watched.

It didn't work. I had to look. Mustering my courage, I turned my head, and my heart began beating faster. There was a young woman sitting on my bed, and she was looking directly at me.

I forced myself to look at her face.

It was me.

I was watching myself.

I closed my eyes and reopened them. I was still there.

I'd done so much acid in Los Angeles, snorted so much coke and smoked so much pot, that my first thought was that I was having a drug-induced hallucination. There was only one problem. I hadn't dropped acid, snorted coke, or even smoked weed that day, and this was different from any acid trip I'd ever taken.

Maybe I was sitting on my bed, I thought. Maybe I was—I am—watching myself at my desk. Looking down, I checked my hands and feet to make certain I was still sitting at my desk. I was. When I looked back at the bed, I was gone.

I tried to convince myself that I was exhausted. Once I got a good night's sleep, everything would be fine. I went to bed hopeful.

The next day wasn't better. Something was wrong. I began feeling as if someone or something was waiting outside my apartment door. I wasn't certain what or who was outside, but whatever was there, it wasn't good, and I couldn't risk opening the door and facing it. The only safe thing to do was to stay hidden in my apartment.

I soon ran out of food except for a single head of lettuce. I took my time eating it raw, as I would an apple, because once it was gone, I knew I would have to get groceries. I wasn't sure I would be able to unlock the door and leave. Late that night, I took the final bite.

The next morning, I got dressed and began telling myself, over and over, that I had nothing to fear. I told myself there was no bogeyman waiting outside my door, poised to attack. I walked to the door but hesitated before touching the knob. When I reached for it, I suddenly jerked back my hand. I couldn't do it. I had to do it. I couldn't do it. I had to do it. It was as if my mind were having its own argument. My rational and irrational selves were wrestling for control. I forced myself to reach down and grasp the knob. With every bit of strength that I could conjure, I turned it and opened the door.

As I forced myself out onto the street, I kept reminding myself that everything was fine, but inside, each step filled me with more and more dread. I didn't relax until I had made it to the store, bought groceries, and returned to the safety of my apartment.

That day, I decided it wasn't good for me to live alone. I needed to be around other people.

I contacted my relatives in Washington, DC, and asked if I could move in with them. They agreed, and at first I felt better. But the change in scene didn't change the problem, which was me. I soon was engaging in more promiscuous behavior, which alarmed my relatives. It was time for me to move on. I had worn out my welcome.

More bad behavior.

CHAPTER THIRTEEN

A *Washington Post* classified ad caught my eye: ROOM FOR LEASE AT POTOMAC LODGE. The vacancy was inside a six-bedroom, million-dollar-plus house within a stone's throw of the Potomac River in Glen Echo, a picturesque hamlet across the DC border in Maryland.

Potomac Lodge? Million-dollar house? It sounded too good to be true.

I drove there and rang the doorbell.

"C'mon in," a husky voice hollered from inside.

I pushed the door, which was lighter than I imagined, and it flew open, striking against an interior wall with a loud bang. The sun shining behind me caused the man standing inside to squint.

"You make quite a dramatic entrance," he declared.

"Sorry," I said in apology. "I'm Jessie."

"I'm James Thompson. Welcome to Potomac Lodge."

He had a firm, confident handshake and was handsome in his tight denim jeans and a polo shirt that accentuated his muscular build.

"Was this really a lodge?" I asked.

"No," he said with a chuckle. "My cousin Roger and I gave it that name. We like to think of it as a retreat from the world."

I liked that.

Cousin Roger was Roger Glen Brown, and he was at work. "He's an analyst for the CIA," James volunteered. Nodding to the east, he said, "The agency is located directly across the river from us."

So much for CIA secrecy, I thought. "What do you do for a living?" I asked.

"I'm a healer," James replied.

"What?"

"I help heal people."

James sized me up as a possible tenant as he showed me through Potomac Lodge, and I sized him up as a landlord. James and Roger were from Texas. Their mothers were sisters, and each of the boys had been an only child. They considered themselves to be more like brothers than cousins. James had gone into the army directly out of high school and fought in Vietnam, returning home in 1967. He'd worked with Xerox Corporation long enough to build up a nest egg and then quit.

"Why'd you quit a good job?" I asked.

"It was interfering with my reading," he said.

"Your reading?"

"Yes."

James was thirty-two years old—nine years older than I was. Roger was about the same age. Roger had earned a PhD from the University of California at Berkeley and had gone to work as a China expert "across the river."

James and I were both Washington newcomers. "I was on my way to India," James confided, "when I stopped a few months ago to visit Roger, and he asked me to stay." Roger was in the midst of a messy divorce, James explained.

"Aren't they all messy?" I asked, making conversation.

It turned out that James and I both were divorced.

James said he and Roger were leasing Potomac Lodge from one of Roger's CIA colleagues, who'd been sent to some exotic capital to be a station chief. They'd rented all the bedrooms except for one.

"We're pretty picky," James warned. He and Roger each had a room; a third was rented to a researcher at the National Institutes of Health, and another was rented to a Securities and Exchange Commission employee. The fifth bedroom, off the kitchen, was going to be used by a housekeeper, whom they hadn't hired yet.

"We've gotten a lot of responses from the ad," he added. Potomac Lodge was built on a hill, with the front facing east and lower level, or basement, dropping down an embankment that led to the Potomac. The downstairs featured a spacious living area, two bedrooms, and a bath.

A large window had been installed in one of the walls to show the soil and rocks behind it. Someone had placed little plastic men in space suits on the dirt behind the glass so it looked as if they were walking on the moon. I loved it.

"Who lives downstairs?" I asked.

"Me," James replied. "And whoever we choose as our final tenant."

I liked James and really liked the house, so I was happy when Roger called me later that night for a telephone interview.

"James already told me that he wants to rent our empty downstairs bedroom to you," Roger announced. "But I feel obligated to ask a few questions."

A few days later, I moved in, and from that moment on James, Roger, and I became best friends. The other two tenants kept to themselves, but we ate dinner together, smoked pot together, and spent hours philosophizing about our future and our lives. Sometimes our discussions turned into loud but good-natured arguments. At that point I would stand on a chair to be taller, explaining that my point of view was coming from a higher perspective. James thought that was hilarious. We would laugh and laugh, and I felt so free, so safe being myself with these two wonderful friends.

The house was much too expensive for them, but James had convinced Roger they could afford it if they rented out the other rooms and got the tenants to pay the lion's share of the rent.

"I call it coasting uphill," James said proudly. "If you use your wits, think outside the box, aren't bound by convention, and are willing to take risks," he explained, "you can live in a million-dollar house without paying much money."

James was smart, unique, and seemed to have life figured out. I admired that, because I was feeling adrift, especially after the Kandy Stroud fiasco and my out-of-body experience. I still felt very much like the lost problem child. Before moving into Potomac Lodge I had sought answers by trying *est*, an acronym for Erhard Seminars Training that its founder claimed was also the Latin word for "it is."

It was the brainchild of Werner Hans Erhard, who'd held his first seminar five years earlier in San Francisco, and the program was sweeping across the nation. Scores of Hollywood celebrities, eager to learn the secret of a happy life, had signed up, including Cher, Cloris Leachman, Joe Namath, Yoko Ono, John Denver, Jeff Bridges, and Peter Gabriel. During Erhard's standard sixty-hour, two-week seminars, attendees were harangued about their empty and unfulfilled lives. Rather than chasing after happiness and success, *est* taught its followers how to live in the moment—or, as Erhard told one of his biographers, "The *est* training offers people the opportunity to free themselves from the past, rather than living a life enmeshed by their past."

Not being enmeshed in my past was one reason I had been drawn to *est*, and when Erhard came to DC to give a lecture, I got James and Roger tickets. They found Erhard interesting but not convincing.

Besides, James had developed his own "coasting uphill" philosophy, which the three of us often discussed late at night while drinking wine and smoking weed.

"A life should be lived in segments," James explained one night.

"What do you mean?" I asked.

"Decide what you want to do—say, during your thirties. Maybe it's travel or living abroad or some other adventure. Then go do it, and when you have done it, move to the next segment—the next thing that you want to experience."

Life wasn't about work or even families. It was about experiences. James had no interest in having children, because they were a complication and an attachment. The same could be said about owning a house and establishing roots in a particular location. They could become encumbrances and could hinder the full enjoyment of life. The only reason to work was to earn enough money so you could afford to do whatever you wanted to do next. Moving up in a career didn't matter. Having a career didn't matter. All that mattered were worthwhile experiences that brought color, enjoyment, and knowledge into your life.

I was enthralled with James's "coasting uphill" philosophy except for one of its core tenets. He argued that an individual should choose when he would die, and he should then end his life on that day. James claimed that if a person chose a specific date, then that individual could optimize his life because he would know exactly how long he had to live. James had chosen his "exit" date. It would be on his fiftieth birthday. He didn't have any interest in growing old or suffering from the various ailments that can inflict the aged.

James asked me why I was searching for answers through *est*. When I told him about my deeply held feelings of rejection and abandonment by my father, he suggested that I free myself from my past in a symbolic way. One of the only belongings that I had brought with me to Potomac Lodge was an old wooden bedroom dresser that seemed to weigh a thousand pounds.

"You should bust it up and burn it," James suggested.

"Are you telling me that as a friend or as a healer?"

"Both."

James helped me carry the dresser up from my bedroom into the foyer. Armed with a hammer, I began busting it into pieces, which James then carried into the living room fireplace to burn.

Roger came home about midway through my healing ritual.

"What the hell are you doing, Jessie?" he asked.

"Getting rid of my past."

He walked into the living room, and seconds later I heard him and James talking rapidly. Putting down my hammer, I hurried to see what was happening.

Huge flames were shooting from our fireplace into the living room, threatening to ignite the furniture and carpet. The dresser had been painted so many times that it had become highly flammable. The flames were so hot that we couldn't get close to them. We threw pots of water into the fireplace, then we simply had to wait for the fire to cool. Later that night, we all laughed because James's healing advice had nearly set Potomac Lodge on fire.

I was falling in love with both Roger and James. But with Roger it was the love of a best friend. With James it was deeper. I was in love with a man for the first time in my life. It was a new feeling for me. Even though I had been married to Brad, I'd never loved him in the way that I loved James. This felt genuine. It felt good.

I knew from our conversations that Roger and James had an ironclad agreement that neither of them would become romantically involved with a tenant, but I wasn't going to let that stop me. After dinner one night, I excused myself to get ready for bed. I took a bath and shaved my legs. I knew James would want to use the bathroom that we shared. When I was finished getting ready, I stepped out into the small hall outside the bathroom just as James emerged from his bedroom. Our eyes locked. Spontaneously I lifted my leg and placed it along a wooden banister that was close by.

"I just shaved," I said innocently. "Feel how smooth this is."

He touched my calf, then ran his warm, dry palm up my thigh. He moved in and kissed me with the softest lips I'd ever kissed. I melted. That night, we became lovers.

During the coming weeks, I fell deeper and deeper in love. James owned my heart. Every sense seemed brighter. One night we walked down to the Potomac River and were mesmerized by the fireflies in the trees. It was as if magic surrounded us.

The yearlong lease on Potomac Lodge was coming to an end as New Year's Day approached in 1977. James and I discussed what we wanted to do in the "next segment" of our lives—a segment that we wanted to spend together. We decided that his savings and my monthly trust-fund stipend would give us enough to embark on a once-in-a-lifetime adventure.

James had been on his way to India when he'd stopped to visit Roger. We decided to go there. I no longer cared about finishing college. When we said good-bye to Roger, I told myself that moving into Potomac Lodge had been one of the best decisions that I'd ever made. As long as I was around other people—people who cared about me and who loved me—I was not afraid to leave my room, nor was I having any out-of-body experiences.

Just as James had said, he was a healer, and he had helped me heal.

As we boarded our flight to India, I was sure of it. Good days lay ahead.

CHAPTER FOURTEEN

If you travel about 180 miles east of Delhi, you'll arrive at the banks of an eye-shaped lake tucked between seven hills in the Uttarakhand state of northern India. The lake is thought to be the home of lake gods and a holy place. In January of 1977, James and I couldn't have found a more romantic locale than Naini Tal, the city of about forty thousand people that formed around the lake's edges. We checked into a hotel and began searching for a house to rent. The hills of Naini Tal are steep. The climb to our hotel was at such a pitched angle that the tops of my feet threatened to touch my shinbones. I wasn't sure I could live there, but that was in the beginning. I soon developed strong legs, but not as strong as the Nepalese men we saw carrying enormous logs up the mountain for fires and construction. I noted how they leaned into the hill, allowing gravity to assist them, and when I tried walking that way it helped.

We found a large house named Pili Khoti, overlooking the city and the lake, and just as James had predicted, we were able to live free of financial burdens on his savings and my trust fund. We were like honeymooners, and our new exotic surroundings enhanced our feelings of romance and magic. I loved the wonderful sense of chaos that was Naini Tal, where simply buying a sari in the market was an adventure. When storms gathered we'd watch the small boats, called pirogues, all swept together in one place to ride out the rain, like leaves on the lake. On beautiful sunny days the sparkles on the water seemed loud. Crows were everywhere. They were huge and made a noise I'd never heard before—deafening, raucous, wonderful.

James and I noticed that each night other strange-sounding birds would begin squawking and continue until dawn, when their incessant sounds would stop. I decided to ask Mukundi Lal, a wiry man of indeterminate age whom we'd hired as our houseman, about the racket.

"Those are not birds, memsahib," he replied. "They are chuck-i-doors."

"What?" I asked, having never heard of such a bird.

"Old men blowing whistles."

He explained that homeowners hired elderly men to sit on their front porches each night to guard against thieves. To keep themselves awake and to stay in contact with one another for safety, the men would blow whistles. This way the sleeping homeowners were not disturbed by the watchmen calling out to one another.

"You must hire one," Mukundi insisted.

James and I didn't think we needed a guard, but after our house was burglarized a few days later, we sent Mukundi to find one. He returned with a relative, one of the oldest-looking Indian men I'd ever seen. The only thing older than he was his rifle, which looked as if it hadn't been fired since the 1800s, when the British first took control of India. James and I doubted our watchman was capable of protecting anything, but Mukundi assured us he could. At dusk, the old man would arrive and sit at the doorway of our house, chirping happily on his whistle until morning, when he would disappear with the morning sun.

I began to understand the Indian caste system and how it permeated everything, especially employment. This was a system of give and take, everyone knowing his or her role. Mukundi Lal made sure every chore was covered. We were required to hire a sweeper woman and her daughter, who used bundles of sticks that didn't look like they were making much difference, although the women dutifully swept the concrete floor each morning. We also had a laundryman who would come by twice a week to pick up clothes and bring back clean ones. My Western clothing soon began to fall apart, so I followed our man one day to investigate how the washing was done. Over a fire sat a huge cauldron of boiling water, where the clothes were stirred before being moved to another cauldron of hot rinse water. Then—and this was the part that amused me—the garments were laid on the ground to dry, the same ground where dogs and children and cows walked. I decided to buy a sari to wear instead of relying on my disintegrating clothes. I walked into the village and purchased a beautiful one, but Mukundi was horrified when he saw it.

"Oh, no, memsahib—no, no!" he exclaimed, raising both arms in alarm. "This sari is only for sweeper women, laundrywomen. You must not be seen in it." Leading me out the door, he took me back to the market, where he directed me to a more appropriate sari. I also had to purchase a maroon slip with a string tie and a top, both made from the same cotton material. He told me that ankle bracelets were usually worn and proudly shepherded me around the bazaar as I purchased other necessary items. When we returned to the house, he began making dinner while I showed James my loot. The sari was peacock blue with a maroon border and gold threads; the ankle bracelets were silver and had tiny silver teardrops hanging from a chain. We had to use pliers to close the latches; they were meant to stay on.

Purchasing the proper sari had been the first step. The next day Mukundi showed me how to wear it. After I had put on my slip and top, he fussed over the folds. He was adamant about my wearing them in front, because women in the cities wore them on the side, but in the country the correct way to fold them was in the front. Once the folds were gathered, they were tucked into the cotton slip. The remainder of the fabric was pulled across my front and then dropped down my back. I felt very feminine in my sari, although it took practice to learn to walk in it. I also wished I hadn't cut my hair very short before we left the States. Short hair while wearing a sari seemed just wrong. The sari wrapped around me, then flowed up and over my shoulder. My hair should have been part of that flow, all mingling together—my hair and the silk of the sari, like the sea.

Every morning Mukundi would wake us by rapping on the door then entering with our morning chai—very strong tea sweetened with sugar and lightened with milk. The beverage was served in small glasses. One morning James was standing naked when Mukundi came into our bedroom. He glanced down at James's penis, his eyes got as round as saucers, and, after putting the tea tray down, he fled. Little wiry Mukundi lost his cool for a minute! We laughed over that one for a long time.

One more person was added to our household—a young Nepalese called Man Singh, who looked like a young, slender Charles Bronson. He was also an untouchable. Hindus could not touch an untouchable without going through a whole cleansing routine afterward. They were considered less than human because they had been born into the lowest caste. Man Singh was in the house to help Mukundi with washing windows, hauling hot water upstairs, and beating rugs. Man Singh came to us for about four hours per day. Once, when he was bringing a pail of hot water upstairs, I touched him on the arm; he snatched his arm away as if burned. I apologized. He looked so scared that my heart went out to him. I began giving him English lessons, and he caught on quickly. But despite his raw intelligence, I knew he was marked for life as an undesirable.

Many nights, the electricity would go off; James and I would peer through the windows to see whether the whole village was in darkness. If not, we would groan and have to replace fuses in our fuse box, risking shock. If the town was dim, we would simply laugh. We discovered that seven was the perfect number of candles for reading. We would arrange them around a plate filled with water. The moths that danced in the flames would fall into the bowl and drown; otherwise it was impossible to read with their flutterings and dusty crawlings. I came to look forward to the power blackouts, when the entire village would go dark except for the moonlight reflecting off the lake and the flickering candles and the fires that dotted the mountainsides.

For James
You are my soul
My ecstasy—
We curl together
Our lake in view
The moon's thumbprint boldly
Shimmering

In 1977, there was no Internet, no cell phones. To communicate with our families we wrote letters and, if need be, sent telegrams. We called

James's mother once from a phone in a neighbor's house. We were cut off, and I loved it. Except when we got sick.

Having lived in Africa, I was in the know about dysentery. But the dysentery I contracted in Naini Tal was above and beyond anything I had experienced before. With a temperature of 104, I tried valiantly to stay seated on our toilet. It wasn't happening. I fell off onto the concrete floor and just stayed there, dribbling blood from one end, vomiting from the other. We were a long way from Delhi, so we had no choice but to stick it out. I remembered my mother's use of the BRAT diet—bananas, rice, apples, and tea—in Africa. That helped. My only positive thought was that I was building my immunities. When I recovered, I asked Mukundi to show me how he was sterilizing our water. He put a pot of water on the coal fire, turned the timer on to twenty minutes, and waited. He was supposed to turn the timer to twenty minutes after the water began boiling. I could have strangled him! I lost two weeks being sick.

When I felt better, I began riding on horseback most mornings. A Muslim man named Abdul would ride to our house with my favorite horse. I generally would ride on the wide dirt path to the top of the basin, called Snow View, and look out to the Himalayas. There was a tea stand there, and dogs. It was almost impossible to find a spot where there weren't any people or tea stands—or dogs, for that matter.

One day Abdul asked if I would like to go farther up into the mountains. We rode together on trails of packed dirt and leaves, the horses' hooves muted, their steps sure. Ravens called, and the air was cool, with a light scent of wood smoke. We passed a woman carrying a large bundle of sticks on her back, a burden that was held in place by a wide strap on her forehead. Suddenly Abdul turned to sit sideways on his horse and began to sing. As our horses climbed higher, his voice carried in the cool air, singsong. I had never truly appreciated Indian music until that moment. When we came to a very steep, narrow trail, Abdul stopped singing and swung his leg back around his horse. The animals carried us up and up until we finally arrived at an open, flat area. I saw a huge tree, its branches spread out wide. Leaning against the tree trunk, legs crossed, was an ancient woman smoking a pipe. Her eyes were white with blindness. A small house was near the tree. We greeted her—*Namaste*—and she slowly nodded her head. We rode just a bit farther, to a place where the trees stopped growing, and dismounted. A huge rock offered sweeping views of the scenery, and I stood on it. Nothing but thick jungle lay at our feet; a hawk flew below us, skimming the trees. Two seeds attached to their cottony parachutes flew toward me, and I caught them. With the seeds in my fist I made a wish that James and I would be together forever, then allowed them to fly again.

James would ride with me some mornings, and we would talk about the books that both of us were going to write. I was keeping a daily journal about our adventure; I wanted to publish articles about our experience in India.

In our memories, we always remember the best of times, but the journals that I was writing were filled with notations about my crying at night or exploding in rages. One moment I was happy that we were in Naini Tal, the next I was furious because I thought I should be doing something grander than living in a house in India with no purpose. My journals contain notations about Valium, over and over again—Valium to get me to sleep, Valium to calm me down. My moods would change from mania and frantic periods to melancholy spells that included picking fights with James and debilitating feelings of mental paralysis. Unknown to me at the time was that my mood shifts were common symptoms of bipolar disorder. Valium and painkillers such as codeine were easily purchased in Naini Tal, and I used them to level my moods. Abdul confided that sometimes it was too cold to sleep on the ground, so he took Valium. I took both Valium and codeine to get to sleep. And I wasn't cold.

James wanted to write a book about Vietnam, which initially struck me as odd because he didn't like to talk much about what he'd done there. Early on in our relationship, he had shocked me awake one night by screaming in his sleep and then bolting upright in bed. He'd been having a nightmare and was covered with sweat. I asked him what he'd been dreaming, but he wouldn't tell me.

Over time, I'd learned that after James had arrived "in country" in 1966 with the 101st Airborne Division, he'd undergone special training and been assigned to a six-man long-range reconnaissance patrol, called an LRRP. They were sent into the jungle to find the enemy. I'd pieced together enough bits of information to know that his LRRP team had crossed the border into Laos when our air force was engaged in a secret bombing campaign there. During a firefight, the five soldiers with him had been wounded or killed. James carried his best friend on his back out of the jungle only to discover that he had died en route. Thinking about how he could tell his story was a way for James to confront his demons. At twenty-four, I was not yet seasoned enough to write about my childhood.

James loved hashish, and Mukundi arranged for a sticky ball—an almost-black wad of hashish the size of a tennis ball—to be delivered to James, who began smoking hash several times every day.

My dysentery was child's play compared to what happened next. James decided to join me on my morning horseback ride, and when his horse began bucking he reinjured his back getting the animal under control. He'd initially hurt his back in the army. Mukundi had a medicine man come to the house to give James a massage. The result was a hot, shooting pain in James's back no matter how he stood, sat, or laid down.

We decided that Mukundi and I would go to Delhi, rent a room, and find a doctor. James would follow. Mukundi and I caught the bus to Kathgodam. The driver, whom we had dubbed Billy because he looked like a tiny Billy Carter, was so short that his feet couldn't reach the pedals. He clung to the bus's large steering wheel with one hand and touched an exposed wire to where the horn should have been with the other whenever we came to a hairpin curve. The sound warned vehicles coming up the hill. Our trip to Kathgodam was like a carnival thrill ride. At the train station there, Mukundi insisted I purchase first-class tickets, and we were soon settled in our own compartment, where everything was green—the seats, the walls, even the four fans that came on once the train pulled away from the station. I was happy that Mukundi insisted on first-class, as people crowded inside the other compartments and even clung to the exterior and sat on the roof. It seemed that all of India passed before my eyes outside the slow-moving train's barred windows: a group of little boys flying homemade kites; a straw-roofed house covered with vultures; a woman with a tiny baby and a small girl breaking rocks in the sun; ponies carrying dirt from the riverbed; a one-furrow plow pulled by oxen and driven by a boy; little temples at every turn; banana trees, mango trees, corn, barley, rice, a tractor next to oxen, brick next to straw.

We had to change trains that night. I slept in a ladies' waiting room with a horrible headache and no food. Mukundi found me tea. Without him, I would have been lost.

After much searching I found a room in Delhi with an ex-general of the Indian army and his wife. From there, I went to the American embassy and picked up a list of doctors. I chose one and sent word to James. He arrived after an excruciating bus ride. I noted in my journal that James was diagnosed as having a pinched nerve in his back on May 18, 1977. That was the beginning of five weeks of hell for us. Knowing that I needed to be there for James, I became hypervigilant. I washed my hands constantly, refused to drink anything but bottled water with no ice, didn't put my hands on my face, and didn't drink any soda. Meanwhile, James tried one failed treatment after another.

I stayed at his bedside in a local hospital, sleeping on the floor next to him. One night after he was asleep, I needed a break and walked to the Oberoi hotel, where I bumped into a couple from Zaire, as it was then called. I mentioned my father and the fact that he had been the president's doctor. Although they didn't know me, they invited me to a party being held that same night at a Ugandan ambassador's house in southwest Delhi. I joined them, and during the festivities I met a handsome British mercenary who had lived in Africa for the previous twenty-seven years. We began drinking, and he urged me to abandon James and return to Africa with him. For a moment, I actually considered doing it and began to flirt with him. But eventually I demurred and returned that night to the hospital a bit tipsy.

An unhealthy pattern was beginning to emerge. I would be satisfied with my life for a brief moment and then become agitated and act impulsively, sometimes hurting people whom I loved. My actions would confuse even me. With James in pain in a hospital, why was I flirting at a party?

I'd pick a fight, flirt, or flee, still confused, until I landed in a depression, filled with remorse, wondering why the hell I had acted so impulsively. The next day, I told James that I'd gone to the party but didn't mention the flirting or the mercenary's offer to take me to Africa. He shrugged it off. It was just how I was, he said.

We could no longer afford to pay for two houses, and James wasn't getting any better, so I returned to Naini Tal to pack and pay our help for a final time. I didn't want to leave, and I found myself becoming resentful of James. I felt guilty because we had promised all our servants that we would keep them employed for at least a year, but we were forced to leave early. Telling Mukundi was the most heart-wrenching. He had tears in his eyes. I wrote him a glowing letter of recommendation and gave one to Man Singh, too. I gave the others—the chuck-i-door, the laundryman, the sweeper woman, and her daughter—all my cash and ended up going hungry during my return trip to Delhi.

Doctors finally decided that James had a fragmented disk and needed surgery. We were nearly broke, so we contacted Roger, who was on vacation in Germany, and he sent us one thousand dollars. I noted in my journal that James went into surgery at 11:00 a.m. After what seemed hours, a surgeon appeared and told me that he had removed a large disk fragment that had been pressing on a nerve, causing intense pain. I sent Roger a thank you note that took weeks to arrive. James and I had returned to our rental flat by the time Roger called.

"I'll be in Delhi in two days," he announced.

"No, it's okay," I said. "James is doing much, much better. He's out of the hospital."

Roger was undeterred. When he got to Delhi and saw how much weight James had lost and how haggard I looked, he insisted that we celebrate our reunion. I took him aside and told him we were broke.

Roger booked us a table in one of Delhi's only five-star restaurants and said he would pay all the bills. Our meal was delicious, and midway through it Roger excused himself from our table. As James and I watched, he made his way to the band that was playing. He whispered to its conductor and handed him cash.

"What are you up to?" I asked as soon as Roger rejoined us.

A Cheshire-cat grin appeared on his face as the band began to play Carole King's 1971 hit "You've Got a Friend."

I started singing softly along. Roger joined in with the next verse, and even James began singing.

By the end of the song we were crying.

Roger didn't want to return to Germany without all of us having a new adventure—especially now that James was feeling better—so he rented a Mercedes, and we drove to Agra to see the Taj Mahal. Before leaving, we bought a tennis ball–shaped wad of hashish and began smoking.

By the time we reached the Taj Mahal, we were more than stoned. Roger left us alone for a few minutes, and when he returned he declared in a loud voice, "God just spoke to me!"

"What?" James asked.

He explained that he had given a holy man inside the Taj Mahal some money, and the oracle had looked him in the eyes and said, "Thou art my beloved son, in whom I am well pleased."

"You're stoned," I said.

"Yes, I am," Roger replied. "But the holy man told me that God wanted him to say it."

The white marble of the Taj itself was cool to the touch and under our feet. Even though the temperature outside was probably near one hundred degrees, each step taken on that marble was refreshing.

James and Roger had invented a role-playing game when we lived together in Potomac Lodge. They called it Triangle, and they decided to play it during our Taj Mahal visit. Each of us pretended to be an ambassador from a particular nation. James was from the Soviet Union. Roger was the US ambassador, and I was from China. In the 1970s, Henry Kissinger was wooing China out from behind its diplomatic walls, so Roger tried to convince me—as China—that he would make the better ally, while James tried to convince me that *he* would be better. We were drinking wine by then, yet Roger and James engaged in a vigorous debate. I ended the game by putting my arms around James and kissing him. "You win," I declared, "because you're mine!"

Late that afternoon, the sun turned red, and darkness began to descend. We sat in the gardens outside the Taj Mahal and watched.

> *An arrowhead of*
> *Snow geese*
> *Shoots into an*
> *Orange globe of*
> *One setting sun—*
> *I rejoice at their fragility,*
> *At the yearning of my soul,*
> *At the intensity of life,*
> *At my existence,*
> *Which is my*
> *Poem.*

There are only a few perfect moments in one's lifetime, and while it may be difficult to remember everything that happens during your life, these perfect moments are forever burned into our memories. When I close my eyes, I can see the three of us sitting on the cool grass, our backs against the wall. We three would always have each other's backs, against a wall or not—or so I thought.

What we saw that evening was a full moon, a luminescent moon, and in that moment all of us felt completely free, as if there were no struggles in our lives. We loved each other. It was as if all three of us could "coast uphill" forever. The moon and the softly glowing Taj Mahal gave me a gift that night. The gift was our adventures in India; the gift was getting through the hell of James's operation and my own personal hell of being at his bedside. The gift was, quite frankly, love.

Back at our hotel, we went for a dip in the pool to help clear our heads, and Roger made another declaration. He'd decided to use his American Express card to buy us airline tickets back to the United States and to give us enough cash so that we could afford to live comfortably in India while we settled our affairs.

A few days after Roger left, I mailed him a thank you letter. He always got a kick out of how we signed them. I put down my first name and James signed his, so our autograph was Jessie James.

In that letter, I informed Roger that we had cashed in the airline tickets that he had bought for us and were using the money to travel overland across India, Pakistan, and Afghanistan, and then fly to Greece. When you calculated all the costs, we would still have enough to fly home, plus we would get to see three additional countries. Roger sent word back that he was delighted that we were continuing our big adventure together.

Near the end of our stay in Athens, James leaned forward while we were eating dinner at a sidewalk café and said, "Let's get married."

James had told me earlier that he didn't believe in marriage.

"You're kidding, right?" I replied.

"No. Will you marry me?"

I looked at his too-thin face and said, "Of course!"

We left the restaurant and found a priest who agreed to marry us if we could find two witnesses. We grabbed a couple from the sidewalk outside the church.

James was crying when he said, "I do."

It was the second perfect moment in my life.

CHAPTER FIFTEEN

James wouldn't come out of the bedroom. He had made a reading nest next to the window and was staying aloof from my family. James and I had returned from Greece to New York and had driven to Greenwich to be with my parents and siblings, all of whom were living at Grandmother Moore's house.

My family had not said anything blatantly negative about my surprise wedding, but from their less than enthused reactions I knew I had disappointed them again. Dad made a point of telling me that he thought the only reason a couple should get married was to have children. When I told him that James didn't want children, he seemed both relieved and puzzled. Why had I bothered to marry him, then?

I was happy when James boarded a flight for Texas, where we had decided to set up housekeeping as husband and wife. I was scheduled to join him a few days later. The only family member who liked James was Granny Close. Being from Texas herself, she enjoyed his Texas accent and southern manners.

In India, James and I had seemed a perfect match. Now our differences screamed out. He was from Texas. My family and I were Yankees from Connecticut. He'd grown up poor. I hadn't. James was an autodidact. My family had sent me to some of the best boarding schools in the nation. Looking back now, I also suspect James was suffering from undiagnosed post-traumatic stress disorder because of his combat in Vietnam—feelings that he didn't feel comfortable discussing with us. He woke in cold sweats, sitting upright and gasping for air, in the years I knew him. And he would never discuss it.

By the time my flight began its descent into the Dallas/Fort Worth International Airport several days later, I was nagged by doubts. Peering through the jet's window at the landscape below, I felt like an alien about to land on an unknown planet.

James was waiting, and he happily announced that he'd found us an apartment in Arlington, a city between Dallas and Fort Worth. After we'd settled in, James told me that he'd decided to postpone writing his book. He had a new plan. He was going to run for the Texas state legislature from Cayuga, in Anderson County, where both James's and Roger's mothers lived.

I laughed, thinking he was joking.

"Are you completely out of your mind?" I asked.

"I believe I can get elected," he replied indignantly.

He began telling me why, and he was convincing enough that even I began to believe he would. The Texas state legislature only met for 140 days every other year. Being a representative was not a full-time job. Because of his injured back, which was still causing him considerable pain, James said he couldn't work at a regular nine-to-five occupation. Being a part-time legislator would be a good match.

I liked some of the ideas that he wanted to implement. What I didn't like was the idea of being a politician's wife. I had my own plans. I wanted to finish college, and I certainly didn't want to move to a tiny Texas town so my husband could get elected.

"James," I said firmly. "Do you really want some local reporter digging into our pasts—especially my past?"

Continuing, I reminded him that he was still regularly smoking pot. "Even though running for office could be a good idea, under our circumstances it's not."

James was adamant that it was, so I asked: "How are you going to finance your campaign?"

His answer was direct: my trust fund.

My body went cold, and I felt nauseated. "But I'm going to be using that money to pay tuition," I replied. I'd already been accepted at the University of Texas at Austin, which meant we would have to move even farther away from the political district that he planned to campaign in.

"There's not enough money for both of us to do what we want," I added. "And I want to finish college."

Our discussion turned into a debate, and our debate turned into an argument, and that argument soon became emotional. James's back was hurting him, and he was lying on the floor in our apartment as we argued.

"You have no idea what it's like to not be able to do things," he declared. Then he yelled, "To no longer be strong; to be old!"

"I'm not going to support you," I snapped.

I went for a walk. I needed to breathe. There was nothing but pavement near our apartment. I could hear the freeway roaring nearby and the cars coming and going from all the carbon-copy apartment buildings surrounding us. I hated Arlington, I hated Texas, and I wanted to return to the East Coast, to Greenwich. Or, better yet, I wanted to wake up from this mess and be in Naini Tal.

By this point, we had been in Texas about six weeks. Two months earlier, we had been celebrating our wedding in Greece, madly in love. Where had the romance gone? My mind was racing. I began to question whether James and I should have gotten married. Had my parents seen something I was missing? Did James love me, or was he simply after my money? Was he using me? Was this all part of his "coasting uphill" game-playing? Was this my first husband, Brad, all over again?

My love for James was being poisoned by my growing paranoia. I couldn't get Brad and his abuse out of my head; couldn't stop thinking about his bullying, about all of it. There was no possibility of my ever becoming a politician's wife, even if I wanted to be one. Some reporter would dig up all that dirt about me, all the drugs, KPOT, all the sexual experimentation. I felt panic and wanted to run far away. When I finally returned to the apartment James was in the shower.

I telephoned Mom in Wyoming.

"I don't know what to do," I explained. "James wants to run for the Texas state legislature. I want to go back to college. We don't have enough money to do both."

"Jessie, your father and I are not going to give you and James money," she declared in a firm voice.

"I wasn't asking you for money!" I protested.

"Oh," she said.

"I just don't know what to do," I said. "He can't work full-time because of his back. I want to continue college..."

"Does that mean you're going to support him for the rest of his life?" she asked, interrupting.

The reality of that hit me. I visualized myself stuck in his political district in a tiny rented house while James schmoozed with voters. I'd have to hide my past somehow. How would I do it? I already hated the fact that everywhere I went in Texas, people asked me, "You're a Yankee, aintcha?!"

"Maybe you need to get out of this relationship," Mom said.

"I don't have anywhere to go," I replied, becoming distraught.

"You can come here to Wyoming and live with your father and me," she volunteered. "James isn't good for you. You need to leave him." Her bluntness surprised me. "If you stay with him," she added, "don't call us asking for help again."

My thoughts and growing anxiety were already churning inside me when Mom told me point-blank that I needed to make a choice: James or my parents.

When she hung up, all I could think about was that my parents finally wanted me to be with them. After years of feeling abandoned and rejected, they were saying, "Choose us." I would feel safe there.

I heard James turn off the shower and began to panic. I had to act. I couldn't stand this anymore. I quickly called a taxi, grabbed a suitcase, and began throwing clothes into it.

"What are you doing?" James asked when he emerged from the bathroom.

"I'm going to Wyoming," I said.

"What? Wyoming? Why?" he replied, clearly shocked. "Jess, if there's a problem, we need to talk about this. I don't have to run for the legislature. We could move to San Francisco—where Roger is—you could go to college out there!"

I paused long enough to glance into his eyes, which were filled with tears. But I heard my mother's voice in my mind, and my heart grew cold.

"No," I said, slamming closed my suitcase.

As soon as the taxi pulled up to our apartment, I bolted out the door and down the stairs, leaving James completely bewildered. He'd not seen this coming.

As the taxi pulled away, I glanced back at our apartment and saw James standing behind our big picture window watching me go. It would be my last image of him.

I ran off the airplane as soon as it landed at the Jackson Hole airport and collapsed into my father's arms, sobbing uncontrollably.

"I've made a huge mistake," I cried. "I need to go back to Texas. James loves me. This is crazy coming here."

Dad gripped my shoulders, looked into my eyes, and said, "No, Jess. You are not going back. You are coming with us."

Although my father was a brilliant doctor, neither he nor I realized that my hysteria was being fueled by my undiagnosed bipolar disorder. Only much, much later would I understand that panic, paranoia, rapid thoughts, confused thinking, and anxiety were symptoms of my mental illness—symptoms that would surface again and again, always causing my moods to swing dramatically from feelings of momentary elation to utter hopelessness.

James called later that night. We could work out a solution to our financial problems, he assured me. I was overreacting. I needed to come home to Texas. James offered to give up his stupid idea about running for political office. We could move to San Francisco, where he and Roger could start a business together.

He was convincing. I wished I had never called my parents. I wished I had not flown to Wyoming. I had been overreacting. I wished James and I had never left India. I wished we could turn back the clock.

My mind was spinning like a whirligig in a windstorm. Think, think, think. I wanted to be with James. I wanted to be with my parents. I wanted to please James. I wanted to please Mom and Dad. I didn't want to be the difficult, irresponsible child anymore.

I hung up the phone and immediately decided that I was not going back to Texas. I loved James, but we were over. I was moving on. I spent the next two days in bed, crying.

Roger called me as soon as he heard that I'd moved out. "If you divorce James," Roger said, "you will be divorcing me too, Jessie. And I don't agree to that. I say no."

I spent another day crying. My parents accused me of being overdramatic. It was time to knock off the theatrics and stop feeling sorry for myself.

At their urging, I filed for divorce. A requirement was that I had to live in Wyoming at least three months, and I also had to have a reason to get a divorce. I remembered that James said he wouldn't raise a child to believe in Santa Claus or the Easter Bunny, so I told my lawyer that I didn't want to have children with him because of that. It was a ridiculous excuse and wasn't my real reason for filing, but it was enough to satisfy Wyoming law.

I began looking for an apartment and gradually turned James and Roger into memories. As soon as I tucked them away, my racing thoughts and panic dissipated. I was moving forward, or so I told myself.

During the following sixteen years, I lost track of James and Roger. I was convinced that I would see James again in an airport somewhere. But I never bumped into him. He did call me once, years later, and we spoke briefly, but I had moved on and so had he. Still, there was a connection.

In early 1994, Roger contacted me. He said that after our divorce James had moved to San Francisco, where they had practiced James's "coasting uphill" philosophy by renting a large Victorian mansion. James's injured back gradually improved, so much so that he went to work at what then was an upstart telecommunications company, MCI, which had been created by the breakup of the AT&T monopoly. James saved enough for a nest egg, then quit and returned to Texas. His mother had died, so he moved into her home and had finally started writing his book. It had not been about Vietnam. It had been about intimidation in the business world—how to use it to get what you wanted. James had told Roger that he would commit suicide on his fiftieth birthday, but Roger said James had agreed not to do it on his actual birthday because he'd wanted to get his book published first. Sadly, no agents bit, and his book went unsold.

Roger spent hours trying to talk James out of his long-planned suicide. He argued that James's life was not his own to take. It belonged to his friends, too. But James was undeterred. A few weeks after his fiftieth birthday, James sat down and wrote his own obituary. He penned a letter to Roger and several of his friends. He put the letters into a briefcase with other important papers and walked across the road to a neighbor's house, where he left the case. Returning to his mother's house, James wrote a note to the police.

"My name is James Thompson. My body is below this note. I have chosen to die this way."

He told the police that there was no foul play at work and that he didn't want an autopsy. He pinned the note onto his shirt and, seconds later, took his own life.

Roger got a phone call from the police at 4:00 a.m. in California. James's suicide was so devastating that after the funeral Roger sold all his possessions and drove to Collegeville, Minnesota, where he entered Saint John's Abbey with the intent of studying to become a Benedictine monk. He was searching for explanations, for purpose, for hope. He eventually left the monastery without taking a monk's final vows. Instead he returned to Texas, where he began writing a book of his own called *Coasting Uphill*, about his adventures with James.

"James died because of his thinking," Roger told me. "He literally thought himself to death."

There was something else Roger said.

"James had other girlfriends through the years, but you were the most important person in James's life—except for me. He loved you, and he wanted the two of you to live like you had in India. He was a pure romantic in that regard. It was the happiest time in his life and one of the happiest in mine."

Roger mentioned that there had been a brief period after the divorce when James and I might have gotten back together, but neither of us had tried. I discovered another irony years later. The last "rejection" letter that James had received had not really been a dismissal. The agent had simply suggested numerous changes that would have made the manuscript more marketable. Who knows? Perhaps James could have sold his book. When Roger sent me that letter, I realized it was from the same agency that would eventually sell the book that I would write years after leaving James.

None of us gets through life without having regrets, without wondering about those roads we did not take. James is my untaken road. I have always wondered what would have happened if I had stayed in Texas with him or if we had moved to San Francisco together. I have always wondered if he would have killed himself if we had stayed married or if he had gotten help for what I am certain was his PTSD. In the end, it doesn't really matter, does it?

What I cling to are my memories. I remember sitting with James and Roger outside the Taj Mahal on that perfect night. I remember how the moon looked above the gleaming white building. I remember the hot, sticky air. I remember lying next to James in the Delhi hospital when he was suffering. I remember James and Roger and me smoking hashish and laughing. I remember how James smelled after we made love and clung to each other. And some nights, even now, after all these years, I cry because of what was and what might have been.

CHAPTER SIXTEEN

I was alone again.

I was twenty-four years old, back living with my parents in Big Piney, getting my second divorce. I had no job, no friends, and no college. I felt like a total fuckup.

I had to stay in Wyoming at least three months to get a divorce, so Mom and Dad spoke to their friends Gordon and Margaret Mickelson, who had sold them their mountain retreat and the land for their Big Piney home, and they agreed to let me live in the "honeymoon cabin" on their ranch while I waited for my divorce to become final.

Although my parents had wanted to "get off the world for a while" after leaving Africa, my father had soon grown tired of being isolated at their mountain lodge. While running an errand one day, he stopped at the Big Piney medical clinic to introduce himself. The nurse practitioner in charge mentioned that she could use a hand, since there was no doctor in town. Before either of them realized it, Dad was working full-time as Big Piney's new physician. Everyone in town soon loved him, referring to him simply as Doc, and he and Mom began spending nearly all their time in their Big Piney house.

Watching my father fulfill his role as the local doctor reminded me again of what a conundrum he was—how could he be such a personable and caring physician yet so uncommunicative and reserved with his wife and children. He never showed much interest in anything his children did unless he thought he could benefit from it. Glenn was beginning to make a name for herself, and when she did become a Hollywood star my father favored her over the rest of us, totally embarrassing Glenn. She was painfully aware that he loved the glow of her spotlight. Tina, Sandy, and I understood our father's coolness, yet even as adults we kept trying in our own ways to win his favor and the same love that he showered on Glenn. My sister Tina and her two children had also moved to Big Piney when I fled there in 1977 after leaving James. Tina's ten-year marriage had ended in a divorce, and I'm convinced now that we both moved closer to our parents because we wanted more time with them as well as their approval. It might be difficult for others to understand, but when you are ripped away from your parents as children, as all of us were by MRA, a part of you feels incomplete and in need of repair. Tina especially wanted her children to have the chance to be close to their grandparents. Sparked by our divorces, our Big Piney reunion enabled Tina and me to grow closer to our mother, but our father remained as self-absorbed and aloof as he had always been. Our best efforts to please him went unappreciated. Tina had become an accomplished artist, but he dismissed her talent and hard work as a hobby. The two of us were aliens to him—mere distractions that took him away from whatever his newest adventure was. Sandy felt as unsettled about our father as we did. He once refused to speak to Dad for more than a year. Dad also mentioned to me that he'd gone to see a family therapist for advice after Glennie lambasted him in a critical letter. She had taken two days to write the letter, and before she sent it she called us—her siblings and Mom—to let us know what was in the letter. It was her criticism that got him to the therapist—not my brother's refusal to speak to him or anything that Tina and I said.

Despite my efforts and those of my siblings, I don't believe any of us ever got really close to my father. We admired him, and I loved him dearly, but when I was with him, I always felt as if he would rather have been somewhere else. The moments of closeness that we did share were always fueled by alcohol; we would have rousing debates and be very pleased with each other.

Why was my father so distant? That question still haunts me. What is easier to understand is my yearning for his approval and attention and the pain that I felt when I received neither.

Heeding my parents' advice, I stopped feeling sorry for myself and decided that a job would help me move forward with my life. I got one easily at the US Forest Service office, where my main assignment was filling out employee time sheets and typing letters for the rangers, hardly an intellectual challenge. I also kept records about the daily temperatures registered at our weather station. I'll never forget seeing the temperature read minus seventy degrees one morning. I'm not sure if that made the record books, but I saw the thermometer with my own eyes. The head ranger picked up a potted plant sitting next to a door, and when he dropped the plant it shattered like glass. We had fun throwing water up into the air and watching it fall as ice. But breathing outside was a chore, and we didn't go outside without a scarf wound around our mouths and noses.

When the temperature climbed up to minus twenty degrees, we shed our parkas and walked down the snow-covered streets wearing only down vests, as if a heat wave had struck town. In addition to the puffy coat my mother loaned me, I began wearing cowboy boots, the footwear of choice in Big Piney.

One afternoon, a male coworker asked, "Where's the flood?"

He was poking fun at me because the cuffs of my denim jeans were so short that he could see my ankles. Pants of the proper length fell on the middle of your foot in front and on the floor behind your heel in back. I immediately went out and bought longer pants.

I soon found myself enjoying the residents of this rugged terrain. They looked after each other and were hardworking people who spoke their minds and didn't put much stock in pretenses. Even though I missed the hubbub of a major city, I found this region of our country reinvigorating, especially after the East Coast snobbery and one-upmanship that I had seen during my brief stint as a Washington journalist.

After about six weeks inside the Mickelsons' honeymoon cabin, I moved into a ratty trailer that sat on concrete blocks under high-voltage power lines that I could hear buzzing above me. The place was in shambles, but the rent was right for my budget. When darkness fell, I would curl up on my couch with a book and a dark beer and pretend my beat-up trailer was a railroad car en route to some exotic foreign location; I chose Bali more often than not. Each morning when I woke, I would still be under those crackling electrical lines on Big Piney's windswept plains.

During very hot days I felt like I was living in a metal bread box, but small joys can go a long way: I heard bird feet going *click-click-click* on the metal roof above me, and that gentle sound would always put a smile on my face.

I was invited to a branding. I wore my new roughout leather cowboy boots and brought matching gloves. This wasn't a spectator sport, but because I'd never helped before, I was given a job that took no skill. Along with a partner I helped pin a calf to the ground for the gruesome job of castration and branding. I got to hold down the calf's butt, and my jeans were soon soaked with scours (the loose poop from a calf). Blood soon soaked into one of my new boots, and the smoke from the branding iron twirled around my head. An old cowboy came up to me as I was struggling to hold a calf and asked, pointing to my scours-soaked pant leg: "Young lady, what do they call *that* in New York?"

I said, "Shit!" and he clapped me on the shoulder and told me, "You're all right!"

I no longer missed city life. I liked these people, and I liked visiting Mom each day. I realized that I didn't have to leave here; I could make a life for myself in Wyoming, with its endless blue sky and hardworking people.

Tina invited me over one Friday night and introduced me to two of her friends, Betsey Greenwood and Corliss Poindexter, who were cousins and had grown up in Big Piney. They knew how to play bridge, and we didn't, but after a short lesson and a lot of wine and laughing, we mastered the game—or at least thought we had.

From the moment I met Betsey, we clicked—even though her family came from a completely different background from mine. Betsey had been reared on a cattle ranch and had been riding horses and punching cows from the moment she'd been big enough to sit on a saddle. When she was a child, she would join her two sisters and brother every morning in the kitchen, where they would eat a hearty breakfast of eggs, bacon, toast, orange juice, and coffee with their parents. They would discuss whatever they needed to talk about that day and then do their chores before the kids went off to school in Big Piney. At dinnertime, the entire crew was back at that table again, finishing their sit-down meal as a family. To me, the Greenwoods represented the cohesive family that I wanted to emulate someday. Her mother was fast in the kitchen, churning out meals that satisfied her family. Her father was tall and possessed a booming voice. He would tease me by saying, "You stay away from my daughter! You're a bad influence!" But he had a twinkle in his eye and a crooked grin.

Betsey had recently earned a bachelor's degree in economics from Grinnell College in Iowa, and she hadn't intended on returning to Big Piney. But an accident had forced her to undergo knee surgery, and she'd come home to recuperate with a large cast on her leg. Despite her bum leg, we began "running the ridges," the term young people in Big Piney used for barhopping along Highway 189, the two-lane road that cuts straight through the high desert, linking Big Piney to the rest of the world. One of our favorite hangouts became the aptly named Cowboy Bar in Pinedale, a popular jumping-off point for tourists heading into the Wind River Range.

Betsey and I made an odd couple. She stands six feet without shoes compared to my five three and three-quarters. We would tell the men who would try to lure us with free drinks to leave us alone. We had such a good time talking that we didn't want to be bothered, although we would sometimes shoot eight-ball pool. Betsey was an excellent player and often left our macho challengers red-faced because they'd been defeated by women. I would hustle players for her, and we kept the table going, small winnings ending up in Betsey's pocket or on the bar for more drinks.

Betsey and I pushed the limits. She owned an Audi Fox at a time when German cars were still rarely seen in Wyoming, and she enjoyed driving it hard through the hairpin turns along switchbacks in the mountains. One afternoon we picked up two hitchhikers. Both of us had been drinking. Betsey decided to see how fast she could drive up to Fremont Lake in the Wind River Range. The hikers had very large backpacks that stuck out from the trunk of the Audi. They kept craning their necks to see if their backpacks were still with us, their faces turning paler and paler with each speeding turn.

We thought it was hilarious as we clutched our booze in Styrofoam cups while the Audi sent roadside gravel spinning behind it. Both hitch-hikers bolted from her car when we stopped, thankful to be alive.

I was just as dangerous a driver. There's a section of road outside Big Piney where the highway rolls up then down then up again. If I pressed the gas pedal down hard enough while I was speeding downhill, my car would gain enough speed for the wheels to seem to lift off the asphalt when I reached the crest of the hill. I felt as though I were flying, with only the sky and Wind River Range appearing in my windshield. It was as if I were rocketing toward them, free of earth and all my problems. More than once, I would do a U-turn and go back for another exhilarat-ing ride.

On Friday nights, Betsey and I would head to Pinedale, a wide spot in the road, to begin our adventures at the Stockman's Bar, where we would down a couple of Bloody Marys before continuing to our Cowboy Bar hangout. I truly enjoyed the taste of liquor. I also liked how it made me feel. I'd drink vodka until I got tired of having a nasty hangover the next morning. Then I'd switch to gin, and when it began getting to me in the mornings, I'd move on to rum. In addition to getting drunk, I was smoking pot and occasionally dropping acid.

I'd been in Big Piney for less than two months when Tina stopped to see me at work.

"Have you seen the new man in town?" she asked, smiling.

"No. Who are you talking about?"

"He works at the Soil Conservation Service office and is easily the most handsome man in town," she announced. "He's too young for me, or I'd go after him!"

I laughed, but I was curious. I wanted to see what she was talking about, so I decided to drop by his office on the pretense that I was inter-ested in getting a job there. It was December of 1977 and freezing, so I put on my bulky subzero-temperature-rated parka and got in my car.

Tina was right. Tom Pick was handsome, with an athletic build, very dark hair, and blue eyes. He didn't have any job openings, but during our brief exchange I learned that he was twenty-eight years old and had moved to Big Piney from Colorado because he loved to hunt, fish, camp, and ski.

By chance, my father actually needed to ask Tom several questions about the soil where their new house was being built, and Dad invited him to dinner, which was the neighborly thing to do in Big Piney when a new resident arrived in town. My parents told me to come, too, and I caught Tom eyeing my figure, no longer buried inside a balloon-shaped parka.

We began dating just before Christmas. It had been only eight weeks since I'd left Texas, yet I was already moving into another relationship.

My parents thought Tom, unlike James, was wonderful. He was quiet, responsible, polite, and thoughtful. He clearly was not the sort of man who would speed around hairpin turns to scare hitchhikers or launch his car over the crest of a hill.

After dinner, I invited Tom to go out drinking with Betsey and me. Instead of driving to Pinedale, we visited a Big Piney bar called the Water Hole #3, and Betsey and I were thrilled when Tom proved to be an excellent pool player. That night, I hustled players to challenge them and we walked away with a pocket full of winnings.

Three months later, Tom and I decided to live together. My contribution to Tom's apartment on Main Street was a ficus tree and my new dog, whom I'd named Gucci. I'd gone to a local landfill searching for an ironing board because I couldn't find one in town and had found a Weimaraner lying on one. I took both the board and Weimaraner home and dubbed her Gucci because her fur looked like faux suede. Years later, I would see a photo hanging in a swanky hotel in Santa Monica taken by William Wegman of a Weimaraner lying on top of an ironing board—just as my Gucci had been!

Tom accepted me, Gucci, and my ficus tree. I felt safe with Tom. He certainly was not abusive, as Brad had been, and he didn't have the emotional baggage from Vietnam that had haunted James, although Tom had served in the army as a dog trainer in Germany. He was a hard worker who made a good salary with benefits.

When a small house came up for sale two houses down from Tina in Big Piney, I snatched it up, and Tom and I moved into it. We discovered that our new house, which was long and narrow, originally had been a chicken house. Tina's children would come over and play in our huge yard. I remember watching them one day and feeling very much at peace.

Still, deep inside of me there remained a yearning. One night, Betsey and I took off, and after hitting our usual haunts I dropped acid. When I arrived at the house at 5:30 a.m. the next day, Tom had locked the door. I didn't have my key, so I pounded on the door, but he refused to answer. I had to sleep in the car. I was furious, but when Tom came outside I felt too guilty and physically wiped out to make a scene.

A short time later, I awoke one morning feeling panicked. I had no idea why. The day before it had been comforting living with Tom two houses down from Tina. This morning, it felt suffocating. What in the hell was I doing? What of Greenwich, New York, Washington, DC? I'd been a world traveler, but now I was frequenting cowboy bars and drinking hard.

I decided to drive to Greenwich, rent a flat, work on improving my French—which I'd spoken in Zaire—become a licensed jet pilot, and find a job ferrying wealthy French businessmen from Paris to New York, where I would help them negotiate multimillion-dollar business contracts.

It made perfect sense to me, so much so that I drove over to tell my mother about my new, exciting plans.

She listened carefully and then said in a gentle voice, "Jess, I don't think you can do that, really, can you?"

"Of course I can," I declared.

I drove back to our house, loaded my ficus tree and Gucci into my car, and started driving east after Tom left for work.

I was so excited about getting started that I only stopped to take potty breaks and for gas, and by the time I reached Greenwich I was confident that I had just made the smartest decision of my life. It didn't take me long to find a boardinghouse, and after hurriedly unpacking I started my search for a French instructor.

As I was checking the Yellow Pages, the feelings of exuberance and grandiosity inside me dissipated. A voice in my head asked: *What are you thinking? You've really screwed things up this time!*

Moving to the bed in my rented room, I curled up in a fetal position, haunted by feelings of doubt and fear. The next several days became a fog as I slipped between reality and fantasy, between feelings of invincibility and crippling vulnerability. At some point, I visited Sandy, who was staying in a Greenwich apartment, and I also remember talking to Glennie in Manhattan on the phone. She offered to call a friend in the radio business to see if he could help me get a job as an engineer. After our chat, I was certain that moving east had been a brilliant move. But moments later, I was crying and wanted desperately to flee back to Wyoming and Tom. My throat all but closed up. I could hardly speak.

The good days and bad days that I had been having became compressed into good hours and bad hours. I couldn't keep up with my own thoughts or moods. Anxious one moment, buoyed the next, I felt as if I were going to burst. Mustering my courage, I used the pay phone in the rooming house to call Tom. My heart was racing with each ring, and when he finally answered, I blurted out in my hoarse, hysterical voice, "Tom, will you take me back?"

"Jess," he replied, "come home."

My aching throat began to instantly feel better.

I hung up the phone, packed, and drove to Sandy's apartment, where I dropped off my ficus tree. I had no idea why, but my brain was telling me that the tree needed to be with him, not me.

Gucci and I began driving west, and as soon as I saw men in cowboy hats and boots again, I felt jubilant. We made the 2,100-mile trip in thirty-two hours of nonstop driving, and when I pulled into the driveway, Gucci and I both burst from the car to inside the house to see Tom.

He was sleeping and was not nearly as excited to see me as I was to be home with him. For a moment, I thought, *What have I done? I should've stayed in Greenwich.* But I pushed that unwelcome thought out of my mind.

"I'm home," I said, crawling into bed with him. "I'm not going to run away ever again."

He hugged me and fell back asleep.

When I began pestering Tom to propose, he dutifully drove to Jackson, where he bought me a beautiful ring. Clearly he was smitten, so he overlooked my erratic behavior. Or maybe he felt he could change me. We were married in February of 1980 at my parents' new house, with a few dozen friends attending. A local woman made my dress from champagne-colored satin sent by Glennie. It was winter, so my bouquet was a bunch of artificial flowers, but it was beautiful just the same.

The local minister, a Reverend Calvin Elliot, spoke the classic lines "in sickness and in health, until death do you part."

There was no doubt in my mind that I was in love with Tom, but when I heard those lines, I realized there was another reason why I was marrying this man.

I was certain Tom would keep me steady, keep me grounded, keep my uncontrolled moods in check. All I had to do was listen to Tom and stick by his side until death did us part. If I did that, the irrational thoughts and exhausting mood swings would be put into a box and locked tight.

Now that I was Tom's wife, I would be normal.

CHAPTER SEVENTEEN

I was about to meet several of my girlfriends at the Water Hole #3 when Tom confronted me.

"I don't want my wife out drinking in the bars," he said.

I was shocked. "I thought we promised we wouldn't ask each other to change," I replied.

"What you're doing is just not right," Tom replied. "I don't want you out there, period."

Secretly, I was pleased. This was the man whom I had harnessed to keep me in check. Just the same, I rebelled—I actually cried and screamed. But he held his ground, and I stopped going out and curbed my drinking after we were married.

I got pregnant as quickly as I could. We both wanted a baby, and I swapped booze and weed for vitamins and exercise. Most days, I felt great, and when I became moody, Tom and I blamed my pregnancy.

Because of Tom's job we moved from Big Piney to Newcastle, Wyoming, a sleepy town along the South Dakota border on the southwestern edge of the Black Hills. I hated it. I hated leaving my mom; it seemed a cruel situation because of my pregnancy. To me, Newcastle was nothing but a dirty little town. We checked into a motel, where we would live while we found a house to buy, and that first night I climbed into the shower and began sobbing. I didn't want Tom to hear me. After my crying session, I decided I would become the best wife, mother, and homemaker I could be.

Tom found us a place, and I quickly made friends with a woman who also was pregnant. She could cook up a storm. I learned how to make bread from scratch and would take loaves to her house, where we would butter the warm slices and eat an entire loaf. Then it would be her turn to bake, and we'd eat another warm loaf at my house. I cooked, cleaned, shopped, and washed and ironed Tom's shirts and pants. I even watched soap operas while ironing. Once in a while I'd wonder how this had happened to me, this life of wifely servitude, but I didn't dwell on it. I loved being pregnant and developed a silent dialogue with my baby. I thought my child would be so special that he or she wouldn't ever give me any trouble or heartache.

One night Tom and I were lying on the couch watching a western movie about Jesse James on television. The young boy who played Jesse James's son was named Kalen. I liked the sound of it, and Tom did, too, so we decided to name our baby Calen if he was a boy. We changed the K to a C because Tom's father was Charles Thomas Pick, and we wanted our son to have the same middle name and initials.

Tom was with me when my water broke. Gucci had been sticking uncharacteristically close to me for hours. My loyal dog must have sensed what was up. Tom took a snapshot of me as I was getting into our Subaru to go to the hospital. I looked so excited. If I had known what an arduous experience I was about to have, I wouldn't have been quite so happy. I went into labor slowly, then hard. After twenty-one hours, the doctor said I still hadn't dilated enough to give birth. When a heart monitor showed our baby was in distress, the doctor performed an emergency C-section. The umbilical cord was wrapped around our newborn's throat, and if we'd waited any longer our baby most likely would have died. The date was June 19, 1981. We just missed the gifts the hospital would have given us if Calen had been the first baby born on Father's Day.

Holding Calen for the first time was magical. He'd come from me, and I was determined to be the best parent ever. I quickly learned that being a supermom wasn't going to be easy. Calen was a fussy baby at nighttime who cried incessantly and for no apparent reason. Because Tom needed to go to work in the mornings, I would get up at night when Calen began crying. I would walk the floor for hours, but nothing seemed to comfort him; it was as if he had a storm raging in his head. Some nights I would become so exhausted that I would put Calen in his crib and switch on

Dashing Granddad Edward Bennett
Close in his pinstripe suit

Handsome Grandpa
Charles Arthur Moore
on the lake

My dad on the porch of our house in the paracommando camp in Zaire

Bettine M. Close, Mom

The plane we took to go into the bush country

Our house in Zaire—this end of the house was Dad's first clinic

A crowd gathered to greet President Mobutu

On our way to Mackinac
Island from John Street. Our
nanny who we called Ma-Ma
on the right and the MRA
nanny on the left

The four of us, me
being a goof

The four of us with Mom
(in the back) and Grandmother
Moore, her mother (in front of
Mom)

The four of us and Ben, our collie, the day we left for Caux, Switzerland.
It was my seventh birthday.

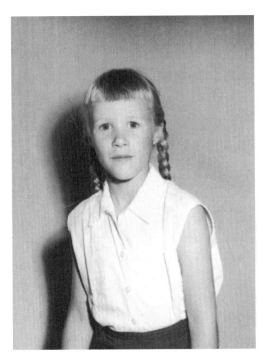

*1960 passport photo
for Switzerland*

*With my beloved
Redstone Rocket*

*Family vacation
in Zaire*

*The six of us on the
front porch of our home
in Zaire circa 1967*

*On President
Mobutu's river boat*

My first and last modeling job, 1969

At KPOT in L.A.

Passport photo, age 22

*Me with my darling
James L. Thompson*

*A week before
leaving for India*

In Bozeman with Wowie, our Samoyed, a gift from Noah Davis

Mom, me, and Glennie in Jackson, Wyoming, early 1970s

With Pop on my
wedding day to
Tom Pick

Tom Pick, me, and two happy
boys, Calen and Sander

Calen with sherry and cookies
for Santa, 1983

HAY
for your
Reindeer

My beautiful eldest sister, Tina Close, in Big Piney in the 1980s

Sandy with Pop Close in the 1980s

Floating the Yellowstone River with family, 1985

Two publicity photos for The Warping of Al, *1990*

Mom, Tina, Glenn, and me circa 1995

Bettine Moore Close (Mom) with her dog pack

Rosalynn Carter with me and Snitz (© Leslie Barbaro Photography)

Calen with Jack

Sander with Joey

Mattie with Wing-Ding

classical music. I would crank up the volume so loud that it would drown him out and I could fall asleep.

Newcastle simply wasn't for us, in part because I had become so homesick. Tom resigned so we could return to Big Piney. Calen, who was then ten months old, was just the right age to make packing a nightmare; I would stuff a box, then he'd come along, supporting himself on the box, his little feet on tiptoes, and pull everything out.

My parents still owned their mountain retreat, and Tom suggested that we turn it into a guest lodge for tourists. My parents agreed. I knew our new project was going to take a lot of work. What I didn't know was that I was pregnant again. When we discovered my pregnancy, I was determined to not let it slow me down.

Neither Tom nor I knew anything about operating a dude ranch, but still we jumped right in and put what we did know to good use. As an outdoorsman, Tom knew a lot about fishing and hunting and offered packages to guests that featured both sports. He was a hard worker and good with his hands. I took charge of overseeing the four guest cottages and turning the ranch into a business. I also cooked and cleaned the main lodge.

I have never worked harder in my life. By 5:00 a.m., I was up preparing breakfast for guests; the first of them arrived in the summer of 1982. I made all the bread from scratch, using my Newcastle training. My specialty became pies, and every night I offered our guests slices of warm homemade pie with ice cream.

Some guests became friends, as often happens in these bed-and-breakfast-style ventures. Julia and Robert Van Nutt of New York told me much later that they were horrified to see me down on my knees, scrubbing the kitchen floor, while pregnant. But I was proud that the state health inspector always gave our ranch a score of 99 percent: he said he always deducted 1 percent because on principle he just couldn't give us a perfect score.

We didn't get to bed until close to midnight each night. With only four cabins and the main house, we needed to rent every bedroom we could, so Tom, Calen, and I slept in an old Airstream camper that was tucked up in the woods next to the laundry house. Tom brokered a deal with our neighbor, Phil Marincic, an old-time Wyoming cowboy, to rent us horses so our guests could ride through the mountains.

I quickly discovered that Tom was a worrier. Unlike me, he became easily tangled in details. We were in the kitchen fixing sandwiches for our guests one morning for a picnic when cowboy Phil came in and overheard us arguing about how to prepare the meal.

"What the hell are you two jawboning about?" Phil asked. "Just slap some bologna between two pieces of Wonder Bread with some mayonnaise. Tell them that's what cowboys eat, and they'll love it!"

Tom just couldn't do it. He fretted over each sandwich.

The tension began building between us. Tom became short with me. Being pregnant and working as hard as I could brought me to tears. We decided that the next summer, we would hire a cook and a maid.

Despite the hardships, living high in the mountains, with all that majestic beauty and vastness, lifted my mood. I didn't find myself getting as depressed as I had been in Newcastle. Instead, I began getting increasingly manic. Tom enjoyed my mania because it fueled a sexual frenzy on my part, but he didn't enjoy the irritation that came with it. I was irrationally irked by him—how he wore his cowboy hat, how he wanted everything perfect for the guests. I got so angry one day that I jumped at him, ready to punch. He stopped me by grabbing my arms. I felt awful afterward. I couldn't understand why I was behaving the way I was, and that frightened me. Although Calen was little, he would later remember seeing me throw a glass at Tom while screaming at him during an argument. Calen couldn't have been more than two years old! I would emerge from those violent moods deeply ashamed of myself and would always beg Tom's forgiveness for my moodiness.

"We have an accordion relationship," Tom complained one night, adding, "Sometimes I think I'm living with two different people."

"What are you talking about?" I snapped.

"I can't seem to ever do anything right. I'm either too possessive or too distant with you. You're either sad and angry or happy and angry."

I didn't know how to respond, because I knew he was right, but I had no idea how to fix my mood problem.

Our goal was to make the ranch profitable enough to be self-supporting, leaving me time to focus on writing and allowing Tom to go fishing and hunting during hunting season and do the building projects he enjoyed. I already had one remodeling idea in mind. An abandoned cabin several hundred yards from the main house would make a wonderful writer's cabin, I told Tom. It would be a place where I could write during the day without being constantly interrupted.

On January 6, 1983, I gave birth to another son, whom we named Sander. We chose his name because it was similar to my brother's nickname, Sandy, yet different. Sander got my father's name for a middle name, William. Back in the early 1980s it was said, "Once a C-section, always a C-section." I didn't go into labor with Sander but went straight to the operating room. Tom drew a dotted line with orange disinfectant across my existing C-section scar and wrote "cut here." The doctors got a good laugh. An avalanche on the road from Big Piney to the hospital in Jackson kept my parents, who were taking care of eighteen-month-old Calen, from coming to see their new grandchild when he was born. When Tom and I and our new arrival did get back to our little house, Calen greeted his new brother by telling me to "put him back" into my body. I told him I couldn't do that, to which he replied, "Get da hamma!"

Because of the hard work that we'd done the first season, we were booked, and our second season started off well until I sensed that our new cook had a crush on Tom. The two of them would sit in the dining room guffawing with guests while I fed Sander and watched Calen in the kitchen. She was a great cook, but I wouldn't hire her again.

When hunting season arrived in the fall, the tourists left and the outdoorsmen arrived. Tom guided them to what was called a spike camp. The Forest Service allotted permits to qualified hunting guides, and Tom was one of them. He and his fellow hunters would hike into the mountains, leaving the boys and me back at the lodge. When Tom was away, I began having horrible nightmares about a strange man, his silhouette darkening my doorway; he meant to kill us all. My body would shake itself awake. I decided to buy a handgun in case my nightmare was a premonition. Tom and I had both heard stories about hunters ransacking unoccupied houses that were used only in the summer. The local newspaper fueled my fears by reporting that some cattle had been found, their throats slit and their tongues cut out for sport as the meat wasn't harvested. I didn't see any point in owning a gun if I couldn't reach it quickly, so I bought a holster and began wearing a sidearm whenever Tom was away from home. My nightmares stopped, but I still felt uneasy living thirty miles from the closest neighbor.

One night I knew someone was watching the boys and me from the woods. I couldn't shake that feeling, and the next morning I called Mom, and she talked me into bringing my sons to Big Piney for a visit. I had just finished packing our truck when Calen said, "Mommy, who dat?"

"Where, honey?" I replied.

He pointed to the woods.

"It a man."

My heart practically stopped. I didn't see anyone, but I hurried the boys into the truck and sped down the mountain.

Tom thought it was just my imagination, but from that point forward I never felt truly safe at the ranch without him around.

When winter arrived, we all had to move to lower ground. The snow and temperature drops were just too brutal, so we'd shut down the cabins and lodge and move into Big Piney. During the off-season, I would focus on building up our clientele. I got an editor of a popular travel magazine in England to publish a flattering feature story about our ranch in exchange for our purchasing an ad.

I felt our second season had been a huge success, but Tom began stewing.

"Jessie, this business just isn't working out," he announced one cold winter day.

I hadn't seen this coming.

He said, "I can't see myself spending the rest of my life trying to make this place work."

"I think we're doing great," I replied cheerfully. "We've only had two seasons, and now we should be getting guests from England. That will be fun."

"We're not doing great," he replied. "To make a decent living, we'll have to increase the capacity here to at least fifteen or twenty guests, and that's going to require us to spend money we don't have to really fix this place up and build more cabins."

Tom's worrier side was coming out again. I realized why, and also realized why I wasn't a worrier. I had grown up with a trust fund. It wasn't huge, but it was enough so that I never really had to worry about being without any money at all. Tom had not had that advantage.

Continuing, Tom said, "We're busting our butts and we don't even own this place—your parents do. We need to move on in our lives. We need to close this chapter."

We argued all that night about the ranch, and the next morning Tom stayed with the boys at home while I went for a long walk in the snow. I didn't want to abandon our ranch. I felt grounded there, despite my worries about being alone with the boys when Tom was gone. The more I thought about it, the more I decided that I could run the ranch by myself if necessary, as long as I kept my gun handy.

As I trudged through the freshly fallen snow, I thought about one evening at the ranch when I was carrying Sander on my hip and Calen was holding my hand. Calen stopped me and said, "Mommy, wook at de tars!"

The three of us looked upward at the stars, and they seemed so bright and close—it was almost as if we could touch them from our mountain lodge. There was nowhere else I could go to be so close to the stars.

I loved Tom, but for the first time in our marriage I thought maybe I should divorce him. Having planted that seed, I began thinking about what might happen if I did. My boys were still little. Tom was a good dad, and they wouldn't lose him if we shared custody. Still, we would become a "broken home." I hated that term. I thought about my parents. They had stayed married, but our home certainly had been filled with cracks and regrets. What to do?

By the time I returned from my walk, I'd decided divorcing Tom would be a mistake—at least for now.

Tom was waiting for an answer about our ranch when I walked in.

"We'll quit the ranch," I said. "We can talk to my parents about it."

A friend suggested we move to Bozeman, Montana, because it would be easier for Tom to find work there and it was a "happening" place.

There was a vibe that set the community of just under twenty thousand people apart. Our friend told us that Bozeman was how Jackson Hole had been before the jet-setters and celebrities discovered it.

Tom went to check it out and returned home gushing about how the community had a vibrant downtown with family-owned boutiques, not having succumbed to the Walmarting and malling of America. He'd already been offered a job selling cars there, which, along with my income, would give us enough money to get settled until he could find something better.

Selling cars? I thought. *That's better than running our ranch?* But I kept silent. Once again, I was walking away from a business that I had helped build and loved, just as I had done when Brad and I had operated our renegade radio station.

I packed up our belongings and, with Calen and Sander tucked safely in their car seats, began the seven-hour drive to Bozeman. We arrived on Halloween in 1984.

I was leaving behind my unfinished little writer's cabin and the mountains that I so dearly loved. I kept telling myself that I wouldn't resent it. I was doing the right thing.

Wasn't I?

PART THREE

MONTANA APRIL,
A FETAL-POSITION MONTH

MYSELF
You were holding something of mine,
Something in a closed, grey box,
And I couldn't see what was inside until
I took it from you and
Laid it on the table.

The light from the window
Illuminated the box on the
Dark wood table—

I opened the lid.
I saw the child.
Burned.
A baby, as long as the inside of the box—
Crisp, dead, like petrified wood.

I didn't want to believe.

I didn't want to take the lid all the way off
And I didn't want to touch the baby

And I didn't know how to look at her.
But I didn't want to give her away.

I handed the baby to
My father
And knew the lid needed to stay on.
He mustn't see it—
This burned child;
He would only turn away in disgust.

I didn't want him to be ashamed of the child,
Of me,
So I took it back.
I took her away from him
Because he really didn't want her anyway.

I blew a small patch of skin onto her face,
And another by her ear,
Near the jawbone.
And I covered her body with a soft blanket.
A grey-blue blanket.

I picked her up
Out of the box,
Inside the blanket,
So I didn't have to touch her burned skin
And I held her
And I knew I didn't want you to have her, either.

I knew you wouldn't know what to do with her.
You made sure she remained burned.
I made sure you kept her like petrified wood.

Where else could she go?
If she wasn't burned,

Montana April, A Fetal-Position Month

If you didn't hold her,
If the lid didn't stay on the box,
If you didn't keep her burned body inside the box
Where could she go?

Would it be all right if I held her?
Would the two of us have to remain alone
Forever?

What else,
My husbands,
My lovers,
What else can I give you
Besides custody of my burned self?
                            —from my private journal

CHAPTER EIGHTEEN

Montana April came, erasing most of the dirty snowdrifts in the street and on the sidewalks. Tom and I and our two boys had arrived and settled into Bozeman during the fall of 1984. In the three years that had passed, I'd come to look on April as my fetal-position month. April light was white, flat, dead. The fields surrounding Bozeman were dormant and wouldn't come alive again until the end of May. April was the month that made it easy to forget which way the seasons were headed: the brown vegetation could have been a precursor to spring or to fall. It was a confusing month, one that found me curled up in a fetal position, deeply depressed.

Calen and Sander, now almost six and four and a half, had grown fast, as little boys do. Sander spoke so quickly he garbled his words. Neither Tom nor I could understand him, so Calen became our interpreter. Whenever Sander wanted something, Calen took Sander's hand, locking their tiny fingers together into one unit. Calen would point and say, "We need…" anything from a Popsicle to a blanket. Calen's hair now was darker, like Tom's, while Sander remained a towhead, their matching cowlicks standing like antennae, streaming backwards whenever they ran. *Did my boys ever walk?*

I loved the bond that had formed between my sons. Calen didn't want Sander near me at first. Jealous. Then the two of them were like two boys with one mind, coexistence in the raw.

I adored being with them, but when my moods darkened and I sank into one of my sad times, I sometimes sought refuge in our bathroom, locking the door. I would sit on the toilet seat with my hands covering my ears, but I could still hear them calling me.

"Mommy! Mommy! Mommy!"

They would stand outside, Calen pounding on the door. *Were their tiny fingers locked into one fist now?*

My relationship with Tom had grown as gray and uncertain as the season. Were we moving forward or backwards? Tom sold cars for about a year after we first arrived but didn't enjoy it. The dealership had required him to watch videos about sales tricks to take advantage of buyers. He found another job at a gun store selling firearms and working on the shooting range. After a while, I'd made friends with several women. We began going to bars together and staying out late. Tom had gotten angry—no, that's not the right word. He'd become furious. Oftentimes he'd refuse to speak to me for one or two days. His "cold shoulder" made me feel guilty, but not for long; it was the price I paid for having a good time. What I hadn't realized was that my actions and his reactions had sown seeds of resentment, like rust gently eating at the metal beams of a sagging seaside pier. Tom had always known that I liked to drink with my girlfriends. Why had he expected me to change?

My dad had recognized my moods as depression and had prescribed an antidepressant, imaprimine, but it was no longer helping. It had only tricked my brain for a short while. Dad called in a prescription for me over the phone: another antidepressant, Zoloft. What I failed to mention to him was that I was also experiencing intense periods of mania along with my blues. Except I didn't even know the word: *mania.*

Depression had been easy to identify. Mania was more insidious. Tom, my friends, and my boys were relieved whenever I emerged from a depression. For several weeks, I would become the perfect wife, pal, and mother. I would play with Calen and Sander and cook actual meals instead of throwing leftovers on the table or ordering pizza.

Tom would always be excited to have me back, because I would be filled with energy. I would be in high gear, but soon my intensity would cause him stress. It would lead to enhanced sexuality, much heavier drinking, more talking, racing thoughts, and hysterical laughing. He hated me going out with the girls and coming home drunk and stinking of cigarettes.

Inevitably, my high-energy phase would peak in a manic rush that would become almost unbearable to me. I would pick fights with Tom, yell at the boys, and begin drinking during the day at home to slow down my racing mind. Rum at four o'clock. I would drive too fast, scream for no reason, and curse wildly. It was as if I was trying to release the energy exploding inside my head. Yet no one understood what I was going through. Not even me. Sometimes I would have thoughts about running away—wild, incoherent thoughts about returning to India and volunteering to become a spy for that government against Pakistan. Hadn't I run away once already, after I'd first met Tom, and escaped to Greenwich only to return to Wyoming?

Tom soon began recognizing a pattern to my mood swings. He would ask me about each phase as he and our boys suffered through it.

"What can I do to help you?" he'd offer. "Do we need to try a different medicine? Do you need to see a psychiatrist here in Bozeman?"

While his intentions were well placed, I didn't want his help. "*I am fine!*" I would tell him and myself, even though I clearly wasn't.

When I first started taking Zoloft, Tom became guardedly optimistic. Perhaps this would be the solution. It was, but only for a while. It tempered the depression but appeared to escalate the mania.

After years of dealing with my moods, his patience had grown thin.

Tom had done well working at the gun store but hadn't seen much future in it, so he'd quit. Although he'd always worked to provide for us, his government retirement and my income gave us enough to squeak by and try something new. I'd started writing a book, and Tom decided he wanted to try his hand at writing, too. It would be something the two of us could share. I liked the romance of the idea. Tom wanted to write poetry and thought he could sell articles about hunting and fishing to outdoor magazines. Tom also had a clever idea. He suggested that we coauthor a children's book about two boys who lived on a dude ranch in Wyoming with their parents. In the back of both our minds, we knew Glenn might be able to help us get a publishing contract, although I was loath to ask. Glenn's film career had taken off shortly after Tom and I had married, and she had lots of connections in Los Angeles and New York entertainment circles.

Tom quickly found that he was more of a reporter than a novelist. He had trouble imagining scenes and crafting dialogue. After several failed starts, we gave up the idea of cowriting a children's novel. Instead, he focused on selling stories to outdoor magazines—without much success.

I enjoyed writing both nonfiction and fiction. Glenn was working on the first of three television movies inspired by the children's book *Sarah, Plain and Tall* and had become friends with its author, Patricia MacLachlan. My sister encouraged me to send some pages of the novel that I was writing to Patricia, and she kindly forwarded them to her editor, Charlotte Zolotow, at Harper & Row publishing in New York. When Zolotow expressed interest in buying my book, Glenn introduced me to Sterling Lord, head of Sterling Lord Literistic, a literary agency, and one of his agents, Philippa Brophy, agreed to represent me.

Brophy handled the haggling, and before I knew it I had a contract to turn my handful of chapters into a book entitled *The Warping of Al*. With Calen and Sander in tow, I flew to Manhattan to meet my editor and sign the paperwork.

Zolotow was an icon in New York publishing, and I was in awe, but she put me at ease right away by ordering pizza for the boys when we arrived. We all sat in her office and ate. When I told her that I felt insecure because I didn't have a high school or college diploma, Zolotow replied that if I had been schooled in writing, I would never have developed the individual writing style that she loved in my early chapters. I have carried that comment with me ever since.

Back in Bozeman, I couldn't wait to get started, but I ran into roadblocks. Tom had given up writing and had gone back to work at the Soil Conservation Service, so finding time during the day to write was difficult because my boys were so demanding, which was their right. The best time was at night. I would get the boys in bed by eight, sit with Tom until nine, and then finally retreat to be alone and write until one or two in the morning.

While I enjoyed the night's stillness and had a deadline to meet, Tom began resenting that I preferred being at my typewriter to coming to bed. I began resenting that he didn't appear the slightest bit interested in my manuscript. He never asked me about its plot or characters. Even if I brought it up, he wouldn't pay attention, and I took that indifference to mean that he didn't care about my book and, by extension, didn't care about me.

Tom and I were living in a farmhouse on the outskirts of Bozeman, and we decided to expand it, so we hired a contractor—let's call him David—who noticed one day that I would rush over to my typewriter whenever I could break away from my boys. I explained that a New York publisher was paying me to write a novel entitled *The Warping of Al*.

"What's it about?" David asked, and with that question he showed more curiosity than my husband had.

"It's about a boy who lives with his sisters, mother, and grandmother," I proudly declared. "The father is gone all the time, and the boy has to learn about life and coming of age on his own."

"You're writing a book about a teenage boy growing up?" he asked, gently chiding me.

"The main character is based loosely on my brother, Sandy," I said.

David seemed genuinely interested. He stopped working, removed his heavy carpenter's belt, poured himself a cup of coffee, sat down at the kitchen table near where I was typing, and listened as I explained that the main character in my novel was the only son of an absentee father who was overbearing and difficult to live with.

"If Al is based on your brother, is this overbearing father your dad?" David asked.

"Actually, he is," I replied.

Before I realized it, I was not only telling David about the characters in my book but also telling him about my family. David poured himself another cup of coffee, and when he finished it, we realized we both needed to get back to work but didn't want to stop talking.

Our relationship changed after that initial conversation. We soon fell into a routine. David would arrive early and begin working, but when Tom left the house for his job, David would take a coffee break and ask me about my book. I would read him paragraphs and explain how the various characters were each finding their own ways to deal with their father. The mother in the story simply bent to her husband's wishes whenever he was at home, I explained. Goopie, the grandmother, closed her door and ignored him. His daughter Dotty learned how to flatter and manipulate her father. A daughter called E—short for Ethel—was rebellious and fought with her dad. Another daughter, Flavia, was sad around him because he intimidated her.

David knew I was basing the characters in my novel after my own dysfunctional family.

"Which one are you?" he asked one afternoon.

"Flavia," I replied. "The daughter who avoids her father and doesn't know how to talk to him."

My chats with David became the high point of my day. I couldn't wait for Tom to leave. I was sharing special moments with David that I should have been having with Tom. But that was his fault, not mine, because he didn't care about my book.

David talked about his background, too. I knew he was married and had a child. Despite that, I found myself becoming romantically attracted to him and began fantasizing about us making love.

I decided one afternoon to just come out and express my feelings. "Would you like to go to bed with me?" I asked.

He wasn't surprised—so I knew that he'd been having the same thoughts—but he balked.

"I'm married," he said. "And Bozeman is a small town."

The next day, David didn't take a coffee break. I'd clearly scared him, and it was awkward. If anything, his resistance made me even more obsessed. I went upstairs and put on a low-cut blouse. He noticed, but only smiled.

I was clearly entering a manic phase, and Tom recognized it. He started to become more attentive now that I was emerging from what he saw as my hostile, sad mood.

But I didn't want Tom's attention, I wanted David's.

I could feel my mania building, too. I liked it. The intensity, the feeling of being alive, the sexuality, and heat of the moment were building inside me. I called my friend Connie, who had a son the same age as Sander, and asked if she would take care of Sander the next day so that I could be free to write. She agreed. Calen would be in preschool. Once Tom left for work, only David and I would be in the house.

Tom wanted to make love that night, but I refused. I was thinking of

David and didn't want to spoil my fantasy. Lying next to Tom, I suddenly felt ashamed. Tom was my husband, and I was planning on betraying him the next day. For a moment in the dark with him beside me, I started having second thoughts about seducing David the next morning. One moment, I would decide to abandon my plan, realizing it was not fair to Tom and our marriage. Just as quickly, I would begin calculating all the real and imagined wrongs that Tom had done to me. David had asked about my book. Tom hadn't. David listened to me. Tom didn't. I barely slept as I went through my list of pros and cons. When the sun came up, the pros had won. I was filled with righteous indignation—coupled with intense feelings of boiling sexuality because of my unchecked mania.

I couldn't wait for Tom to leave and David to arrive.

CHAPTER NINETEEN

I was frantic with arousal.

My face was flushed, my heart was pounding, and I was tense with anticipation when David came through the door and went directly to work on our remodeling project. I tried to appear calm when he broke for his morning coffee. Sauntering toward him, I asked if he would come upstairs to check on a room that his construction crew had completed the day before.

When we entered it, I faced him, put my arms around his neck, and kissed his lips. He was taken aback, but didn't pull back, and within seconds we were on the floor, pulling at each other's clothes.

David quickly entered me, and during that brief moment, we looked into each other's eyes and I realized that his body was a stranger to me, and that made me even more excited. I was the aggressor. I had forced myself on him, and for a split second I thought about Brad and how he had forced himself on me. *What am I doing? Why am I doing this? I'm married. I have children.*

Within minutes, it was over, and we got up from the floor and faced the awkwardness of our situation. I told him that I had to go fetch Sander from Connie's house but wanted to take a shower first. David kissed me tenderly and walked downstairs without saying a word. *What have I done? There is no way to undo it, is there?*

The next morning arrived, but rather than stopping we repeated our infidelity. Every morning after that when Sander was gone, we would have sex. After a while it began to feel normal, as if we were making love, not two animals in heat. But I hated myself. I knew I was jeopardizing my marriage with Tom, but I couldn't seem to stop. *Why? What is driving me into another man's arms?*

David and I began using the *love* word, and it soon became terribly difficult for me to be in the same room with both David and Tom. I hated deceiving Tom but had no choice. Did I?

David had called Bozeman a small town, and word of our illicit rendezvous made it through our circle of friends and reached David's wife. Furious, she told Tom. He was caught completely off guard.

"Are you having an affair with David?" he asked. "I need to know!"

My mouth was a dark, locked space that wouldn't open.

He asked again. "Are you having an affair?"

My body began to shake. Tom wasn't supposed to ask direct questions like that. He was supposed to leave me alone, as he always did. I suddenly felt cold, and vomit tried to rise up my throat. I'd been caught.

"Are you?" Tom asked, raising his voice.

I had to force out some kind of answer from my constricted throat. I lied.

"No," I said, trying to sound a bit indignant.

Tom searched my eyes for a sign. "Is that the truth?"

I felt myself sinking into a black hole.

"Yes."

"Do you know I love you?" he said. "Do you know that even if you're having an affair, I'll still love you? So don't lie to me. Please, tell me the truth."

The truth. It was under my tongue, under my fingernails, under my crazy, pounding heart. If the vomit came, Tom would stop asking questions. But why would I vomit if I were innocent? I desperately wanted it to be night, the boys asleep in bed, the pony safe in the barn, the dog on her bed in the kitchen. I wanted to be in Tom's arms, safe from what I had done. I wanted it to be the way that it should have been but was no longer.

I couldn't tell him. The truth wouldn't come out of my mouth. Instead, I snapped: "There's only one answer you'll accept!" It was as if he were the one at fault for daring to question me.

I hoped my anger would make him go away and prevent him from seeing through me and knowing what I had done.

"That's not true," he replied. "You're just not willing to tell me the answer that is the truth!" He turned to leave the room.

I stared at his back. *Don't walk away! Save me! Please make all this just go away; make everything right again, make our family right again, make me love you again.*

He knew.

I started to say something but couldn't. Instead, I hurried into the kitchen, where I opened the refrigerator, took out a bottle of vodka, and took a long swig, the liquid burning as it went down.

I was looking for liquid courage, and I kept drinking until I found it.

Tom was in the living room, glancing at a magazine. How could he just be sitting there as if nothing had happened? I knew I was drunk, and I wanted it to be that way.

"Tom," I said. "I am going to tell you the truth, all of it."

I did. I apologized. I cried. I begged him to take me back and forgive me. We talked for hours about our marriage and about what I had done and why. Incredibly, he told me that he loved me and that we would get through this. He didn't want a divorce. I was overwhelmed with gratitude and relieved. *Forgiveness is possible in a marriage!*

David's wife was not so forgiving. David telephoned and said she had filed for a divorce. He asked if we could talk about what had happened between us. He was losing his marriage over me. It seemed the least I could do.

We met in an out-of-the-way bar. It started with conversation and drinks and ended with our having sex. *Why am I doing this? Especially after Tom forgave me. Am I really in love with David? Why else would I be doing this to Tom? Can I be in love with both of them?*

As before, I began making a mental list of all of wrongs that Tom had committed to justify my double betrayal.

Tom's mother happened to arrive in Bozeman for a visit. After dinner, I excused myself, saying that I needed to go out on an errand. Instead, I met David, got blindly drunk, and fell asleep in his arms. I didn't make it home that night. Tom was humiliated. My risky behavior was ruining my life, and even I didn't understand why I was letting it. It was as if there were a demon inside me.

I knew Tom still loved me, but I seemed determined to make it impossible for him to keep loving me.

After Tom's mother left, I told him that I had been meeting with David and having sex with him. Tom was dumbfounded and asked me if I really loved David or if I was doing this because I hated being married to him.

"I do love you," I said.

But I also loved David, although I wasn't sure whether it really was love or simply that I wanted that intense feeling of being in love, the romance and passion of an illicit affair.

Tom was as confused as I was. He didn't want to break up our family, but I'd destroyed all trust between us. How could he not suspect me of cheating each time I went out? I couldn't blame him.

While we were talking, I felt as if I were having another out-of-body experience in which I was floating above myself, watching quietly, knowing that I was participating in a conversation yet having little control of my words.

Our gut-wrenching conversation ended with Tom deciding that we were done as a married couple. He wasn't going to live with someone whom he couldn't trust. I didn't believe him at first. Then I realized he wasn't kidding. Our marriage was over, and it was my fault.

When Tom told our boys that Daddy and Mommy were getting a divorce, Calen screamed and bolted through the farmhouse door toward a hill near the barn. He wasn't wearing a jacket, and it was winter.

Screaming "No!" Calen collapsed in the snow, spread-eagle, like a face-down snow angel.

I thought, *What am I going to tell his teacher?* I thought, *Calen must be cold lying in that snow. He should have a coat on.*

I felt invisible and had no idea what to do.

Sander didn't run away. He crawled into my lap and began to cry. He wrapped his tiny arms around my neck and asked, "Where is Daddy going? What will Daddy do?"

I said, "I don't know."

Tom went to fetch Calen, picking him up from the snow. He brought him into the kitchen. My older son was clinging to Tom and refused to look at me.

All I could think about was how I had betrayed all three of them. I should have remained in my marriage even if Tom never asked me a single question about my book. It would have been better than the numbness I was feeling now. There could be no pain like the pain of breaking your children's hearts. My choices had done this. *Why? And for what?*

I wanted to die.

I moved out of the bedroom that night into a tiny room off the kitchen. The deadline for my book was approaching, and I couldn't miss it. Tom stayed in the bedroom. A few days later, we tried to mend the damage. We decided that we needed a new interest—something that would bring us together—so we went out and each bought Harley-Davidson motorcycles so we could go on rides. When I crashed mine and couldn't walk for a while, Tom put a chaise longue next to my desk so I could keep on working. He was being sweet, and it looked as if he was willing to forgive me yet again.

I wanted his forgiveness, but part of me seemed blocked, and I found myself unable to return his love.

When I finished my book, I thanked my boys in the acknowledgments, writing, "To Calen and Sander, my favorite human beings, who have given me the privilege of being a mother." I did not mention Tom.

By the time my book was published in 1990, I knew there was no turning back. A divorce was inevitable. What of David? He was nothing more than a sad memory.

Because the characters in my novel were based loosely on my own family, I was not surprised when my siblings, parents, and readers who knew us began speculating about who was who. Mom and Dad were the easiest to recognize, although I suspected that both of them dismissed my less-than-flattering portraits of them. It was easy to identify Glenn as a character, because she was the daughter who was most cherished by her father. As the only boy in the novel, everyone assumed Sandy was Al. Much to my irritation, the character whom I'd patterned after Tina had been cut from the book by Charlotte Zolotow. That left two daughters for readers to choose from when it came to identifying me.

When writing the novel, I'd always pictured myself as Flavia, the depressed daughter who avoided her father by hiding in her room. I thought it was painfully obvious to anyone who knew my father and me.

Who, then, was E—Ethel—the feisty daughter who fought with her absentee father? In my book, I described E as a child who couldn't "talk about anything without getting all worked up about it. I mean, she's one of those people who seem to think that every thought should be paraded around until there aren't any sides of it left to look at. Talking to E is kind of like trying to peer into an unlit tunnel: You're never quite sure what's coming at you."

I'd pictured E this way: "Her hair's shiny brown and straight but looks reddish when she's out in the sunshine. She gets very tan during the summer; a lot of freckles pop out all over her face, like they were there all the time but appear only under heat, like lemon juice invisible ink. Her eyes are such a dark blue that sometimes they look like they're all pupil. I'd use crimson red and midnight blue to paint E, if I were going to paint her..."

One of my girlfriends took me aside and said, "I figured out everyone but E. Who is she supposed to be?"

"No one," I replied. "I made her up. She's not a thinly veiled character of anyone in the Close family."

Years later, I gave a therapist a copy of my book, and after she'd finished it, we talked about how I had modeled my fictional characters after Dad, Mom, Glenn, Sandy, and myself. Was that really so odd? Many first novels are autobiographical. Curious, the therapist asked me to identify each family member, and when I explained that I was Flavia and that E was a made-up character, she stopped me.

"Don't you see what you did?" my therapist asked.

"What are you talking about?" I replied.

"Flavia, the depressed and afraid character, is definitely you," she replied. "But so is E. You are Ethel, too. Flavia is your depressed side, and E is your manic side."

I had never made the connection. Without realizing it, I had created two characters in my book that both represented me. The therapist was seeing what I had missed and what Tom had been forced to live with during our twelve years together. With my highs and lows, I really was two different personalities—the frightened, insecure Flavia and E, the confident, ballbusting spitfire who recklessly raced through life angry at the world, destroying relationships.

I had unknowingly described my still-emerging bipolar self.

CHAPTER TWENTY

One of the symptoms of mania, according to the American Psychiatric Association, is overindulgence in "enjoyable behaviors with high risks of negative outcomes." The World Health Organization defines one of the signs of a manic episode as "behavior that is out of character and risky, foolish or inappropriate that may cause a loss of normal social restraint."

Those definitions pretty much described me at the arrival of the 1990s.

The Warping of Al didn't hit *The New York Times* bestseller list, but it did sell enough copies for my publisher to ask me to write a second novel. I was on my way to becoming a notable author—at least that's what I thought.

I came up with a new plot for a second book: a young teenager lives with her mother and abusive father. She decides to run away and joins an itinerant camp of the Grateful Dead's hard-core fans. I started writing and really liked the beginning, where the main character hears her mother being slapped and punched then goes downstairs to help after her abusive father leaves the house. My editor liked the first few pages, too, but when I started writing the book's second chapter, the flow of words stopped. I had fallen victim to the infamous writer's block.

Frustrated, I decided to take a break and focus on something else. I didn't need to lose weight. I was thin. But I decided I needed to build much-needed muscle. I went on a health kick. To purify my body, I stopped taking all medication, including Zoloft, and joined a local gym.

From the day I first slipped on spandex, I began pushing myself harder and harder. It wasn't uncommon for me to spend two hours in the gym six days a week. I wasn't the only gym rat. Noah Davis was a trainer, and we immediately noticed each other. I liked Noah instantly, in part because he was big and strong but also because of his banter and charm.

Noah told me that he'd been drawn to weight lifting because it required him to push himself without forcing him to compete with anyone else or depend on other people. Mind over his own body.

"It is all about you testing yourself," he explained. "I've never been interested in team sports."

Noah had come from a military family that had moved constantly, and his father, like mine, had been a largely absent figure who'd always been at work. After graduating from a suburban Washington, DC, high school, Noah had gone to "find himself." Eventually, he'd ended up in Manhattan, where he'd become a close friend of Fabio Lanzoni, the Italian fashion model whose physique and long locks had inspired hundreds of romance-novel covers. Noah and Fabio shared mutual interests in weight lifting, riding motorcycles fast, and bedding equally fast women. A motorcycle collision in Manhattan had sidelined Noah and prompted his move to Bozeman, where his parents had retired. At age thirty-seven, he still viewed himself as a drifter, much more comfortable being a "voyeur of the world" than getting locked into a daily grind.

I'd just finished doing a series of gut-punishing crunches one afternoon when Noah strolled over and ran his finger up the back of my leg, from my knee to my butt.

"Nice hamstrings," he said.

I smiled.

He smiled back, with a twinkle in his eye.

We continued to flirt whenever I was in the gym. Noah and I decided to rent a room at Chico Hot Springs, a resort about an hour and a half away from Bozeman in Paradise Valley, just north of Yellowstone National Park. It was a romantic spot with two natural hot springs. After a soak, drinks, and dinner we called it a night and fell into bed.

I knew I was ovulating; I could tell from the sharp pain in my abdomen. I told Noah, and he joked that we'd make a daughter and would name her Doom.

We both giggled, but the next morning I told him: "I think we made a baby last night," and I wasn't kidding.

"That wouldn't be good," he replied in a serious voice.

I was surprised. "I told you I was ovulating," I said. "And you knew we weren't taking any precautions!"

A horrified look swept over his face. While he enjoyed my company, he wasn't in love with me, and he certainly was not in a position to become a father. "I can't even take care of myself," he admitted. Our night together was the result, he joked, of a "hormonal collision."

Not for me. I was in love and determined to make him love me. His casualness about our night of passion became a challenge. We continued to date during the coming weeks, and in my journal I wrote long passages about how much I loved Noah, as if I were a schoolgirl having her first crush. I wrote poetry about him and couldn't think of much else except him. Neither of my sons liked Noah when I introduced him. And Noah, from his perspective, instantly recognized how unprepared and uncomfortable he would be playing the role of father. Being a dad was just not something Noah wanted or was ready for.

There was another problem besides my sons' negative reaction to Noah. When he'd asked me out, I actually was seeing someone else, a Bozeman businessman. He'd taken my boys and me back east to meet his parents on Long Island and to attend a New York Rangers hockey game at Madison Square Garden. If I were going to be dating anyone, Calen and Sander would have preferred him.

On January 17, 1991, the same day Operation Desert Storm was announced, I discovered life-changing news. At age thirty-seven, I was carrying Noah's baby.

Because I had wrapped myself in a puppy-love cocoon, I was thrilled, and I immediately began fantasizing about marrying Noah and raising our love child with my boys. We would all be one happy family.

Noah wasn't thrilled.

"How do I know it's mine?" he asked.

"Because I haven't fucked anyone else since my last period!" I said angrily.

Noah was convinced that the best course was an abortion, and he offered to help pay for one.

"Maybe I don't want an abortion!" And again, "I told you I was ovulating!"

I remember him mumbling, "All the other girls had them."

"Well, I'm not 'all the other girls,' you jackass!"

It turned out that Noah was dating someone else on the side and had no interest in stopping. My big announcement turned into a gigantic screaming match that ended with Noah storming out and Calen hollering and covering his ears.

Once again, "Jessie the fuckup" was at work.

Rather than walking away from Noah, I dug in my heels. With time, I thought, he would get rid of the other woman in his life and realize how lucky he was to have me. That fantasy gave me hope.

I'd aborted Brad's baby during my first marriage—under pressure from his parents—and terminating this pregnancy would have been the simplest step to take, although I didn't tell Noah that. It was what several of my friends were urging me to do and clearly what Noah had said we needed to do. Although I was pro-choice I didn't like the idea of abortion as birth control, especially when both parties knew that the chances of getting pregnant were good.

But still, I made an appointment with the local doctor who performed abortions. I canceled it the next day. Then I made another appointment but canceled that one, too. Then I made yet another appointment, and this time the nurse on the other end of the line told me to come in right away so the doctor could pack my uterus with seaweed.

"What?" I asked.

She explained that seaweed would begin opening my uterus. I'd have to leave it in for twenty-four hours.

I couldn't do it. I couldn't bear the thought of some man putting his hand in me, either to pack my uterus with seaweed or take the baby out. I canceled that appointment, too.

My father and Tina were just as alarmed as Noah was. They recognized that I wasn't in the best shape financially to take on the raising of another child, especially if I were unmarried. Plus, my erratic mood swings were becoming more and more obvious to everyone.

My mother surprised me, though. When I called her back to tell her I had canceled my appointment for an abortion, she let out a sigh of relief and said, "Oh, thank God!"

Sandy got angry and told me that I was lucky to be having another baby.

I poured out my heart to Glenn. What should I do?

By 1991, Glenn had a three-year-old daughter of her own, Annie, whose father was John Starke, a producer whom she'd met while making her first movie, *The World According to Garp*.

"If you really want to have this baby," Glenn replied in her calming voice, "I will take care of the child if you decide you can't. I will raise the baby as if it were mine."

My eyes filled with tears, and my voice cracked. "You'd do that?"

"It's what sisters do," Glenn said quietly.

The next day, however, she called me back and said, "Never mind!"

"What?" I replied.

"You'd always be telling me how to raise your child—this simply wouldn't work."

Suddenly, we both broke into laughter.

"You're right!" I told her. "It was a terrible idea. I would always be telling you!"

Because I'd already had an abortion, I wondered why I was dragging my feet. The answer finally came to me. I had two sons. The first time around, in Los Angeles, I had not been a mother. Now I was, and that made all the difference. I made a decision. I would have the tests I needed to make sure the baby was healthy, and in the meantime I would allow things to take their own course. If I spontaneously aborted, then it wasn't meant to be. If this baby grew without complications, then I'd have it.

Pretty simple. This was my pro-choice baby, on my terms.

I was going to have Noah's baby regardless of what he wanted. When I told him my decision, I fully expected him to run away. Much to my surprise, he didn't. He wasn't happy about my decision, but if I had the baby, he promised to "do the right thing" and not turn his back on his child.

I wasn't certain exactly what he meant by that, and because I was the one who'd decided to go ahead, I needed to get ready, both physically and financially. I immediately stopped drinking and started a vitamin regimen. I also started looking for a job. I had launched a renegade radio station with Brad and had managed a guest ranch with Tom, so the idea of running a business didn't intimidate me. Besides, it would help me get my mind off Noah. I was still hoping that he would marry me.

I learned that a downtown coffee shop called the Leaf and Bean was up for sale, but I knew it would be too pricey for me alone, so I telephoned Glenn and asked if she might be interested in investing in it with me. If she would provide the capital, I would put in the sweat equity.

Glenn is a Yankee who appreciates the value of a dollar, so she listened politely to my plea but warned that she would only invest if I had a business plan that made sound economic sense.

I started working on one with the same exuberance that always came to me when I was entering a manic mood. Not only was my plan persuasive enough for Glenn to invest, she also brought in a friend as a partner.

It felt good to be a partner with Glenn. There had never been any jealousy between us, although I did envy her financial success. I had proudly followed her career. She had been nominated for an Academy Award for best supporting actress after she appeared in *The World According to Garp* in 1982. The next year, she had been nominated for another Academy Award for playing Sarah Cooper in *The Big Chill*. Glenn had been generous when it came to including us in her Hollywood adventures. While she was filming *The Big Chill*, I had been pregnant with Sander, and actor William Hurt's partner, Sandra Jennings, had been pregnant, too. The cast and crew put down bets on which baby would be born first. I don't remember who won, but I enjoyed the camaraderie. Glenn seemed to make friends so easily.

The Big Chill led to a starring role for Glenn, who played Iris Gaines opposite Robert Redford in *The Natural* in 1984. The following year, she appeared in *Jagged Edge*, a thriller that kept me on the edge of my theater seat. And in 1987, my sister played the starring role of a lifetime in *Fatal Attraction*.

Tom and I had gone to see all Glenn's movies, but I will never forget sitting in the Bozeman movie theater watching her performance in *Fatal Attraction*. Right before my eyes, Glennie turned into this terrifying, obsessed female predator who quickly became every cheating married man's worst nightmare. She was wonderful in that part. In real life,

Glennie couldn't be further from her terrifying character, Alex Forrest. Yet on-screen she became this psychopath.

For better or worse, that role became linked to Glenn. I was grocery shopping with my two boys when I spotted a tabloid newspaper at the checkout counter. A banner headline screamed: THE MOST HATED WOMAN IN AMERICA! A photo of Glennie was directly below it. That headline upset me until I realized the paper was about her character. Still, my boys wanted to know why people hated Aunt Gi.

We didn't see much of Glenn because she was so busy, but when there was a holiday our entire family would congregate in Big Piney at my parents' house, and Glenn would fly in. She was always the same Glennie that all of us knew. No snobbery, arrogance, or superiority about her.

I remember walking with her on a sidewalk in Bozeman once, and a complete stranger charged up to us, jabbed a pen and paper under her nose, and barked: "Give me your autograph!"

He didn't say "please," and I wanted to smack him, but Glenn was gracious and signed it.

I don't think Tina or Sandy or I would want the attention that she received.

You would have thought that after Glenn starred in *Fatal Attraction*, our family would have had a serious discussion about mental illness. Everyone knew I had been taking antidepressants and was subject to wild mood swings and strange thoughts. My father had admitted to me that he had depression, but none of us brought it up. Ever. Even Glenn didn't see any connection between the crazed Alex Forrest character she'd portrayed and me. She thought I was irresponsible and impulsive. Mental illness just didn't happen to us. It was unthinkable.

Thanks to Glenn's purse strings, I signed the sales papers and was handed the key to the front door of the Leaf and Bean, on Bozeman's Main Street. I was five months pregnant, and my first thought when I opened that door was: *What have I done?*

The Leaf and Bean had been in operation since 1977 and was well known downtown, but I immediately began putting my personal touches on it. A travel guide once described Bozeman as a charming town "in a John Wayne, Norman Rockwell, Bob Marley sort of way." That fit in 1991. Bozeman's residents were a curious blend of western ruggedness, apple-pie goodness, and northern funky chic.

Because my sister Tina was an artist, I knew how willing most painters were to show their work. I invited local artists to display their paintings for sale in the coffee shop. I built a stage in one corner and invited local musicians to play on weekends. When classical guitarist Stuart Weber, a native of Montana, played for us, he donated a couple of professional stage lights. No one had brought entertainment downtown before, and the renters in the apartments above "the Bean" began complaining to city officials about the noise. I rallied other downtown merchants, and a fierce battle broke out, in which renters fought any sort of live entertainment. We won and kept the music going. I also added a bakery to the coffee shop so we could sell our own baked goods. My mom chipped in for a large new espresso machine, and I contracted with a company called Montana Coffee Traders to provide us with all the coffee beans we used in the drinks. I even invented my own drink, which I called the Tornado. It was a double shot of espresso in coffee with cream, with a shot of steam from the wand to blend it all together.

The Starbucks phenomenon was spreading outside Seattle at about the same time as I was giving the Leaf and Bean a face-lift. We were attracting a variety of customers with different tastes. In the mornings and at lunch, we drew the business crowd. In the afternoons, teenagers began showing up because they didn't have anywhere else to hang out. At night, we attracted younger adults out for the evening who wanted a place to relax and talk. I loved being in the center of the action.

Managing any business, especially one that offers food and drink, is grueling work. Noah offered to help out at the Leaf and Bean as part of his new "do the right thing" stance. I gave him a desk near mine in my downstairs office but got angry when I caught him talking to another woman on the phone. That's when I realized he was still seeing the same woman whom he'd been dating when I got pregnant. What happened next made our already dysfunctional relationship even more prickly. Noah began dating one of my new employees. When I confronted him, he openly admitted it, but said he still cared about me, too. He simply was not someone who wanted to settle down with one woman.

The Leaf and Bean was going so well that when a store immediately next door to it, called Poor Richard's, came up for sale, I got Glenn to buy it, too. Poor Richard's sold magazines, newspapers, tobacco, and candy. I put Calen and Sander to work behind the counter but got worried when I realized they had front-row views of the soft porn available in the store in the form of *Playboy* and other men's magazines. I didn't like my boys being introduced to women who assumed such humiliating poses. I called Glennie, and we decided to eliminate men's magazines from the store. I had two male customers holler at me. Somehow a reporter from a British paper heard and tried to tie Glenn into the flap—"Hollywood Star Refuses to Sell Smut"—but I didn't bite. I told her it was my decision because of my sons, and that killed the story.

In September of 1991, I gave birth to a beautiful baby girl, Matheson Sinclair Close-Davis. Noah was involved in choosing the name, as were Calen and Sander. I was still clinging to the idea that someday the five of us would become a family, despite Noah's girlfriends.

I was so happy that I finally had a daughter. Jessie the fuckup had made the right decision in not getting an abortion. Mattie was beautiful. I put a crib in my office in the Leaf and Bean and brought her with me each morning to work.

Mattie had an immediate impact even as an infant. The other women who worked there, including the one who was dating Noah, bonded with her and wanted to help me. Mattie even had an effect on our customers. I published a monthly newsletter to promote a sense of community and to alert regulars about upcoming special events. The paper was called *The Leaf Tribean*, and I began penning a feature under Mattie's name, giving customers musings about the coffee shop from a baby's point of view. Everyone loved it—and everyone loved her.

During our first year, I had doubled revenue and made the Leaf and Bean more profitable than it had been. We were still the only coffeehouse in town—no kiosks, no other stores.

Unfortunately, my personal life was not going nearly as well.

CHAPTER TWENTY-ONE

Journal entry, December 1991
Giving birth has kicked my moods into high gear. Depression isn't just about walking around in a black cloud; it's the physical heaviness, nausea, and exhaustion that become a black cloud within you. I am the black cloud.

Journal entry
I felt betrayed yesterday because Noah said he would take Mattie to his house on Sunday, just the two of them. When he arrived, he'd changed his mind and was going to church with Cherie. If he can't be a dad without his girlfriend's help, then his time with Mattie will be limited.

I am tired of being nice, of trying to not admit my rage. I will not have him play happy little family with Mattie and Cherie. What both he and Cherie put me through when I was pregnant with Mattie has not led me to be generous and loving toward them. If my rage includes payback, then that's the way it is. I will no longer subject myself to his verbal abuse, his pretending with Cherie, his parading around with Mattie, as if he is some type of New Age sensitive guy.

Journal entry
God grant me the ability to forgive, to love, to let go, to grow. I am my own prison. I am my own pain. Why do I still believe there is someone out there who will love me, understand me instantly, someone who will see beyond the surface parts of me, someone who will trust what

I say and tell me the very truth without hiding? I hide. I confuse. I get attached to surface. Is it possible to love without fear and have someone love me in return without fear? I want to forge ahead in my life with what I want to do.

Journal entry

I spoke to Glenn tonight. She asked me: "What is it that you want for yourself?"

It is courage, humor, flexibility, patience, love, faith, honesty, generosity. Maybe I just haven't been alone long enough. I need to take care of myself. I need to stop throwing myself into the pain and then wonder why I hurt. I need to take things slowly. I want to know that I can count on myself and trust my own judgment. I feel like I'm getting there, but I'm scared that I will slip back.

Journal entry

I am writing tonight from Glennie's place. I told Noah over the telephone that I didn't want him coming to my house anymore. I really did it! I was scared to do it. I feel guilty, but I did it. Here in New York, I have found an enormous relief being away from him and Cherie. I am grateful that I have finally given myself permission to say "NO" to him. I need to protect myself from him and my feelings of love toward him. Just because I wasn't protected as a child doesn't mean that I can't do something to protect myself now.

Journal entry

It is 12:30 a.m. and I am letting Mattie cry herself to sleep in Glennie's cottage. It is nearly Christmas and I feel very cruel and sad, but I do need her to put herself to sleep. I've been feeling very brain-dead from sleep deprivation and I know that she needs to learn to deal with this by herself. It has been almost twenty minutes of crying.

To be here in Glennie's place is a piece of heaven, sanctuary without any men around. I am sitting here staring into the flames that have now died in the fireplace and thinking about my request to have Noah stay away from Mattie and me for now. I am nervous that he won't respect my request and I will acquiesce. I become sad very easily and quickly when Noah is in my house. I wish I didn't have to go home. Bozeman feels like a burden to me right now. I feel empty inside when I'm in Bozeman.

A poem about Noah.

EVER
I hear her soft breathing
And know her small face is lying next to mine
In the dark.
And I think of you and how she
Resembles you and how she
Is an explosion of us
And I think how I'd like to reach across her
To find you there
And play out my passion for her
By touching you
By feeling you inside me like I did when we made her
And I'm glad I can admit to loving that part of her again
The part that is you
Even if we don't listen to the sound of her soft breathing
In the dark
At the same time.
Ever.

Journal entry, Christmas Day, 1992
I have written a letter to Cherie. "My wish for the coming year is that the pain will dull, that the lessons learned in 1992 will settle themselves comfortably in the folds of my heart, and I will be able to accept you living with Noah without fear of me—this is sent to you with the glimmer of light in my darkness."

My goal for myself is to face my fears, to stand up for myself, to protect myself, to love myself, to love my children, and to love life. I need to move on. I need to let go of Noah and my dream of us as

*family. I love my family. My family is my children and me. We are
four and we love and have fun and feel complete when we are together.*

I don't need a man to feel this way.

Journal entry

*Noah no longer haunts my heart. I am in love with a writer and it
feels warm and right. I wanted him from the first minute when I saw
him, which was a year ago, when the first full moon was out. With
him my life is full. He has promised to leave his wife. I tell myself I can
wait for him to get a divorce. I need strength. I feel as if I am pedal-
ing just to keep my head above the blackness. He is the light drawing
me out.*

*I know how difficult it is to leave a family. I have done it. I left Tom
and it has taken me two years to no longer feel guilty.*

If he loves me, he will do this for me now.

Journal entry

*I am angry. "Quality men" is a contradiction in terms. I need to pro-
tect my heart from now on. I need to be satisfied with me and mine,
and not indulge in flirtation. There's no one around here in Bozeman
who I would flirt with anyway. There is only a huge group of very
mediocre men or maybe men as a group are inherently mediocre.*

Journal entry

*Tom is staying in my house tonight to see the boys. I feel guilty about
our marriage not working out. I feel guilty about me and how I hurt
him, and it doesn't seem to matter how much he hurt me. I remember
when my dad was away from me as a child. I didn't love or know my
dad the way that Calen and Sander know and love their dad, and now
he is not with them. It hurts them.*

*I'm scared. I'm scared that I am a bad mom. I am scared that I
scream too much, that I won't listen to my boys, that I will want to hit
them when they are rude. Why am I like this??? Why does life have to
be so damn difficult? Why do relationships have to be so hard? I want*

another adult here to help me, to balance my life, to be my partner. The stress on me is not a myth. I want someone who I love to actually love me.

Journal entry
I feel defeated, like crying, like giving up. Calen can be so cruel. I was sad and too tired to go to the market tonight and he got angry. He whines if he doesn't get his way. He says insulting things. I feel I simply can't ignore him. I cannot not react. I feel like I can't live like this. This little man in my house trying to boss me around and not obeying what I say.

Sometimes I hate all males, no matter what age. They think you are their slaves. I can't handle a relationship right now with anyone. Just leave me alone. Maybe Calen will have to live with Tom in Utah because I won't have him constantly being rude to me.

How can I write that? I love Calen so much. Why do we have to go through this? What am I doing that causes him to be so cruel? What do I do when he is so wonderful, which is more than half of the time? I feel that he is a time bomb ready to go off any minute.

Journal entry
I am ending it. I was stupid to get involved with a married man, the writer. Why do I do this to myself? Why did I do it to him? It isn't working. I am not waiting for him any longer. I am tired of being the one who has to wait.

Journal entry
He came to the Leaf & Bean today to tell me that he is leaving his wife.
  Now what?

Journal entry
I have been lying to myself for so long. I need to find myself. I need to know who I am before I can truly love someone else. I need to love myself first if I want someone to love me. I began drinking and began getting involved with men on my 15th summer and drinking and men

have been inexplicably intertwined ever since. I still can't handle either. They are a deadly mix, so deadly that they make me want to die.

1. Men
2. Failure
3. Want to die
4. Drink to not feel

It is a destructive pyramid, a wheel with me in the center keeping it spinning. I keep praying to be free of my obsessions with men. I need to release myself from the bondage that is me.

Journal entry

I wanted my dad to love me but don't know how to make him. Getting men is easy. Simply spread my legs. Sex seemed to be proof of love. I seduced them so I could reject them to punish myself and to punish them. Why?

Now I have a daughter. How will I protect her from them? How will I protect her from my own self-destructive behavior?

I feel so alone. I feel unloved and unlovable.

I want to die.

CHAPTER TWENTY-TWO

Coffee had become cool, and the Leaf and Bean was benefiting from a growing national fascination with specialized coffee shops. We were now earning enough for me to hire a full-time manager and spend more time at home with my children.

I'd taken Mattie to work with me every day since her birth, but she was walking now, and I couldn't keep an eye on her and conduct business. We kept open bags of beans on the floor near the espresso machine, and one of her favorite tricks was to reach into those bags and throw beans everywhere.

I worked out an arrangement with one of my best employees, who agreed to take care of Mattie at my house in the mornings and then work the rest of her shift that afternoon at the Leaf and Bean.

The investor whom Glenn had brought in initially wanted out, so Mom bought her Leaf and Bean shares, making our store a family-owned operation. I decided to drive with my manager to Whitefish, Montana, to visit the company that supplied our coffee beans. It was a five-hour trek to Montana Coffee Traders, but it was well worth it. I liked R. C. Beall, the company's owner, from the moment we shook hands. I'd never met anyone so passionate about coffee. He imported his beans from growers whom he knew personally in Monteverde, Costa Rica, a mountain community where he helped growers establish a cooperative so they could earn fair prices for their beans. If you listened to R. C.—and it was hard not to, because he liked to talk—you would think coffee was the most important product in the world. He saw it as a way to bring people together to resolve their differences.

R. C. explained that only about 1 percent of all the coffee beans in the world were air-roasted. Most beans were baked in a rotating drum, but air-roasting—which required suspending the beans on a bed of extremely hot air—allowed each bean to be roasted evenly.

During our tour of his air-roasting operation, R. C. mentioned that coffeehouses in Montana had been created and run almost exclusively by women, because females had been prohibited for years from operating bars.

R. C. and I hit it off so well that we began talking about various ways I could expand sales at the Leaf and Bean, and I came up with what I thought was a clever idea—selling bags of Leaf and Bean coffee in Montana grocery stores.

R. C. thought it was brilliant and immediately offered to join me in a distribution partnership if I could recruit other investors. As soon as I got home, I telephoned Glenn, and she liked the idea. I suggested we sell the coffee in a package that had a photograph of Mom, Glenn, and me on it, since we were the owners of the Leaf and Bean. Paul Newman was making a fortune selling salad dressing, and I felt that having Glenn's endorsement would give us a similar edge.

Glenn talked to her business manager, and he agreed that the idea of selling Leaf and Bean coffee in stores had potential. He suggested that we begin approaching major coffee companies. I balked. I wanted fresh, air-roasted beans from R. C., not beans from some conglomerate. I needed to learn more about coffee so that I could defend my stance, so I called R. C., and he suggested we visit his growers in Costa Rica. We left immediately, and when I returned, I convinced Glenn and Mom that we needed to use R. C.'s beans.

Glenn arranged for us—R. C., Mom, and me—to meet with her and her business manager in Los Angeles to discuss how we would take the next step. Before we were scheduled to meet, however, my mental illness kicked in. I went from being manic one day to depressed the next and then manic again a few days later. My erratic mood shifts alarmed R. C.—so much so that he pulled out of our deal.

I was determined to make this happen without him. If R. C. didn't want to roast our coffee, the Leaf and Bean would begin roasting its own beans—or so I thought, until I found out how much it would cost to set up an air-roasting system.

After months of planning and high hopes, I was forced to give up my distribution idea.

In the midst of this turmoil, Noah left his longtime girlfriend, Cherie, for another woman. His new love was Jean, a woman who worked for me at the Leaf and Bean as my baker. Why was he always dating people whom I knew? The situation became even stranger when I invited Cherie to move in with me, because after she broke up with Noah she needed a place to live, and I knew Mattie adored her. By this time, I'd gotten over Noah and no longer cared if he was seeing someone else. Just the same, I dubbed Mattie "my little peacemaker." Her smiles and energy ended up bringing Cherie and me together as friends.

By 1993, the Leaf and Bean and our adjoining news shop, Poor Richard's, had twenty-five employees. Everything was going well with both businesses.

Sadly, I wasn't doing as well. My up-and-down cycles, which had helped destroy my marriage to Tom, were back with a vengeance. I would wake up one morning and find myself slipping into a depression that could last for days or even weeks. Then I would begin to emerge from the darkness, have energy, and be my happy self. My manic phase would arrive next, pushing me over the edge, confusing my thinking, terrifying me with strange thoughts, and turning me into an angry, short-tempered monster.

The signs were obvious to anyone who knew me well. When depressed, I would stop paying bills, not open mail, and stay home rather than reporting to work. I would sit in a chair and stare at nothing for hours. I would avoid answering the phone and talking to people, including my own children. I just wanted to be alone—yet being alone made my mood even worse.

When I became sad, Calen would get angry with me. At age thirteen, he didn't understand why his mother wasn't doing her job. Because he was the oldest child, he would be forced to take charge. We would have nasty fights, and he would call me horrible names. Calen was rebellious, emotional, demanding. I think both boys were relieved when their father asked them to live in Utah with him during the 1993–94 school year. When summer rolled around in 1994, Calen wanted to stay in Utah with Tom. I knew he missed his father. I had missed my father as a child, too. Still, his request broke my heart.

I talked to Tom, and both of us felt trapped. I decided Calen could stay in Utah with his dad and I would return to Bozeman with Sander, who wanted out of Utah, but Tom said no. He didn't want his boys separated, so he told Calen that he had to return to Bozeman. Calen felt rejected by Tom and returned for the summer deeply hurt and angry.

I realized that Calen and I both wore our hearts on our sleeves. I couldn't read Sander as easily as I could read Calen. I suspected that both my boys were disappointed in me as a mother, with good reason.

The stress of overseeing the Leaf and Bean and Poor Richard's, taking care of three children, and dating a series of men who ended up as disappointments began to close in around me. I woke up one day with a migraine headache that completely zapped me of my strength and made it impossible for me to function. Over-the-counter medication didn't ease the pain. I couldn't get rid of these recurring headaches. The throbbing would be accompanied by what doctors call scintillating scotoma, which causes the field of vision in a person's eyes to flicker and actually compress, making it difficult to see. Whenever this happened, just keeping my eyes open became a huge chore because they were supersensitive to light.

My doctor gave me shots of Imitrex, a drug that actually reduces vascular swelling in the brain, and they seemed to help. One night I was on my knees in the bathroom giving Mattie a bath when I got such a powerful migraine that I crumpled over on the floor. I yelled to my boys, and they brought me an Imitrex injection. All I had to do was place the syringe against my skin and press a button. When I hesitated, all three of my kids, including little Mattie, standing naked in the tub, began screaming, "Push it, Mom! Push it!" I did, and after lying for several minutes on the floor I was able to get up and function again. I was embarrassed that all my children knew how ill I was.

Although the shots helped, I began self-medicating with my old friend alcohol. I started drinking every day, often hiding hard liquor in sodas—Dr Pepper was my favorite—so no one would realize how much I was drinking.

Vodka and gin helped dull the pain, but the migraines proved relent- less. Desperate, I went to see a Bozeman psychiatrist. He prescribed Adderall, a strong stimulant normally used to treat attention deficit disor- der and attention-deficit/hyperactivity disorder but sometimes prescribed off-label to individuals who'd been diagnosed with bipolar disorder. A stimulant is supposed to help you get out of bed in the morning and make it easier for you to stay focused and active. What I didn't discover until much later was that many psychiatrists refused to prescribe Adderall to anyone who has bipolar disorder because when their "up" feelings begin to wear off, patients sink even lower into depression than they had been before.

The Adderall caused me to fall into a seemingly bottomless pit of despair, and when that had run its course, I would blast upward into a supermanic period. Even though I would be manic, feelings of emptiness would rise in me. I would feel incredibly lonely and ashamed. The shame would always spark thoughts of suicide.

During a migraine-driven manic moment, I telephoned Glenn shortly before Christmas in 1994 and announced that I wanted out of the Leaf and Bean and Poor Richard's. *Immediately!* I wanted her to sell both busi- nesses, and she needed to sell them *now!*

Glenn called Mom, who was equally surprised by my demands. As soon as she hung up with Glenn, Mom called me.

"Jess," she said, "I thought you loved running the coffee shop."

I had no patience and couldn't understand why Mom was question- ing me.

"I can't. I can't do this anymore!" I told her. "I just can't. I'm so tired. I never have any time with the kids, and my headaches are terrible. I just can't do it."

When Mom suggested that I take a few days to think about selling, I exploded and launched into a tirade about how I wasn't going to be trapped any longer. I was the one doing all the grunt work and putting in the sweat equity. If I wanted out, then they needed to sell.

"I can't stand working there another day," I moaned.

Because of my obvious inability to cope, Glenn and Mom agreed to sell both businesses. We found a buyer, but as soon as the paperwork was signed, I immediately regretted what I had done.

I loved the Leaf and Bean, and I knew selling it had been a huge mistake. What was wrong with me? Why did I behave this way? I quickly slipped into another funk. What was I going to do now? I felt worthless and ashamed, and once again I reached for booze.

Although they didn't say anything, I suspect my parents realized that I was feeling overwhelmed, because Dad called me with a proposition.

"Your mother and I would like to pay for Calen and Sander to attend boarding schools back east," he explained. "They'll need a good education if they are going to get into the right universities."

"I'm not sure they want to get into the right universities," I replied.

"It's a family tradition," Dad continued. "You want the best for them, don't you?"

I wondered but didn't ask: *Do I have a choice?*

"I need to speak to Tom," I said, demurring.

Tom was dead set against it. He knew enough about my family history to realize that this "family tradition" was one reason why I believed my father was emotionally crippled and distant.

"I don't want someone else raising my kids," Tom declared. "Besides, the kids I know who grew up in boarding schools are not the kind of kids I want mine to be."

I should have agreed with his stance, but I didn't want to disappoint my dad, and I also, deep down, knew that I couldn't keep taking care of my boys. They were becoming difficult to handle, especially when I was depressed. Because Tom was away I would call my big brother, Sandy, and he would zoom over to help. Inevitably, Sandy would get us all laughing.

I told Tom, "The boys want to go. They want to follow in my dad's footsteps."

Tom and I argued, but in the end he relented.

Calen and Sander were both excited. I suspect they were tired of my moods.

Dad was all smiles when he arrived in Bozeman to take my sons back east to visit schools. The trio went first to his alma mater, St. Paul's

School, which dated back to 1856. Dad and his twin brother had attended St. Paul's after his parents returned to the United States from Paris, and my mother's father and her late brother also were St. Paul's alumni along with several male cousins.

Dad loved walking them around the now co-ed campus, singing the school's praises. Sander ended up at St. Paul's, and Calen enrolled at the Holderness School in Plymouth, New Hampshire.

Calen was fifteen and Sander was fourteen in 1995, when they left Bozeman. Mattie was four, and I was forty-two.

PART FOUR

THE MONSTER WITHIN ME

I've been known to complicate my life.

—from my private journal

CHAPTER TWENTY-THREE

It was just Mattie and me—or it should have been just the two of us—but being me, I couldn't simply leave it that way for long.

A local newspaper asked me to write a column called CloseShots, which would contain a five-hundred-word profile of someone local along with a photo that I took of that person. For one of my first columns I chose an old cowboy who lived about fifty minutes away from Bozeman. Actually, he lived in McAllister, which was named after the local family who'd settled there before Montana's statehood. But it never caught on as a town and wasn't recognized as one when the federal censuses were taken. The closest "big" town was Ennis, which boasted 838 residents.

The cowboy's ranch was in the foothills, and after I finished interviewing him and snapping photos, I headed west toward McAllister and the highway back home. Somewhere I got off track, and as I was rounding a turn on a gravel road I saw a cottage with a good-size outbuilding near a creek shaded by cottonwood trees. A For Sale sign stood at the entrance. I decided to investigate.

A real-estate agent would call this listing "charmingly rustic," which meant it was pretty run-down. Peering through its windows, I counted two bedrooms, a tiny kitchen, and an equally small living room. The lot contained two fir trees, flowering crabapple trees, and a lawn that took me down to a creek. That creek was what captured my imagination. Clear water flowing over and around multicolored stones made a gentle trickling sound that was sweet to me. I leaned against the house and took it all in—the creek, the hills, the dots of bright yellow and blue wildflowers—all leading to a backdrop of blackish-blue mountains that jutted from the earth like a giant's backbone. When a blue heron circled over me, eyeing the cool creek waters, I took it as a sign. This would be a good place for Mattie and me to live.

I'd stumbled on this adorable bungalow by chance, but my decision to buy it was not based entirely on serendipity. I had met a man who lived in McAllister—let's call him Phillip—and my newest infatuation clearly was influencing my desire to leave Bozeman. I called a real-estate agent and told her that I wanted to purchase the bungalow in McAllister and sell my home in Bozeman.

As soon as I listed my house for sale, I began having second thoughts. I found myself in yet another familiar place, making another rash decision. Although my boys were attending boarding schools, this was their home, and selling it would make them feel as if they were strangers when they returned for holidays and summers. I pushed those thoughts away.

Because I'd already signed contracts, I couldn't back out. I had reached a point in my life where I could recognize the mistakes I was making while I was manic. Recognizing a problem, however, is not the same as fixing one. I left my Bozeman house feeling sad about what I had done but also excited to start over. Again.

Mattie and I dubbed our new home the Mouse House, not because of all the mice who lived with us but because Mouse was Mattie's nickname. We both settled in nicely. I especially enjoyed listening to the water in the creek as it gurgled by us. In the summer, the creek became a wonderful play area where Mattie and I could wade, sail miniature boats, and search for fish. In the winter, it would gorge from its banks and freeze inches from the retaining wall. Mattie loved skating on this ice while I slid around, trying to keep from falling, and our dogs scratched at the ice with their paws for footing as they slipped over it. At this time we had Mattie's little white dog, Murray, Sander's dog, Joey, and my dog, Wowie. Joey was a cattle dog whom we'd rescued down in Utah at a shelter, and Wowie was a Samoyed whom Noah had given us, a dog he had raised. Wowie guarded Mattie at all times, and the wildness on the ice worried him. He stayed very close to his little girl.

I learned that our Mouse House had been built in 1901 as a school-house for the local ranch children, and now that Mattie was nearing five I decided to turn one room into an impromptu classroom so I could homeschool her. I sent off for materials from the Calvert School correspondance course, and we both would get excited when boxes arrived with textbooks and instructions. I found a long-forgotten book of mine, in Old English, about Robin Hood, and I read that to her, too. Mattie loved that story so much I decided we should perform it. Mattie always got to be Robin Hood; she would protest if I insisted that I wanted to be Robin Hood, so I adopted Little John as my character, although she would have preferred that I play Maid Marian.

Those moments with Mattie were some of my happiest, but there were black shadows in between this light like the strips of dark and light in winter woods. I began drinking more and more as my moods began making me anxious and the migraines continued to torture me. I reached a point where I couldn't face taking the garbage outside without putting the tied bag down at least ten times to do something else. It was a personal victory for me to get the garbage bag tied in the first place. I struggled over the decision about whether to use a tie or to simply grab the sides of the large bag and tie the tops together. I knew there was some evil force lurking outside, and I was afraid. I didn't believe the market was really at the end of the road, so I didn't buy food regularly. Looking back now, I believe my paranoid delusions—e.g., that the market wasn't there—were spawned by my fear of actually having to go inside the market. From the time I parked outside it until I finished shopping and braving the checkout line, I would feel dizzy and nauseated. It was easier to leave the garbage in the kitchen by the door and easier to eat all the food that was in the cupboards, no matter what it was.

If I did get outside the house, I would generally be okay. But sometimes not. This was always much easier when Mattie was with me. She was my ground, the simple reason why I persisted in living. This little girl was the person who held me on this earth at this time.

Alcohol obliterated my cyclical moods, both the terrifying, sad ones that kept me prisoner inside my house and the manic ones that electrified me with energy. I drank myself into oblivion many times over and explained my hangovers to little Mattie by telling her I had the flu. Too many times Mattie found me on the couch, pretending I was sick. I was sick a lot. She would find something to eat or protest the lack of food loudly enough to get me up and into the car. Many times, after shopping, we'd stop at the local bar, the Bear Claw, on the way home. She was allowed to sit at the bar and eat her dinner until 8:00 p.m. Then she sat near the pool table. Mattie learned to play pool from the old cowboys there. I would drink along with everyone else. It was always a relief to feel the vodka warm my body, and the fellowship of the bar warmed my heart. My hands would stop shaking, and the nausea I always felt by afternoon was quelled by the alcohol.

I realized I was a functioning alcoholic but had no interest in changing. My parents and siblings had no idea that I drank so much because I hid it from them. Only my friends and Mattie knew. Alcohol defined my life and, sadly, Mattie's, too.

Mattie told a friend of mine, who offered us her guest room one night to keep us from sleeping in my car, that "when Mommy has one drink, we go home; when she has more, we sleep on a friend's couch." When my friend told me this the next day, I was deeply ashamed.

Having settled into the Mouse House with Mattie, I was free to begin pursuing Phillip, the man who had first attracted me to the area. We became drinking buddies, then lovers, and we decided to marry but not actually live together, because we both wanted to keep our houses. He owned a house in McAllister near the Bear Claw, and I had no interest in abandoning our Mouse House. It was a union doomed from day one for a variety of reasons.

At first, Phillip was understanding. When I fell into one of my down periods, he would help out with Mattie and try to lift my spirits. But he quickly realized that I was a closet drunk and tried to get me to curb my drinking. For a while I did, and the three of us were happy. But when my migraines came back with a vengeance, I started hitting the bottle again.

I was driving home from the grocery store in nearby Ennis one afternoon when a migraine headache became so horrific that the solid white line at the edge of the road became a series of dashes. I couldn't bear to keep both eyes open, so I covered my left eye in order to continue driving.

Feeling desperate, I called Dad, and he set up an appointment for me with a neurosurgeon friend of his in Salt Lake City. Although Dad didn't tell me, he suspected that I might have a brain tumor. As soon as he shared his suspicion with Glenn, she offered to meet me in Utah so I wouldn't have to go through a battery of tests alone.

I felt better the moment I saw Glenn at the Salt Lake City airport. She had dropped everything to be with me. As we were walking to a cab, I reminded her that in the 1970s we had been together in Central Park on a stroll and I'd told her that I no longer needed her to be a mom to me. I was big enough to handle my own problems. Or so I'd thought. Here she was again doing just that—being a mom to me. She laughed and said she wouldn't want me to be alone during my tests.

The neurosurgeon ordered an MRI, and I was told to lie on a pallet that would slowly roll my body into the center of a doughnut-shaped machine. As soon as my head hit that pallet, I began feeling panicked.

"I don't know if I can do this," I told Glenn. "I'm claustrophobic."

She suggested I close my eyes and think of something pleasant. I did, but when the pallet under me began inching forward into the machine, I had to open my eyes.

"Get me out of here!" I screamed, my entire body shaking. I felt as if I were being buried alive. The technicians stopped the test and wheeled me out. I was covered with sweat.

Glenn calmed me down and got them to give me a sedative. When I was knocked out, they put me back into the machine. The tests showed that I didn't have a tumor, much to Glenn's and my dad's relief. However, it left the big question unanswered.

What was causing my migraines?

The psychiatrist in the same hospital interviewed me next, and when I asked him why I couldn't control my moods, he told me that at my level of intelligence, if I had been able to do something about them I would have. That sounded comforting.

"You need medication," the psychiatrist explained.

He already knew that I'd been taking Zoloft for depression. When he heard about my manic periods, he came up with a different diagnosis.

"I believe you have bipolar disorder," he said.

He explained that bipolar disorder is considered a severe mental illness, as serious as schizophrenia. The difference is that bipolar disorder and depression are "mood disorders." Schizophrenia is a "thought disorder" that causes people to hear voices, see things, or think things that aren't real.

The hospital psychiatrist prescribed Tegretol, which he said would stabilize my moods. To deal with my depression, he prescribed Celexa, an antidepressant. He warned: "You need to stop drinking."

I smiled and nodded and assured him that I would follow his orders, but I didn't mean it. I was psychotic, a symptom that this doctor didn't address, and I thought the psychiatrist and my dad were trying to poison me with medication. I probably wouldn't have taken either prescription if Glenn hadn't urged me to take my pills.

"Richard Dreyfuss has bipolar disorder," Glennie said.

She'd worked with him in a Broadway play called *Death and the Maiden*, and he'd talked openly to her about his mood swings. Because Richard Dreyfuss was able to control his moods, my diagnosis seemed less frightening. If he could do it, so could I!

Glenn said good-bye at the Salt Lake City airport, and I returned home to McAllister determined to get better.

My enthusiasm quickly waned. My new medications left me lethargic. All I wanted to do was sleep. At times, I felt as if I were riding an elevator. The Tegretol brought me down; the Celexa brought me up. I stayed off booze for about a week, and then one afternoon Phillip, Mattie, and I stopped at the Bear Claw. It took only one drink to get me tipsy, thanks to my new medication, and I thought: *Think of all the money I'm going to save buying drinks!*

I soon discovered that nothing is simple with medication. Not long after beginning my new regimen, a nasty rash appeared on my arms. Red spots quickly spread over my entire body. The ones on my arms itched so terribly that I scratched them, and they soon turned into nasty, weepy pustules. I kept scratching until the pustules became ugly open sores. They became so painful that I drove myself to a local emergency room one night.

"I have no idea what's causing this," the emergency room doctor told me. "You'd better go to a dermatologist—and fast, before they get any worse."

Worse? Was that possible?

When a dermatologist examined me, she immediately asked me about my meds.

"I'm taking Tegretol and Celexa," I replied.

"This is a Tegretol rash," she declared. "If these pustules are already showing on your skin, you can be sure they're on your internal organs, too. You need to stop taking it immediately."

I telephoned the psychiatrist and told him what I knew already, that I was being poisoned by my pills. From his voice, I could tell he wasn't convinced. When he'd interviewed me, I'd showed signs of paranoid thinking—after all, I thought he and my dad were trying to poison me—and he must have thought I was exaggerating about the medication, even though I told him about the red sores on my arms and what the dermatologist had said. The more I tried to explain, the more frustrated I became. *Why don't doctors listen?* Our call ended with him telling me that he couldn't treat me if I didn't take my medication.

Ignoring him, I stopped taking Tegretol, and my rash began to disappear a few days later.

I wouldn't let it go.

As soon as the wounds on my arms were nearly healed, I would begin scratching them open again, keeping the sores going. I knew this was going to cause scarring, but I couldn't help myself. Before long, my arms looked like the lines of a crossword puzzle had been drawn on them. I started wearing long-sleeved shirts to hide the scabs and scars. I had been reintroduced, subconsciously, to my old "worry spot"—which I'd discovered as a young girl at the MRA compound in Dellwood. It was there where I learned how to stifle anxiety by rubbing the skin between my thumb and finger until it bled.

Intellectually, I knew what I was doing was foolish. But that didn't stop me from doing it. Within days, I had sunk into one of my depressed moods. I went into my bathroom one morning, picked open a sore on my arm, and poured hydrogen peroxide on it, scrubbing it open until blood began oozing from it. The stinging pain calmed me down. It was as if opening that wound allowed all the tension, anxiety, and bad feelings welling up inside me to escape. I think my brain needed physical pain in order to free me from my anxiety.

In the midst of all this, I received a phone call from one of Calen's teachers at Holderness.

"We need to send Calen home," he announced. "I'm sorry, but I'm worried he might be suicidal, and we can no longer be responsible for him."

Suicidal? Calen?

Calen's teacher told me that there were only two weeks left before school would adjourn for Christmas break, so he wouldn't miss much if he came home early and got patched up before returning after the New Year.

I picked up Calen at the Bozeman airport, and he immediately claimed that the teachers at Holderness were overreacting. He was not suicidal. He simply needed time to think. I brought him to the Mouse House, where I settled him into my "studio"—the one-room outbuilding that came with the property and was about forty feet from the main house. I'd lined it with bookcases and equipped it with a kitchenette and a tiny bathroom for guests. I'd planned to do my writing there, but I had not written anything for quite some time and had abandoned work on my second novel.

Calen went directly to the studio and fell on the bed. He was exhausted, so I left him to sleep, but when I looked out my kitchen window a few minutes later, I could see him through a studio window, pacing the floor, chain-smoking cigarettes.

Now what? I asked myself.

Calen told me his experiences at Holderness had been horrible. The hazing by upperclassmen had gone beyond words and involved physical assaults. I certainly was not sending Calen back. Instead, he would live in the studio, where I could keep an eye on him and help him heal. He would get his GED by taking online classes.

I was determined to help Calen, but the truth was that I was in as bad shape as he was. I began rapid-cyling, a condition that caused me to feel mania for about half an hour, become depressed for half an hour, then start the cycle all over again.

My instability and Calen's problems scared Phillip. He retreated to his house and stopped coming over as much. When he did come over, we argued. I would scream at him in a depressed mood, then moments later turn manic and become apologetic and laugh. To him, my laugh became as irritating as my sadness.

Phillip called two friends who were psychologists and told them that I had been diagnosed with bipolar disorder. Their advice was simple.

"Get away from this woman ASAP," one of them said. "If she is bipolar, she will ruin your life. And it sounds like she's rapid-cycling—not something you want to be around!"

Phillip and I both filed for divorce almost a year to the day after we walked down the aisle. This was my fourth divorce. Mattie was crushed. She loved Phillip, and she felt abandoned. Guilt folded me inside its thorny arms. I knew my mood swings had driven Phillip away.

I didn't want Calen sitting around all day, so I pushed him to get a job. Handsome and personable, he found work at the only restaurant in McAllister. Two weeks later, he quit, explaining that he didn't like being around so many other people.

I suggested he attend an acting camp just for fun. He did and ended up playing a major role in Shakespeare's *Hamlet*, which was being performed during the summer festival in Bozeman called Sweet Pea. Glenn used her influence to get Calen a bit part in a television movie that she was co-producing and starring in for Hallmark Hall of Fame. That role earned him a Screen Actors Guild card, and he decided to follow in Glenn's footsteps. He landed a second job, appearing in a movie called *Bad City Blues*, being shot in Kalispell, Montana.

Although Calen was able to memorize lines for the movie, his behavior started to become bizarre. Voices began taunting him, and many days he would appear on the movie set completely lost in his thoughts and voices. When filming finished, he came home. I began to notice that most of his friends were distancing themselves from him, so I was happy when Calen decided to get a border collie for company. He named his dog Jack. I would watch Calen put Jack in his gray truck and take off for the mountains.

I always felt better knowing that Jack was with him. Calen would sit for hours on a rock simply staring straight ahead while Jack sniffed and ran around close by, searching for squirrels, chipmunks, and rabbits. One afternoon as the two of them were returning home Jack leaned too far out of the truck window. Calen made a sharp turn, and Jack went flying out from the truck, hitting the loose gravel with a crack, completely shattering one leg. Calen hurried Jack to a vet, who put Jack's leg in a cast, but the healing didn't happen; a month after the accident Jack's left hind leg was amputated.

When they came home after Jack's operation, I realized that Calen and Jack made quite a pair. Both were broken in their own way— although Jack, taking easily to having only one rear leg, didn't miss a beat, whereas Calen was lost.

I also realized that I didn't know how to help my son. How could I, when I didn't even know how to help myself?

CHAPTER TWENTY-FOUR

It was time to move again. Mattie and I were arguing about everything, mostly because of my frequent "flu" spells. There was no way I could continue homeschooling her in the Mouse House in my condition. I decided we had to return to Bozeman so she could enroll in the same elementary school that the boys had attended.

Suzy Nixon, a friend of mine, said her boyfriend wanted to hire me. He lived in California and was the absentee owner of two Bozeman businesses that were hemorrhaging cash. Suzy had bragged about how well I had managed the Leaf and Bean and Poor Richard's, so he hired me by phone. He told me to start work the next morning, because the sheriff would be escorting his shops' current managers, a couple, out the door at 9:00 a.m., and he wanted me there.

I told Mattie and Calen that I had no intention of selling the Mouse House and the adjoining studio, where Calen stayed. We could use it on weekends as a getaway.

Suzy invited us to stay at her house with her three children until we could find an apartment. In addition to my kids, I brought along three dogs. Suzy had dogs, too, as well as cats. We had two women, five children, five dogs, and seven cats all under one roof. It helped that Mattie was close friends with Suzy's daughter, Madison, who was the same age. Suzy's sons, George and Tommy, were friends with Calen and Sander, although Sander was still at boarding school.

I jumped right into my new job and quickly deduced that both businesses were heading for bankruptcy. Suzy's boyfriend asked me to keep them open as long as possible so he could consider his options. I spent most of my time fending off creditors. It was exhausting, and by the end of each workday I was badly in need of a drink—or so I thought.

Suzy and I soon developed a routine. I would come home from work in my business clothes, briefcase in hand, and yell, "Honey! I'm home!" She would laugh and pour me a large goblet of red wine. Suzy would cook dinner, and afterward I would wash the dishes while she gave our girls and Tommy their baths. I would read to them and put them to bed. We worked well together, but the stress of so many people living under the same roof and the pressure from my job soon got to all of us. After several weeks, Mattie, Calen, and I moved into an apartment over one of the stores that I was overseeing.

Living downtown without a man in my life caused me to fall into my old habits. Each evening, I would meet my girlfriends at a restaurant and bar called Boodles to let off steam. Suzy would join us. We would congregate at the end of the bar, where there was a group of green-velvet-covered stools unofficially reserved for us. Liza Hella, a concert pianist and former San Francisco model and actress, Suzy, and I were the regulars. Sometimes my friend Pam Roberts, who produced documentary films, would be there, as well as some other women who owned downtown businesses. On some weekend nights, after the bar closed, we would move to Suzy's house. The three of us were blondes, and we began getting quite a reputation for our antics and partying ways. At Boodles, I made fast friends with several men, as only drunks can do, over many drinks. Most were local businessmen who stopped in for a nightly drink or two. I told myself that I needed the adult company, but I was really after the alcohol.

As I had predicted, the two businesses that I was managing had to be shut down, and I was out of work. Because we were living above them in a tiny apartment, I needed to find a new house for us. I was tired of walking everywhere and tired of living with three dogs and two children in such close quarters. I had to walk the dogs very late at night so no one would see they were off lead. Through a friend, I met Mike Shafer, a roofer with broad shoulders, huge biceps, and wild, long hair. We decided to share the cost of renting a house. I developed an immediate crush on him and started acting seductive. I would find one of his T-shirts lying around the house and breathe in his scent. I decided to try to get him into bed, but despite my efforts Mike spurned my advances. That had never happened before, and I was incredibly frustrated, but I learned that I could actually become friends with an attractive man without bedding him.

Seven-year-old Mattie adored Mike, especially when he would hoist her up onto his shoulders and "gallop" from our house down the street to a Dairy Queen for ice cream. He taught her how to ride a bike. She also continued to see her father, Noah, who took her out for meals and on jaunts to visit his family.

Mike tolerated Calen but mostly avoided him because his actions were growing more and more bizarre. One afternoon Mike and I were in the kitchen discussing whether or not we needed a new refrigerator when Calen burst in and lunged toward me.

"What the fuck are you saying about me?" Calen screamed.

Mike stepped between us. I couldn't physically control Calen, who by then was six feet tall and weighed more than 175 pounds. Mike could, if he needed to. Calen glared at us and left the room without saying another word.

Mike and I decided to buy a house together on Rouse Avenue because I had good credit and he had the cash. Calen moved into a loft above a garage next to the house. Mattie, Mike, and I each got our own bedroom.

Almost immediately, Calen's moods worsened. He looked haggard and was lost in his own thoughts. By the fall of 1998, nearly all Calen's friends had stopped coming to see him. Even his three-legged border collie, Jack, seemed to sense something wasn't right and began hanging out in the house with us instead of in Calen's garage-loft bedroom.

The Bozeman psychiatrist treating Calen prescribed a strong anti-psychotic, Seroquel, commonly used to treat bipolar disorder. But it didn't seem to help.

Unsure how to help Calen and with no job to keep me occupied, I began spending my days watching the clock, anxiously waiting for happy hour at Boodles. It was my escape. But my coming home late, drunk, and noisy soon got on Mike's nerves, especially since his roofing job required him to leave the house before daybreak. I promised that I would be quiet when I came home, and I meant it, but I was always tipsy when I got in and I was always loud.

Calen recognized that he needed help, and he asked me to take him to a naturopath in Bozeman because he had become suspicious of his psychiatrist. The naturopath told Calen that his body was out of harmony physically, mentally, and spiritually. The first step to getting in sync was to stop taking his antipsychotic medication and begin using only natural plants and minerals as remedies. This naturopath further advised Calen that his mental confusion was being caused by his liver, which had fallen out of whack because of the deep-seated anger that Calen felt toward Tom and me for divorcing.

Calen bought it hook, line, and sinker and immediately stopped taking Seroquel. He went on a strict natural diet, as prescribed by the healer. Within days, Calen was in even worse mental shape.

Frantic, I persuaded Calen to visit a counselor, since he didn't want to return to his psychiatrist. He didn't like the medication his psychiatrist was prescribing for him. He hated how drugged it made him feel. The counselor told me that he thought Calen would benefit from going on a "personal vision quest." Calen would be left in the mountains with only the barest essentials. Surviving on his own for three to four days would force him to take a hard look at himself and eventually help him stop his "negative behavior." Thank goodness Tom and I refused to allow Calen to go on this "quest." We realized that this counselor knew nothing about serious mental illness, even less than we knew, which was not much.

One afternoon when Calen and I were sitting in the living room, my friend Pam dropped by for a visit. Calen was sitting on the couch, rocking back and forth while keeping his feet frozen in one spot. The pupils in his blue eyes were so dilated that they looked jet black. Pam saw him and asked me to leave the room.

Then, when Pam asked Calen if he was feeling okay, he burst into tears and told her that he was hearing voices.

"What are they telling you?" she asked.

"That I don't know anything. I'm stupid. I'm a piece of shit."

"Calen. Don't listen to them. You're not stupid."

"They're watching me, too," he added.

"Who? Who's watching you?"

"Them. They have eyes everywhere. They've hidden cameras in the walls."

Pam took me aside. "I think Calen has schizophrenia," she said. "You need to get him help, get him to a psychiatrist."

I didn't know what schizophrenia looked like, but my firstborn could simply not have it.

My father also was concerned. "Jess," Dad said during a visit, "you've got to do something."

By Thanksgiving, everyone in my family knew Calen was mentally unstable. Yet no one seemed to know what to do about it, or if they did they didn't tell me.

When I mentioned that Pam thought Calen might have schizophrenia, the reactions in my family were pretty much the same. Schizophrenia? That was an illness for other people, people we didn't know, people locked up in asylums. It wasn't something that could happen in our family and definitely not something that could happen to my son. There were two cases of schizophrenia in the Moore family, but we didn't talk about them. These individuals had been sent to live in asylums, and one, younger than me, had died. I remembered this cousin and had loved her when I was young. She had been a sweet girl. Schizophrenia? No. This couldn't be something Calen would be saddled with. Not Calen.

CHAPTER TWENTY-FIVE

I needed to check on Calen. I'd not seen him all day. Living with him had become a torment. Every encounter between us sparked an argument. I drank a glass of vodka to steady my nerves and started toward the garage.

Mike had installed pull-down steps that led upstairs, and as I started to climb them I called out softly, "Calen."

He didn't reply, and I felt a pain shoot through my stomach. A few days earlier, Calen had asked me to watch his dog, Jack, while he went for a drive. As soon as Calen drove away, I had a terrifying thought. *Oh, my God, he's going to kill himself!* He never left Jack behind. I kept imagining the worst; I had never felt so out of control. I didn't know where he could have gone, but I didn't want to call the police, so I spent hours pacing, calling friends, and screaming out loud in our house in total frustration. Calen came home hours later, completely unaware of my anguish. I could feel those same fears bubbling within me now.

I had not been to the loft for some time, and when I peeked through the trapdoor, what I saw shocked me. A single dangling bulb gave the room an eerie glow, and as my eyes adjusted, I noted that Calen had painted on every wall. He had covered one with bright red paint, turning the untouched white drywall into giant letters spelling out the words *lunatic red.*

Two grotesque figures—neither male nor female—decorated another wall. They reminded me of scary monsters.

"Calen," I called.

The Monster Within Me

No reply, but I saw his stocking feet sticking out from under a blanket on the futon that served as his bed.

"Calen," I repeated, this time a bit louder. "It's Mom. Say something."

He raised his head and looked at me. The rings under his eyes, along with his blank expression, hollow cheeks, and distant stare, gave me an instant chill. He looked like a living ghost.

"Are you hungry?" I asked, trying to be as nonthreatening as possible.

Calen sat up, snatched a cigarette from a half-empty pack on the nightstand, lit it, took a long drag, and then defiantly blew the smoke directly toward me at the other end of the loft.

I asked, "What are you doing? Are you okay?"

"Get out!" he snapped.

"Excuse me?" I responded. I hadn't said anything that warranted his disrespect.

"Get out of my room, you *bitch!*"

"Calen, please, Calen..." My body was shaking.

"Get the fuck *out* of here!"

"Calen! Don't talk to me like that!" I yelled.

He glared at me and snapped: "Get the fuck out of here, *now!*"

I was watching my son, but I told myself that it really wasn't Calen. I didn't know who this boy/man was.

"*Stop it, please!*" I screamed. "Why are you acting like this? Please, please, please just *stop this!*"

His face was filled with hate. "*Get out now!*"

I backed my way down the stairs and returned to our house. There was nowhere to put this pain. Nowhere to release it or vomit it up—nothing. Nowhere. I poured myself another vodka.

"Mommy," Mattie said. "Is Calen all right?"

"No," I said. "Get to bed."

"But Mommy," Mattie said, her voice a whine, "I don't want to go to bed right now. Mikey and I are watching a show!"

"I don't care," I said, louder. "Just get in bed."

"I need to brush my teeth first."

"No. I told you to go to bed. Now!"

211

Mike came into the room. "I'll get her in bed; it's okay."

"No," I told him. "It's not okay. I don't know what to do for him!"

"I don't know, either," he said. "But I'll get this girl to bed."

I called Calen's father, Tom. Because of his job, he'd moved from Utah to Helena, Montana, some two hours away.

"Calen's worse," I reported. "He was screaming at me now. Telling me to get the fuck out of his room. I can't do this anymore. I'm afraid."

I could tell from the tone of Tom's voice that he assumed I was being melodramatic. This was not the first time that I had called him about Calen, and I suspected he knew I'd been drinking.

"I'm sure he'll be fine," Tom said reassuringly.

"He's sick!" I exclaimed.

Our call ended moments later in anger and frustration.

Sander and two friends from St. Paul's School were going skiing in the Austrian Alps during spring break, and they invited Calen to go with them. Two adults would be chaperoning three sixteen-year-old boys and Calen. I felt relieved when my sons boarded a flight for Europe. I was emotionally devastated, and I have no idea why I let Calen go except for some kind of magical thinking on my part—that this trip would cure him.

When Glenn learned that Sander and Calen would be gone for several days, she invited Mattie and me to fly to London, where she was finishing shooting a sequel to the 1996 Disney movie, *101 Dalmatians*. The new film, aptly titled *102 Dalmatians*, had Glenn reprising her role as the villainess, Cruella De Vil.

Mattie and I were having a wonderful time with Glenn when I received a panicked call from Sander in St. Anton, Austria. Calen was having a mental breakdown. He believed that Sander and the others were trying to feed him "alien meat" and that St. Anton was actually a Hollywood movie set. Calen didn't want to leave the hotel room. One of the chaperones, who had a relative with schizophrenia, was using her experience to keep Calen calm, but Sander was scared.

I telephoned Tom in Montana. It was 3:00 p.m. in Helena on a Friday when he answered.

"You're closer to Austria," he said. "Sounds as if you need to go get him and bring him home."

"Tom, I can't do this!"

I was hysterical and in no condition to rescue Calen. Besides, Glenn and I were worried that if I did go, I wouldn't be able to handle him.

"Jessie," Tom said, "I don't have a passport."

"I'll talk to Glennie," I said. "She'll know what to do."

Within a few hours, Tom was booked on a flight to Los Angeles that Glenn had arranged. From there, he boarded a red-eye to New York's JFK airport, arriving Saturday morning. A courier met him with a passport, and he boarded a jet leaving for Austria that same afternoon. Glenn had arranged everything from London. She'd gotten Tom a passport, fast, by calling US Senator Ted Kennedy, who had pulled the necessary strings.

At some point during all this, Tom spoke to Sander, and they came up with a ruse to get Calen to the airport. Tom landed, passed through Austrian customs and immigration, and walked into the terminal, where Sander and Calen were waiting. He walked up behind Calen and said in a casual voice, "Hello, Son," as if nothing were amiss.

Tom told Calen that they needed to go home. Although Calen didn't want to leave his brother, he went with his dad. Miraculously, they returned to Helena without incident, arriving on a Monday. Mattie and I left for home, too.

To this day, I'm amazed at how smoothly our family rescue operation went, and I give all the credit to Sander, Tom, Glenn, and Senator Kennedy. We were lucky to have the connections to make it happen.

Rather than staying alone in the Bozeman loft, Calen stayed with his father in Helena and agreed to see a psychiatrist there. The doctor put Calen on a cocktail of mood stabilizers and antipsychotics. Tom also persuaded Calen to join several community youth sports teams to keep him busy.

Tom telephoned me with updates, and we assured each other that we were doing everything two loving parents could do, but as the days passed it became clear that nothing was working. Tom told me that Calen would pace endlessly, smoking and talking to himself. He would drive around searching for a "portal" in the mountains that would take him to another dimension. His doctor upped the medication, but it only seemed to make him more distant.

Tom read an ad in the Helena newspaper about a group called the National Alliance on Mental Illness (NAMI), whose members were mostly parents of children with mental illnesses. He went to a meeting and called me afterward, excited about what he had learned. A father whose son had schizophrenia had spoken during the meeting about how his son had to be repeatedly hospitalized until he eventually had gotten better. It was a "lightbulb" moment for Tom. He realized that schizophrenia was not like a cold, which you could recover from after a few days. It was a serious and debilitating illness, but with treatment you could get better.

Tom felt that Calen was so sick that he needed to be hospitalized, but he was afraid that Calen wouldn't agree. Under Montana law, Calen couldn't be forced into a psychiatric hospital unless he posed a danger to himself or others or he became so incapacitated that he couldn't care for himself. Despite his odd behavior, Calen wasn't violent. Tom decided to talk to Calen about going into a hospital, but Calen didn't believe he was sick. Instead, he announced that he had been chosen to participate in an epic battle between good and evil. He spoke about different realities, alternate universes, and kept mentioning the Real World as opposed to the world that he was currently stuck in.

When Tom asked him what he meant by the Real World, Calen explained that "they" were trying to keep him from getting into the Real World. They were trying to keep him confused in his current world.

"Who are they?" Tom asked.

Calen eyed him suspiciously but didn't respond.

Tom kept talking to Calen and eventually wore him down. He agreed to go to St. Peter's Hospital, which had a small, locked inpatient behavioral health ward. Tom had called the staff about Calen, and when they arrived a hospital psychiatrist greeted them at the door. The doctor explained that he wanted to do a series of tests to determine if Calen had a brain tumor or another kind of physical ailment that was interfering with his thoughts. Calen agreed to be tested and voluntarily signed himself into the hospital, much to Tom's relief. Calen would later tell us that he had agreed to go to the hospital because he thought the portal to the Real World—the portal he was searching for—might be inside it.

While nurses took blood samples, Calen counted the squares on the wallpaper, repeating out loud, "Red square, white square, red square, white square."

He told the nurses, "Christ's blood is different from everyone else's blood. It's different from aliens' blood, the Real World blood."

Tom called me after he left Calen, and for only the second time in my life I heard him sobbing. My eighteen-year-old firstborn was locked in a hospital mental ward. I felt as if all this was my fault. I felt like I was carrying several hundred pounds of guilt on my shoulders. I had struggled for years with my own mood swings, and I knew intuitively that I was responsible for passing along my flaws to my son. Science might not be able to specify what causes severe mental illnesses such as schizophrenia, but there was no question in my mind that Calen had inherited a damaged gene that had been embedded in our DNA and could be traced back to "crazy" Uncle Seymour Hyde, who had taken hostages at gunpoint in Manhattan and rode naked through the Greenwich countryside. This was not my crazy uncle, though. This was my son, and I had done this to him. It was the worst feeling a mother could have.

Tom visited Calen daily, and I called Tom for nightly updates. He told me Calen had made a friend in the locked ward, another young man his age who was equally psychotic. The two of them were spending hours sitting in front of an erasable whiteboard explaining paranoid theories to each other, egging each other on with their delusions as doctors tried to determine what medications might help free them from their own thoughts.

After three days, Calen decided that the doctors and nurses were plotting to kill him. They were not going to allow him to enter the Real World. Calen began planning an escape, and when two sheriff's deputies came onto the ward with a patient, Calen darted for the open doors.

Both deputies snatched Calen as he attempted to run by them. Joined by the psych ward orderlies, the officers slammed Calen onto the floor. He fought back, swinging wildly and kicking as they pinned him down. When one of them finally got Calen in a choke hold, a nurse hurriedly injected him with Haldol, a major antipsychotic that literally knocked him out.

When Tom told me what had happened, I called the Helena hospital and told them that I was coming to see my son. I drove up as soon as I could get away. Calen was standing at the nurse's station, and I could see that one side of his face was red and scabby from the nasty carpet burn he'd received while fighting the deputies and orderlies.

A big grin swept across Calen's face when he saw me.

"Hey, Ma," he called out as I came through the door, as if nothing bad had happened to him. He gave me a big hug.

We settled into two chairs, and I listened patiently as Calen explained why he had fought the officers.

"I was trying to get my contacts out, and they were holding me down," he said. "They were holding my arms, but I knew that if I could get my contacts out, I could be in the Real World."

I held his hand and peered into his eyes. He was being given Haldol and because of that he was cognizant. But he couldn't stay on Haldol all the time—it is a good drug but a dangerous drug for side effects. There were other anti-psychotics out there but what would work?

I didn't know what came next. All I knew was that my heart was breaking, my son was hurting, and I needed to pull myself together and do something to help save him.

But what?

CHAPTER TWENTY-SIX

We're talking about Calen," Mom said. "Anything he needs, you just let me know."

I felt grateful and relieved. I knew Calen was going to require long-term care to recover. Thinking back, I realized it had taken him about three years to reach the point where he was now. Three years of watching him get progressively worse—even though I had taken him to a psychiatrist, a naturopath, and a counselor. If it had taken him three years to get here, it was going to take a while for him to get better.

Although he was getting good care at St. Peter's Hospital, our insurance company wasn't going to pay for him to stay there longer than two weeks, even though the hospital's doctors warned us that it might take five or six weeks for the medications that they'd prescribed to fully kick in. That just didn't make sense, but it is how our system operates.

I didn't want him getting a Band-Aid at St. Peter's only to be discharged and return a few weeks later.

Asking my mom for financial help made me feel guilty, but not guilty enough to keep me from doing it. A private hospital would be expensive. Many of them didn't accept insurance, and neither Tom nor I was in a position to pay for the high level of care that Calen required.

With Mom on board, I began searching for psychiatric hospitals. I searched the Internet, called friends, and learned that several other parents I knew had children with mental illnesses but had kept quiet about it. They had been afraid their sons and daughters would be stigmatized. I'm sure that part of my determination to get Calen the best care possible sprang from guilt. I had wasted so much time taking Calen to men who didn't know what they were doing.

I began attending NAMI meetings, just as Tom did, and soon learned that other parents felt guilty, too, because they had been unable to help their own children. It was as if I were suddenly a member of a secret club. I felt immediate relief after my first meeting. I had no idea that mental illness, schizophrenia, bipolar disorder, and schizoaffective disorder were as prevalent as they are.

Every waking moment was consumed with something to do with mental illness. I ended up selecting McLean Hospital, outside Boston, for Calen. For starters, it was affiliated with Harvard Medical School and was identified by *U.S. News & World Report* magazine as the nation's number one psychiatric hospital. Located in Belmont, a Boston suburb, the hospital dated back to 1811. Seven years after that, it had switched from being a general hospital to one specifically designated an "asylum for the insane," only the fourth such institution in America at the time. Seventy-seven years later, it had dumped its "asylum" tag and was reborn as McLean Hospital, named after a Boston merchant who died in 1823 and left the hospital the equivalent of $3.5 million in today's dollars. A list of its former patients reads like a who's who. Musicians James Taylor, Rick James, Steven Tyler, Marianne Faithfull, and Ray Charles; actor Billy West; poets Anne Sexton, Sylvia Plath, and Robert Lowell; mathematician John Nash—even Zelda Fitzgerald, wife of F. Scott Fitzgerald— had all sought help at McLean.

As soon as my dad realized McLean was affiliated with Harvard, he made a few calls to medical colleagues back east, then gave his approval.

When I spoke to the hospital, I was told that Calen would be evaluated for two weeks in a facility called the Pavilion. He would undergo a slew of tests, all known by their abbreviations—MRI, EKG, CAT—as well as blood work and psychological evaluations. He would be assigned to a psychopharmacologist to help him with medication. Calen would not be under lock and key. He would be permitted to walk outdoors and roam the hospital's grounds. He was free to leave the hospital at any time. Just the same, security guards could respond in less than a minute if a problem arose.

Tom didn't want to send Calen to McLean, but I insisted, and he finally gave in. Calen was still visibly confused when he was discharged from St. Peter's Hospital, and I was nervous about flying with him to Denver and then Boston. United Airlines discounted Calen's ticket because his trip was deemed a medical necessity, but it wouldn't cut the cost of mine. The ticket agent looked at us suspiciously when we appeared at the airport. I could almost read her thoughts: *What could possibly be wrong with this seemingly healthy, good-looking young man—so wrong that he deserves a discounted medical-necessity fare?* If Calen had been in a wheelchair, the agent wouldn't have given us a second glance, I thought, but because his was a mental illness, I was certain that she suspected we were trying to cheat the airline.

Getting through the airport's security, especially its metal detector, was the next step. Calen slowed his pace as we neared it, but I took his arm and assured him it was okay. He made it through but began to feel anxious again when we started to board and he was surrounded by a throng of other passengers. Inching forward in a line of strangers was difficult for us both. I tried to distract Calen by asking him to locate our seats, hoping he would concentrate on finding each row's number rather than on our turtle-like boarding pace. I held my breath, hoping he would not explode when a man in front of us took forever to put his bag in the overhead compartment then slowly remove his jacket and fold it. When we finally slipped into our assigned seats, Calen whispered to me. He said the other passengers were listening to his thoughts, but if he remained perfectly still, didn't make eye contact, and stared out the window he'd be able to minimize the thoughts he was broadcasting. I touched his arm reassuringly and tried to get him to eat or drink something, but he refused. He didn't want to interrupt his vigilance. Finally, he fell asleep, and I began to relax. A vodka helped.

McLean had a car waiting at Boston's Logan International Airport, and we soon arrived at the Pavilion, a brick building with a modest white portico at the entrance and a long veranda. I later learned that Wyman House, where the Pavilion is located, was named after the hospital's first superintendent, who'd believed in "moral treatment" for patients, which included making them feel as if they were living in a home rather than in an impersonal, antiseptic ward. All the buildings were designed to look like houses, not institutions.

Calen and I were taken to his room, which contained a double bed, a sofa bed, a wooden writing table, an armoire, and a television. The walls were painted a soothing blue and had white chair rails and ornate ceiling moldings. It was quite a contrast to the off-white walls and institutional furniture at St. Peter's Hospital.

While Calen was unpacking, I whispered to the male nurse: "You know, TV scares him a lot. I wonder why there's a TV in his room. We've been pretty careful to keep him away from it since he left St. Peter's."

"Some patients are okay with it, others aren't," the nurse, who was big enough to physically dominate Calen, replied. "The ones who aren't can learn not to turn it on. Your son will learn about choices here. It's not easy but it's necessary."

I didn't particularly like his answer, so I said, "The TV makes me nervous because he's just beginning here, and he's probably not even on the right medications."

"Don't worry, ma'am, we'll keep an eye on him," he replied.

I needed to check in at a nearby hotel but was worried about leaving Calen.

The nurse told me to go. "Take your time and come back whenever you're ready. He's not going anywhere."

I hailed a cab, checked into a hotel about five minutes away, tossed my bags onto the hotel bed, and raced back to McLean, surprising the nurse because I'd only been gone about twenty minutes.

"Sorry," I said, out of breath. "I forgot to give you Calen's medicine earlier."

"It's okay," the nurse replied. "Our doctors already have spoken to his doctor in Helena, and we've given him his pills. You can relax."

After hearing that, I wished I had stopped at a bar after checking in at the hotel. I could have used a couple of shots of vodka. I found Calen lying on his bed in a fetal position with the TV on.

"I saw a vampire," he whispered. "First on TV and then outside, at the window."

Damn it!

I unplugged the TV, put an extra blanket from the armoire over it to block the screen, drew the curtains, and sat next to him on the bed. So far, I was not impressed with McLean!

Calen said, "Don't tell them, okay?"

I stroked his arm. He was almost a fully grown man, but his illness made him as vulnerable as a child.

"I'm going to sleep on the pull-out bed here tonight in your room," I said. "Not at the hotel."

"Thanks, Mom."

It was getting late, so we both went to bed. Calen was still sleeping when I woke up and tried to smooth out the linen blouse I was wearing. By the time I came out of the bathroom, he was sitting up in bed and began laughing at how disheveled I looked. At least he was smiling.

We both spent that morning meeting separately with psychiatrists. While I talked about Calen, he was being interviewed. Getting a correct diagnosis and determining what medications could help alleviate his symptoms could take months, I was warned. Months? At least they were going to be thorough.

Midafternoon, I ducked into the Pavilion's kitchen and was eating a piece of coffee cake when Calen came in. He said he wanted to show me something important. Calen led me out the back door onto a lush lawn of grass.

"I saw squirrels and chipmunks earlier," he said excitedly.

"Let's bring cake out here and throw it to them," I suggested.

Within minutes we were feeding the squirrels. Calen had another appointment, so I waited for him on the lawn, and when he returned we went for a walk. We'd gone about a hundred yards when Calen spotted a short stone wall and suddenly took off running toward it. Leaping up on the stones, he let out a loud *Whoop!* I chased after him, noticing that there were no thistles in the grass, as there were in the West. The lawn was cushiony, as the lawn in Greenwich had been when I was a girl. By the time I reached the wall, he had spotted an abandoned building from the old asylum days near a cluster of trees.

"Let's look at it," Calen said excitedly.

We hurried down a gentle hill to the house, which had tall white double front doors covered in chipped paint. "This is where the horse-drawn carriages used to stop," Calen declared at the entryway. Scrambling up the worn front steps, he peered inside through a dirty window. I joined him, pressing my face to the glass. Leaves covered the floor, tables lay on their sides, and file cabinets were empty, their drawers hanging open like hungry mouths.

Without warning, Calen jumped backwards, as if he had accidentally stuck his finger into an electric socket. He caught himself before he could topple down the front steps.

"What's wrong, honey?" I asked.

"I heard them," he replied. "A woman. A man. Don't you?"

"No," I said.

"There's pain here...."

We walked back, our jubilant mood replaced by an emerging sadness. We were not here for a vacation. We were here because he was sick, just like the hundreds of others who had passed through this hospital. I told Calen that I was going to sleep at the hotel that night.

I called Tom from my room. "The first day went okay, but this is hard on Calen. I wish we could just come home."

The next four days came and went quickly as I accompanied Calen to his MRI and other medical tests. The high energy that he had felt when we first arrived was gone. There were no more gleeful runs down the grassy slopes or whoops from atop stone walls.

I, too, was emotionally drained by the end of the first week. It was time for me to go. I'd done all that I could as his mother, and now it was up to him and the doctors. I packed my suitcase, checked out of the hotel, and had a taxi drive me to the Pavilion so I could say good-bye.

Calen was between therapy sessions, sitting outside feeding the squirrels and chipmunks coffee cake. As I approached him, I thought: *I should be leaving him at college.* I fought back tears and told myself: *No crying now. Buck up, Jessie. This is what's best for him and for you.*

Calen smiled when I sat down next to him and then turned back to feeding the squirrels and chipmunks. They would watch a piece of cake hit the grass and then eyeball him and each other before scampering forward to claim it. I noticed Calen's lips moving, but no words were coming out. *Where are you, my son?*

I wanted to wrap my arms around Calen and hold on and cry, but I couldn't do that. Doubt washed over me. *Can I really trust these people to take care of my child?*

I said, "Sweetie, I have to leave. I have a ten thirty a.m. flight home."

"I wish I was coming with you," he replied.

We sat for a few more minutes until the cake was gone and then walked together to the front of the Pavilion, where my taxi was waiting. I'd promised myself that I was not going to make a scene. Calen didn't need that. Yet I grabbed his arm tightly when we reached the cab and said, "My God, I don't want to leave you." Panic and sorrow grabbed my chest.

"It'll be okay, Ma," he replied, gently touching my hand with his. I felt its warmth. He was reassuring me!

"I'll be home soon," he added. "Say hi to everyone for me. Good-bye, Ma."

"I can't say good-bye," I said. "I'll just say, 'See you later,' like Uncle Sandy and I would say when we were separated. Okay? I love you more than anything in the whole universe, more than tongue can tell."

Calen turned and walked into the Pavilion, and for a moment I felt disappointed, hurt. He didn't seem that upset that I was going. The taxi started down the driveway. As we turned a corner, I spotted Calen. He came bursting out the building's back door and was running across the grass toward my cab. My first instinct was to tell the cabbie to stop, to fling open the door, and to grab Calen and escape together. Instead, I dug my fingernails into my purse and began to cry.

When Calen reached the road, he stopped and waved enthusiastically at the back of our departing cab. That was my parting image of him.

I cried, intermittently, all the way to the Denver airport, where I hurried into a bar to wait for my flight to Bozeman. I cried so much that I wondered if a person could become dehydrated simply by weeping. Several vodkas made me even sloppier.

When I got home, I collapsed in bed, but I was awakened early the next morning by the phone.

It was Calen calling.

"I want to come home," he said.

"You can't, honey," I replied.

"I hate you," he said.

Before I could reply, he hung up.

CHAPTER TWENTY-SEVEN

As always, when I was under extreme stress, my shifting moods sent me into the arms of a new man and another bottle of booze.

Mark Sovulewski provided me with both.

At age thirty-eight, Mark was nine years younger than I when we met in 2000. He was ruggedly handsome, with ink-black hair, a handlebar mustache, and mischievous amber eyes. He'd recently arrived in Montana from California, but acted very much like a local cowboy, right down to his big silver belt buckle and scuffed boots. His mother's people, the Bakers, were Montanans, so Mark felt he had every right to wear this cowboy costume.

We were introduced through my friend Pam, whose husband, Dave Sovulewski, was Mark's older brother. Pam thought we might make a nice couple and invited us to join them for dinner at her house. From the moment we shook hands, I was smitten, and Mark was just as taken by me.

After dessert that night, Mark and I excused ourselves and spent the next several hours getting to know one another better while sitting on the front porch steps. Mark asked me about Glenn, and as usual I was proud but annoyed. It was celebrity-mongering, but I quickly got over it. How could I reject him because of some innocent questions about my movie-star sister?

Mark was enrolled at the University of Montana's College of Forestry and Conservation in Missoula, some two hundred miles northwest of Bozeman, and was starting a new chapter in his life. Because he was much older than other college students, he wasn't interested in most college events and spent weekends in Bozeman working at his brother Dave's construction company. Mark had two daughters in California from a previous marriage. He told me that he'd had two serious relationships in the nine years since his divorce, including one with a woman who'd committed suicide.

"I tend to attract women who need saving," he warned.

I thought: *Well, that's definitely me.*

Mark said his hobby was barhopping. He liked hanging out in them. I told him about the Bear Claw, my favorite, and the only, bar in McAllister, and we instantly made a date to visit it ASAP. I'd hit the jackpot—an attractive man who enjoyed drinking as much as I did.

A week later, Mark and I got drunk when he came to Bozeman and ended up tangled together in the guest bedroom in the Sovulewskis' house, where we attacked each other like wild animals, making so much noise that we got well-deserved lectures the next morning from Pam and Dave. Our lovemaking had awakened their seven-year-old daughter.

Mark was the perfect antidote for the pain and ongoing guilt I was feeling about Calen. My son was calling nearly every day from McLean Hospital to ask if he could come home. Each time I told him no it was as if a piece of my heart were being ripped out. Calen would get angry and argue with me. I don't think he had anyone else to vent his anger on. Many nights, I hung up in tears, knowing that Calen had intentionally said things to hurt me.

After his two-week hospital evaluation, Calen moved into Appleton House, a residential facility on the hospital campus, to live among thirty other "residents." The hospital staff didn't like using the word *patients.* Like him, Calen's housemates had been diagnosed either with schizophrenia or bipolar disorder, arguably the most serious mental disorders. When Calen was in a good mood, he would tell me about the others in his recovery program, especially a woman his age named Katie, whom he liked.

I could tell from our talks that Calen was still struggling to control his own mind. Voices continued to tell him that he was stupid and needed to hurt himself. After about eight months at Appleton House, Calen missed a bed check at night. Hospital security was called, but before the guards could find him Katie and another friend of Calen's from Appleton House found him sitting on the steps of the campus chapel holding a knife. Katie talked him out of using the knife to harm himself. When security arrived, Calen admitted that he was having suicidal thoughts and was moved for his own safety into a room on a locked ward.

I'd decided that Mattie and I were going to move to Missoula to live with Mark. I should have recognized mania, but I didn't. Once again, I was manic and chasing a man.

Mattie and I moved into Mark's two-bedroom apartment, and I enrolled Mattie, who had just turned nine, into third grade. This school had many more services than her former school, and her new teachers discovered she had dyslexia. I had known she was struggling with reading and had tried to help by homeschooling her those few months, but I didn't know what else to do for her. This school in Missoula was just what she needed.

But besides Mattie finding some important answers, here we were in Missoula living with a man whom we barely knew and who had a serious drinking problem, just as I did. It wasn't unusual for Mark and I to go through a half gallon of vodka in a few days. Meanwhile, Calen was in a mental hospital. Little Mattie was dealing with a learning disability in a new school and now had limited contact with Noah, her father, back in Bozeman.

If that wasn't stressful enough, my continuing mood changes made me feel as if I were on a playground teeter-totter. The drinking helped, or so I believed.

Calls from Calen tapered off after Mattie and I got settled in Missoula. He returned from the locked ward to his room at Appleton House and fell into a routine as doctors continued with medication trials, searching for just the right cocktail of drugs to keep him stable and silence the voices without turning him into a zombie. Tom and Sander went to visit him, and so did Glenn and her daughter, Annie. All of them reported that Calen appeared to be getting better.

Mattie got help for her dyslexia both at school and at home. It turned out that Mark had been diagnosed with dyslexia as a child and had lived with it for years. He began helping Mattie with homework.

What didn't improve was the amount of drinking that Mark and I were doing. Whenever we traveled between Missoula and Bozeman we stopped at a bar near the highway turnoff to Warm Springs, which was not actually a town but rather the location of Montana's only state psychiatric hospital. The asylum had been built in 1877, before statehood, near a natural spring that spewed out scalding water. The outlaw Jesse James reportedly visited Warm Springs, and Mark and I both got a kick out of hoisting drinks near where famous outlaws and Indian tribes had once congregated. Whenever I thought about the nearby state hospital, I thought of Calen and was happy that he was at McLean and not squirreled away in a state facility where the staff was under constant pressure to treat and discharge patients.

The Warm Springs bar was about midway to Bozeman, so Noah would often come to retrieve Mattie there when it was time for her weekend with him. Mattie would stick quarter after quarter into a shuffleboard game while she waited for her father.

Initially, Mark and I enjoyed our honeymoon phase. When Mattie was staying with Noah, we would take road trips across Montana filled with binge drinking and lovemaking. Montana is home to dozens of historic bars, many dating to the Wild West days, and we were determined to visit as many as we could. I remember one weekend when we drove to Lincoln because we'd heard it was home to the oldest bar in the state. It was also where the Unabomber, Ted Kaczynski, had been caught four years earlier by the FBI. After hitting the town's two watering holes, we drove to the place where Kaczynski had lived in the woods only to discover that the FBI had dismantled his cabin and taken it somewhere else to use as evidence. His entire cabin was gone, and that struck us as hilarious overkill. I knew that Kaczynski had been diagnosed with paranoid schizophrenia, and it scared me that Calen might have that same illness.

A few months after moving to Missoula, during a manic moment, I began getting anxious and decided it was time for Mattie and me to return to the Mouse House. Almost overnight, I wanted out of Missoula and Mark's apartment.

Mark decided to quit school and move back with us. We settled into the Mouse House.

Our drinking quickly became out of control. If I didn't have a drink by the afternoon, my hands would shake and I'd feel sick to my stomach. The sound of ice going into a glass and the sound of vodka and tonic following it became a siren song. I loved it and couldn't wait. But I also didn't love it. With the drinking came suicidal thoughts—of how I would do it and where—and these thoughts began to scare me.

Mark found work with a fence-building outfit in McAllister, and I took another stab at being a homemaker. It wasn't easy, because I was drinking so much at night that getting up in the morning became pure torture. As soon as Mattie left for school, I'd reach for the bottle to "steady" my nerves.

Not long after we returned to live at the Mouse House, my telephone rang.

"Mom," Calen said. "I just saw a vampire."

I'd been drinking and wasn't feeling well. I really didn't want to deal with this.

"Oh, Calen," I said.

"She had bloody fangs. She turned her head and looked at me, and I could hear her hiss!"

"Where are you?" I asked him.

"I don't know—somewhere."

I was frustrated and tired and let out a loud, exasperated sigh as I girded myself for what I knew would be a long conversation. Instead, the phone went dead. I assumed Calen was angry at me, so I mustered my strength and called Appleton House to tell them about our conversation and ask a staff member to get Calen back on the line.

When the night-duty counselor answered, I said, "Calen's not okay. He just called to tell me he saw a vampire. Would you send someone to his room to make sure he's all right?"

"Calen's not here, ma'am," the counselor replied.

"What are you talking about?" I replied. "I just talked to him."

"He's not here."

I felt as if I had just been doused with freezing water. I snapped out of my alcoholic fuzziness.

"What the hell is going on?" I snapped.

The nurse explained that Calen had taken a bus into Boston earlier that evening with three of his friends from Appleton House but hadn't come back to the hospital with them. They said he had been fine when they had first gotten off the bus in Harvard Square, but moments later Calen had bolted from everyone.

"You have no idea where he is?" I asked again, stating the obvious.

"Boston's a big city, ma'am, but we are looking for him."

I slammed down the receiver and called Tom. That's when I got a second jolt. Tom already knew. The hospital had called him as soon as officials realized he was missing, but Tom and Calen's doctor had decided not to tell me because they didn't want to "upset me."

I was furious but also understood why they had kept me in the dark. I had told Tom and Calen's doctor that my own mental illness seemed to be mushrooming as a result of all Calen's calls and the stress that a parent feels when a child is sick. Just the same, I was angry that I wasn't called.

I quickly told Tom that Calen had telephoned me and that if I had known he was missing I might have been able to persuade him to return to the hospital.

Angry, I slammed down the receiver and started toward the cabinet where Mark and I kept our vodka. But when I got there, I hesitated. What if Calen called again? I needed to be sober. When my hands began shaking, I decided to compromise and pour myself a modest drink.

I imagined the worst. I couldn't stop thinking about Calen roaming Boston alone, psychotic and frightened. I imagined him hurting himself or others hurting him.

There are twenty-four hours in a day, and each hour is sixty minutes long, but when one of your children is missing and you know he is psychotic, those sixty minutes drag and the twenty-four hours seem longer. There is nowhere to rest, no calming of your mind. Knowing Calen was away from his evening medication added to my fear. He'd been so fragile for so long that missing even a single dose of medication might cause him to act out.

Around midnight McAllister time, I called Appleton House. It was 2:00 a.m. in Boston.

"I'm afraid we haven't found him yet, but we will," the night-duty counselor said calmly.

"I'm afraid because he obviously missed his nightly meds," I said.

"Well," the counselor replied, "it might be worse than that. One of his friends said she thinks he has been 'cheeking' his meds and then spitting them out later. We don't know how long he might have been doing that, but I'm sure we will find him. Don't worry."

I wanted to scream: *Don't worry? My son may have not been taking his medication for days and is now missing on the streets of Boston and you tell me not to worry?*

I bit my tongue and got another drink after hanging up. That drink was followed by another and another. Calen's dog, Jack, seemed to instinctively know something was wrong, because he came over and sat at my feet while I tried to picture a happy ending to this emergency.

In my mind, I pictured Calen suddenly pulling up outside the Mouse House in his gray pickup and jumping out, the way that he used to. He would hurry into the house yelling, "Hi, Ma!" and I would know that he was safe and give him a hug.

I ran that fantasy clip over and over in my mind until I blacked out.

CHAPTER TWENTY-EIGHT

The phone rang early.

Calen had returned to McLean Hospital on his own, stopping occasionally during the six-mile walk from Harvard Square to Appleton House to duck into an alley or crouch behind a bush so that he could avoid anything and anyone stalking him.

The image of my nineteen-year-old son hiding from imagined vampires and other phantoms made me physically ill. Again I wondered: *Is this going to be his life—our life?*

About two months after Calen moved into Appleton House, one of his doctors called to tell me that Calen had been diagnosed with schizo-affective disorder. I was told that the diagnosis meant that he had elements of bipolar disorder and schizophrenia—both a mood disturbance and a thought disorder. A double curse. My heart sank. It had been clear from the start that Calen was deeply troubled, and various scary-sounding diagnoses had been tossed around, but this one had finality to it.

I called my parents in Big Piney to tell them. When the word *schizo-affective* passed my lips, I burst into tears and crumpled to my knees. All I could think about were the homeless people who roamed the cities, dirty and delusional, screaming and acting oddly. All I could think about were the movies in which mad-dog killers escape from mental asylums. That wasn't my son!

Mom tried to console me, but my own fragile mental condition made it impossible for me to imagine anything but the absolute worst future for my son. He was cursed to live life tormented by his own mind—alone, scared, and scary. I became so distraught by my imagination that when

I later called McLean to speak to Calen, my call was directed to one of his doctors instead. After listening to me for several moments, the doctor advised me not to speak to Calen. It wasn't because he was worried about how Calen would react. It was because I was so emotionally upset that the doctor thought talking to Calen would be dangerous for my stability. I wouldn't be able to handle it.

Calen's illness locked its jaws on me and began gnawing, chewing slowly. I could think of little else. I already knew Calen's behavior had cost him most of his friends. *Who would want to hang out with a madman?* Now his friends were moving forward with their lives, earning degrees, going to work, and getting married while he was trapped in a mental hospital. *What sort of future will he have after he is discharged? What college would want to admit someone with his diagnosis? What young woman would risk dating him? What employer would hire him?* It was as if he had become his illness, and I felt sure that his illness would crush his dreams and rob him of all hope. *Would you want someone with schizoaffective disorder teaching in a classroom? Would you want to hear a pilot before takeoff announce that he has schizoaffective disorder?* I had taken Calen to McLean so that he could get "cured," but the books I read said there was no cure for schizoaffective disorder. It was a lifelong sentence. *What if he never does get better, never is able to leave the hospital, never is able to return home?* Now that his symptoms had a label, I knew he was no longer Calen. He had become his illness, and I hated that.

During a visit to a Bozeman grocery store, I found myself telling a clerk that my son was in a mental hospital and had been diagnosed with a severe mental disorder. A repugnant look took shape on her face. It was as if I had given birth to the Antichrist. Driving home, I decided I had to do something to fight that look. Would that clerk have reacted as she had if I had said my son was in the hospital fighting cancer? Of course not. She would have been sympathetic, understanding, and probably would've tried to console me. Instead, she glared at me with contempt. My son was one of "them," and that made me suspect as well. The apple doesn't fall far from the tree, does it? Did she think mental illness was catching?

I thought about the fact that gay men who had become sick with the HIV/AIDS virus had been viewed as lepers. Over time and with education, that viewpoint changed. The same couldn't be said about bipolar disorder and schizophrenia. Those diagnoses turned you into lepers. Calen's friends had abandoned him. I had been afraid that Mattie's little friends wouldn't be allowed over to our home to play if the parents discovered I had bipolar disorder. Even if the parents hadn't been afraid, I was. That needed to change.

What could I do? I was only one mother living in rural Montana, and I was struggling with my own issues. Still, I had to try. When I got to the Mouse House, I drank a couple of vodkas to calm my nerves and reached for my phone.

"Glennie," I said when my sister answered, "you will never have to buy me another birthday present or Christmas present or anything else for that matter if you can do me one favor."

Glenn was busy shooting a made-for-television movie version of *South Pacific* with Harry Connick Jr., but had taken time to answer my call.

"What?" she asked me quietly.

"Can you do something about the stigma, the stigma that people with schizophrenia and bipolar disorder face?"

I was worried that Glenn would assume I was drunk, so I explained to her how the grocery clerk had reacted when I'd told her that Calen was in a mental hospital and had schizoaffective disorder.

"It's just awful," I said. "This is Calen."

Glenn promised to think about it, and when I hung up I felt better. If anyone could do something about the stigma, it would be my sister. I knew she would want to learn about mental illness before she did anything. Glenn is an avid reader, and she doesn't do anything without thoroughly researching it first, especially when it comes to lending her name to a social cause. If Glenn is going to promote something, she has to believe in it. Her integrity is not for sale and never has been. If anything, I suspected she might wait to make sure that my request was genuine and not sparked by my drinking and guilt about Calen.

By Christmastime, the doctors had put Calen on a new regimen of medications, and he was stable enough to come home for a visit. I was thrilled but also a bit apprehensive. I wasn't worried about how he might act: I was worried about how my family would treat him. Holidays had always been a tough time for me emotionally. I kept telling myself that everything would be okay as long as I didn't drink in front of Calen. I had gotten good at hiding my drinking from my parents and siblings. Now I would hide it from my children as well. Sander was coming home, too—from the University of Colorado at Boulder. My boys would bunk in the studio while Mattie, Mark, and I were in our cozy Mouse House.

Christmas Day went well. We exchanged presents, and everyone had a good time. I should have been happy, but during the short period between Christmas and New Year's I slipped into a funk. To steady myself, I began drinking, and on New Year's Eve, I was rip-roaring drunk by midnight. I needed the booze to cheer me up and block out the suicidal urges that had been popping into my thoughts more frequently.

Killing myself seemed like a reasonable answer to all my problems. With death, I could finally be released from myself. I believed that if I shot myself, I would release my blood, which would, in turn, heal me. My thinking was completely illogical, but it made sense to me.

I awoke in the wee hours of the morning on January 1. Mark was sleeping soundly next to me, and I didn't want to wake him, so I slipped off our bed quietly and made my way out into the kitchen. Mattie was asleep on the top bunk in her bedroom, and the house was quiet. I turned the knob on my kitchen door, stepping outside into the chilly black morning air. My kitchen faces the studio, but the lights inside it were dark, so I knew Calen and Sander were sleeping. I was alone. No one was aware of what I was about to do.

Being an avid outdoorsman, Mark owned several guns, including a pistol that he kept in his pickup truck. When we had started dating, I'd gotten him to promise that he would keep his guns locked up. I didn't want Mattie to accidentally shoot herself, and I didn't think it was smart to have loaded weapons lying around when both Mark and I were intoxicated. Mark had kept his guns secure, but I'd noticed earlier in the afternoon that he'd left a pistol on the front seat of his truck without locking it into its case behind the driver's seat. It was what I was now after.

I was going to do it. I was going to kill myself.

As I made my way to his truck, I imagined the scenario. I would open the truck's door and retrieve Mark's handgun, checking to make certain it was loaded. I would raise it with my right hand and use my left hand to guide the barrel into my open mouth. I could almost feel the cold metal touching my skin and tongue. The next step would be easy. A final thought, a squeeze of the trigger, and it would be over. I would be dead. I would be healed.

When I grasped hold of the truck's door handle, I had another vision. I could literally see the back of my head exploding as the slug from Mark's gun ripped through my brain, spraying gray matter—like pudding—and blood onto the ground. My body would collapse.

Had my image of the future ended there, I would have been okay with it. But it hadn't.

Mark would hear the gunshot and realize I was not in bed. In my mind, I could see him awakening Mattie as he turned on lights and called my name. Calen and Sander, both groggy, would hear the gunshot, too, and step outside. By this time, Mark would be next to the truck, looking at my lifeless body. He would see that it was his gun that I had used. I envisioned little nine-year-old Mattie staring out the kitchen window. Would she realize I was dead on the ground? What would she think? How would Calen and Sander handle my suicide?

Touching the cold handle of the pickup truck's door snapped me back to reality. I could see Mark's pistol on the seat, just as I remembered it, a glint of moonlight reflecting off its chrome barrel.

I reached for it but stopped when Mattie's face unexpectedly flashed in front of my eyes. I couldn't shake the image of her running from the kitchen, screaming hysterically as she reached my dead body. I could see tears flowing down her soft cheeks. Mattie already had been through so much. How could she possibly understand why her mother had killed herself and abandoned her?

My hand jerked back, and I slammed the truck door shut. Like

Charles Dickens's Ebenezer Scrooge, I had seen enough. I couldn't do this to Mattie and Calen and Sander. They needed me. It wasn't right. Crying, I stepped away from the truck and walked back into the Mouse House, slipping inside its kitchen as quietly as when I had left it only moments before. Instead of returning to bed with Mark, I crawled into the bottom bunk in Mattie's bedroom. I wanted to be close to her. Lying there, I thought about how she and her brothers had saved me from myself without ever waking up. I cried myself to sleep.

The first morning of the new year brought with it a new resolve on my part. When Mark emerged from our bedroom, I told him what had happened during the morning hours. He was shocked, sad, grateful, but thankful that I hadn't killed myself, especially with his handgun. He promised to keep it locked up in the future.

"I'm going to stop drinking," I said. "I can't keep doing this."

To my surprise, Mark agreed. We both realized that alcohol had taken over our lives. What better day than New Year's Day to start our new life of sobriety together?

Excited yet scared, we decided to attend an Alcoholics Anonymous meeting. We were going to need help to stop drinking. This was not the first time that I'd tried AA. Ten years earlier, when Tom and I had been going through our divorce, I'd attended AA meetings for a year. Although I had mouthed all the correct words at the time, I had never believed that I was an alcoholic. I told myself that my drinking was "situational," caused by the stress of a divorce and my emerging mental illness. At least, that's what I told myself. I'd spent twelve months sober and then, as they say in AA, "went back out."

Bozeman was much too far for Mark and me to drive to an AA meeting, so I telephoned a friend who I knew was an AA regular. Juliana was tall, loud, and had a laugh that could skin a cat. We'd met and become friends in—where else?—a bar a few years earlier. I'd been on a date with a cowboy named Max when we stopped at the Blue Moon Saloon in a nearby town. I'd ended up on a stool next to Juliana, and we'd spent all afternoon drinking together.

When I reached Juliana, she told us where to find an AA meeting and offered to meet us there. New Year's is an especially difficult time for recovering alcoholics, she said, so finding a meeting was easy. We settled on one that night in Ennis.

Juliana gave me a big hug after Mark and I parked outside the Madison Valley Medical Center, the Ennis hospital. We followed her downstairs into a room whose walls were lined with AA posters. The twelve steps to recovery were listed on one, the twelve traditions on another. A coffeemaker in one corner of the room offered both regular and decaf and was flanked by stacks of mismatched mugs.

I doubt many people want to attend an AA meeting for the first time. It's embarrassing to walk into a room of strangers and admit that your life is completely out of control because of booze. I excused myself to use the bathroom, located in another corner of the room, before the meeting began, only to realize that it didn't have a ceiling fan and that every noise that I made would be clearly heard in the room just outside the door, where everyone was taking seats at a table. I turned on the water to help cover the sound of my peeing and swept a cold, damp paper towel across my face before emerging to meet my fellow AA attendees.

There were about seven of us, including Mark and me and Juliana, and although AA is based on anonymity, in a town the size of Ennis everyone is recognizable. Juliana and I were the only women, and our meeting began—as I assume all AA meetings begin whenever someone new "darkens the AA door"—with what is called a First Step meeting. One by one, each AA member takes a moment to recall how alcohol abuse nearly destroyed his or her life. Mark and I were supposed to listen for three commonalities: denial, powerlessness, and unmanageability. The purpose of First Step stories is to make newcomers realize they are not alone and to remind AA regulars that all of us have hit bottom at some point—that we have experienced a feeling of "incomprehensible demoralization," which is how AA describes it when you reach the end of your rope and think about wrapping it around your neck.

An old cowboy began the First Step meeting, explaining how he'd almost killed a man during a drunken rage. The cowboy's intended victim was his wife's new lover, which added some justification to his story, but not much. He was not a murderer, he explained, and yet alcohol had nearly led to him fatally shooting someone.

His story caused me to think about my near suicide less than forty-eight hours earlier. What had I been thinking?

Perched around the table, I realized that my First Step story—while different—was strangely similar to everyone else's. Like them, I'd denied my addiction and hidden it until I could no longer function. I felt tremendously guilty for all the times that I had almost let Mattie go hungry because there was hardly any food in the house and had refused to drive her to a friend's house because I was drunk on the couch.

Mark and I left that meeting feeling resigned, sad, but also determined. I was certain I could go cold turkey because Juliana had done it. Juliana warned me that alcoholism is a physical addiction as well as a mental one, which meant I was going to feel physical withdrawal symptoms as I weaned my body away from booze. That night, Mark and I both braced for the worst, and I envisioned myself breaking out in cold sweats as my entire body trembled uncontrollably.

For some reason that didn't happen to either of us.

Two days after that first AA meeting, both of us were craving a drink, so we decided to attend another meeting to help us stay sober. We got into our pickup truck and headed for the highway, but as we were driving to the Ennis hospital, Mark glanced at me and I looked at him, and simultaneously we both said, "Screw this."

Instead of going to AA, we made a U-turn back to the Bear Claw and spent the rest of the evening drinking there. The next morning, guilt set in, so we decided to drive into Ennis for another AA meeting.

This time we made it to the basement room and discovered some new faces sitting at the table. Still, I already knew most of the members from our first session, including the older cowboy who'd nearly shot and killed his wife's lover.

The man running the meeting asked, "Is there anyone here for the first time since their last drink?"

Mark and I sheepishly raised our hands.

"We need to do a First Step," he announced.

One by one, each of the members recalled how alcohol had taken over their lives, and I got to hear that old cowboy talk again about how he had nearly killed another man during a drunken rage.

Mark and I left that meeting determined to stay sober. This time, we lasted about three days before we fell off the wagon again. When we returned to AA, I was in no mood to hear another First Step.

"I'll admit to drinking again," I announced. "But I don't want to go through another First Step. I mean, this is our third time, and I already have heard your stories."

The old cowboy stared at me, leaned forward, and said, "Well, isn't that just too bad, missy!"

If I wanted to stay in AA, I would be required to follow the rules. No exceptions. The cowboy started his First Step story, and I heard for a third time about his and everyone else's grim descent into addiction.

For Mark and me, the fourth time was a charm. I began keeping track of how many days had passed since my "sober day," when I had stopped drinking. Day by day, week by week, month by month, the length of time when I could declare myself sober began to increase, and I became prouder and prouder of keeping track, saying, "It has been..." (a week, a month, a year) since my last drink.

During the ensuing weeks, I discovered that for me, the most difficult challenge was not physical withdrawal from alcohol; I never felt the delirium tremens—DTs—that I'd feared. What caused me the most distress was the reaction of my friends and fellow bar-stoolers. Nearly every event that Mark and I were involved in centered around drinking. We had built our days and relationship around a bottle and bars. I foolishly believed at first that I would be able to simply go on living my life just as I had done. That was not to be. Getting sober meant I couldn't go barhopping with Mark or my girlfriends.

Even my own parents found my sobriety awkward. My father knew I was attending AA but said, half joking, "You won't mind if I have a drink, will you?" He then poured himself one and put the bottle down in front of me.

Being sober wasn't what I expected—at first it was simply awful. One night, I went outside the Mouse House, looked up at the beautiful stars, and began screaming. *How am I supposed to enjoy anything in life? How am I supposed to be? I don't know how to be without alcohol! I don't know how to be angry or happy without it!*

One evening Mattie called me into our tiny bathroom. "Mommy," she said, looking very serious, "you were more fun when you drank."

I was stunned. Her little face looked up at me, and I could see her chin trembling.

I said, "Oh, sweetie, I know. I know...we'll just have to figure it out." We gave each other hugs. "It'll be better after a while," I told her.

I realized that even her plea didn't make me want to pick up a drink. AA was working.

Juliana was a big help at moments like that. She brought me a present that she had found in a store that sold secondhand books. It was a copy of *Twelve Steps and Twelve Traditions*, the original book published in 1952 by the founders of AA. The book had been owned by a young man who, Juliana said, had killed himself because of his addiction. Without alcohol, he felt socially isolated, like an outcast. He'd lost all his drinking buddies and ended his life.

When she handed me the book, Juliana said, "Don't you ever forget what brought you to AA."

I thought about Mattie, Calen, and Sander.

When I began reading the book, which opened with step 1 ("We admitted we were powerless over alcohol—that our lives had become unmanageable"), I noticed its previous owner had underlined key paragraphs, including steps 8 and 9.

8. Made a list of all persons we had harmed, and became willing to make amends to them all.
9. Made direct amends to such people wherever possible, except when to do so would injure them or others.

The first thought in my head was about Tom and our divorce. Then my boys and Mattie and all the times when the "flu" had kept me in bed. Staying sober was going to require a lot of work on my part. I was going to have to make a lot of amends.

PART FIVE

FINDING MYSELF

It's a curse knowing what hands tell at a glance. I rarely look to faces anymore for my first impression. Hands hold the truth— faces turn to masks too easily. Hands eliminate words.

—from my private journal

CHAPTER TWENTY-NINE

My world became brighter. Without booze dulling my mind, it was as if I were being reintroduced to brilliant colors and delicious aromas that had been blunted by years of alcohol abuse. Slowly, I began to feel free of my addiction, especially in the late afternoons, when in the past I would have had to have a drink to stop my hands from shaking or to prevent nausea. Mark and I attended AA meetings faithfully, and life seemed good and full of promise.

We bought a house in Bozeman so that Mattie, who had turned ten, could enroll in public schools there. Mark began working regularly at a construction job, and I resumed taking photographs and writing.

My mental illness, however, had not forgotten me. Being sober didn't stabilize my moods. If anything, the alternating bouts of depression and mania returned unchecked and with renewed ferociousness. The only positive was that the mood stabilizer I was taking seemed to end my migraine headaches, and I was grateful to be done with that torture. When I complained about my continuing mood swings, the local psychiatrist treating me tweaked my medications, but it didn't help. I felt as if I were a tiny boat being whipped by waves, completely at the mercy of an angry sea.

Two years after Calen checked himself into McLean Hospital, he decided to come home. The doctors wanted him to stay longer, but he was weary of the place. He landed at the Bozeman airport in March of 2002, sporting shoulder-length hair and appearing overweight. The extra pounds were a common side effect of his medication. But his appearance didn't concern me as much as his demeanor. I felt Calen had become institutionalized. He seemed incapable of making the tiniest decision on his own and waited for me to tell him what to do and when to do it. He was afraid to leave our house, and the thought of him bumping into his old friends frightened him. They had rejected him and weren't interested in giving him another chance. It was heartbreaking.

I had to get Calen involved in life, so I began taking him with me on errands. Initially, he would sit in the car and wait for me. After several weeks, he finally came into a store. He walked in, looked around briefly at the items nearest the door, then walked back out to the car. It was a victory.

Mark was good with Calen, but having a twenty-two-year-old man freshly discharged from a mental hospital living in our home soon became an issue. In addition, Mark's two teenage daughters from his first marriage decided to move in with us. The two girls, along with Mattie (now eleven), Calen, and an assortment of dogs, all living in the same house with Mark and me became too much. My psychiatrist had warned me, saying, "No, Jessie. No, no, no!"

But whom was I going to turn away?

I loved Mark's girls and was determined to not let my mood swings affect us one way or another. I'd just have to focus.

All of us did our best, but there were simply too many of us— a fact that Calen was the first to realize. He didn't like commotion. He decided to move out, and he used money that he had inherited from his great-grandmother Moore to buy a one-bedroom condo. I was worried, but I told myself that living independently would help him regain his self-confidence.

It did. At first. But the transition proved too overwhelming. One evening when I went to check on him, I found Calen cowering on the kitchen floor with his back braced against the corner cupboards. He was rocking back and forth.

Judging from the empty bottles in the house, I knew he'd been drinking, and his apartment reeked of pot. Calen also told me that he'd stopped taking his medications.

I couldn't ignore the irony of the moment. My son was following in my footsteps, trying to deal with his mental illness just as I had done—by self-medicating with booze and pot. He was in such fragile shape that I was afraid to leave him alone. I urged him to take his meds, but he refused.

I decided to call Katie, the woman Calen had befriended at McLean. She'd been discharged, too, and was living with her parents in a southern state. Just as my AA sponsor could talk to me—one drunk to another—Katie could talk to Calen as a peer. When she answered the phone, I explained that Calen was refusing to take his pills. She began speaking to him and eventually suggested that the two of them take their medications together. I handed Calen his pills and watched as he listened to Kattie's voice.

"Okay, are you ready?" she asked Calen. "Let's do this together. One, two, three, go."

Calen swallowed his meds at the same time she took hers. It was cute and effective. I felt relieved, but I wasn't about to leave him alone. I slept on the floor of his apartment that night. Fortunately, Calen seemed better when he got up. He agreed to take his medication again. He called Katie to tell her.

I liked Katie and thought she was good for Calen. The two of them continued to talk each day, and before I knew it Calen had invited Katie to come to Bozeman to live near him. I was apprehensive but felt mostly relieved. They seemed good for each other, and having Katie in Bozeman would free me to deal with my own mounting problems.

By this point, Mark and I had been together more than three years as common-law husband and wife, but he was growing tired of my mood swings. I couldn't blame him. One night when he came home from work, he found me hiding in our bedroom closet. I was lying on our shoes underneath rows of hanging clothes.

"Jess, what are you doing?" he asked.

"Hiding," I said.

"From what?"

"Everything."

"Oh, honey, come on, let me help you get up. You can lie on our bed, and I'll close the door."

Mark helped me get settled on the bed. He lay down next to me, holding me tight, and whispered, "I want you back."

"I'm right here," I said, instantly angry. I pushed him away. "This is me, too! Why can't you see that?" I looked into his eyes and saw only sadness.

Because Mark left early in the mornings for work, he went to bed at nine o'clock. I stayed up until 2:00 or 3:00 a.m., watching television or reading. We became ships passing in the night.

In the spring of 2004, our relationship reached a breaking point. Two incidents caused it to snap. During a manic mood, I decided to trade in the Dodge Durango SUV that served as our family vehicle; we never seemed to go anywhere together, the five of us, and I thought it was a waste of gas to drive it when hardly anyone ever used it but Mattie and I and perhaps Calen. Besides, I could justify anything when it came to purchasing a new car. I loved buying them. Calen went to the dealership with me. When Mark saw a new car, he freaked out.

I hadn't bothered to tell him I was going to buy a new car, and I certainly didn't feel that I needed his permission. He disagreed, saying, "We're married, and a decision like that should be done together!"

I felt as though his hands were around my neck, choking me.

The next incident happened when Mark went to California to attend a family reunion. He got drunk and called me. I was disappointed in him and scared, especially when he announced that he wasn't going to continue going to AA with me. He missed drinking and felt he could control it. Maybe he could, but I doubted it, and I didn't want his drinking to drag me back into an alcoholic abyss.

I decided Mattie and I were going to move out, but we couldn't return to the Mouse House because I'd rented it to tenants. I needed to stay in Bozeman anyway because Calen and Katie were there and Mattie was now entering middle school. I telephoned Mom, and she understood the situation. She offered to buy a house in Bozeman for Mattie and me to live in. We found a perfect house except for one thing: I suspected the basement was haunted. We decided to buy it anyway because of the location and the price. This situation was perfect for both Mom and me. When we finally moved out and put the house back on the market, Mom made a profit.

Mark didn't put up much of a fight when I announced we were leaving. He admitted he couldn't handle my unpredictable moods anymore. Living with me was like living with two different people. Without realizing it, Mark was echoing what Tom had said about my moods when our marriage had ended in divorce.

I slipped into a depression after separating from Mark—only this one was different from all my earlier ones. It brought a new element with it: a demonic Creature that had settled inside my brain, taking root just behind my left ear.

At first, I couldn't make out what it was. I just knew it was there and that it was small, deadly, and very real. I knew it had planted roots and didn't plan on leaving anytime soon. Slowly, it began to reveal itself.

The Creature had two burning red eyes—tiny things that seemed to glow and were simply terrifying. I was afraid to look at the Creature's body. I didn't want to irritate it. But I had to know what it was. When I finally forced myself to look I realized the Creature resembled an angry grayish squirrel, but this was not some cuddly rodent.

It spoke to me but said few words:

"Kill yourself."

It repeated them over and over and over and over until I had trouble thinking about anything else. My earlier attempts at suicide had failed because I hadn't planned them well. With the Creature coaching me, I began considering ways to end my life. They had to be quick and foolproof. I needed a method that wouldn't allow me to change my mind at the last moment. And I knew, this time, that the Creature wouldn't allow me to think of my children and put them first.

I was soon spending my days thinking of suicide, considering each possible method and then rejecting each plan until I settled on one in my mind. I had it figured out. I would drive to the Mouse House, which I loved dearly, and walk down to the creek that flowed through the property. Dropping to my knees, I would position a 12-gauge shotgun between the ground and my chest. I would reach forward and pull the trigger. The shotgun blast would shred my heart and spill my blood.

My plan would guarantee the spilling of blood, which was important to me. The image of my blood flowing from my body was incredibly soothing. I wanted to be baptized in my own blood because I continued to believe it would somehow heal me. Releasing my blood would free me and silence the Creature in my skull.

All I needed to do was choose a date to die. I thought of James, my second husband, who had committed suicide. He had chosen when to end his life. I would follow his lead.

It had been several years since I'd reached for Mark's unlocked handgun on New Year's. I'd stopped myself because of my children. They had needed me then, but not now. Calen had Katie. Sander was in college. Mattie was thirteen, but she had her father, and I knew that my parents, Tina, Glenn, or Sandy would look after her. My children would be hurt by my death, but if anyone understood the anguish that my mental illness was causing me, it was they. They had experienced my depressions with me, had been dragged along during my bursts of mania, and had found their own ways to handle their mom and her quirks. I knew they were survivors, and I had reached a point where I no longer wanted to be one.

I had been sick for so many years that I didn't really think I was that sick; I was the way I had always been. At one point Moo offered to send me to McLean but I had refused. I didn't think I was that sick. I had learned how to hide, how to fake it. At least I thought I had.

"Kill yourself."

Mattie and I were scheduled to go on a road trip to Denver to visit friends. Our return would take us through Big Piney for an impromptu family reunion. Glenn had flown into Wyoming, and Tina and Sandy had agreed to drive to Big Piney so our family could be together. I had no intention of telling any of them that I was going to kill myself, but the family gathering would be a good way for me to see everyone one last time. Perhaps the Creature had known about Glenn's visit. Maybe it was karma.

When we arrived at Big Piney, Mattie and I settled into the two-bedroom guesthouse. It was about fifty yards from the main house, which was a beautiful stone-and-timber home with a high-ceilinged living room that my father had decorated with souvenirs he and Mom had collected in Africa. The guesthouse had Tina's paintings hanging on its walls—

intricate botanical drawings of flowers and lichen. Adjacent to the guest cottage was a third building, another two-room structure that Dad used as his office. One room, designed to be my mom's art room, was cluttered with papers and boxes of photographs of our ancestors.

Glenn had arrived fresh from a studio where she'd done voice work for a character in a new Disney movie. Her latest motion picture, *The Stepford Wives,* was about to be released. My father quizzed her about both as soon as we got together in the main house for one of Mom's meals. It felt good to be among them, but I didn't say much. The Creature talked to me incessantly.

"Kill yourself!"

On the morning when Mattie and I were planning on returning home, the Creature woke me up. He was more frantic, more insistent.

"Kill yourself! Kill yourself! Kill yourself!"

I covered my ears with the palms of my hands, but he kept screeching, his voice growing louder and louder. I felt defeated, totally helpless, and utterly hopeless. He was winning, and he knew it. That gave him power.

Mattie and I lugged our suitcases from the guesthouse to our Subaru, then Mattie walked up to the main house to say good-bye to her grandparents. I wondered if anyone could hear the Creature's screams. He had started spinning in a circle, doing somersaults at a frenzied pace.

"Kill yourself!"

I felt as if my head were going to explode. The Creature's hollering was becoming unbearable. I wasn't certain I would be able to drive. I had to do something to shut him up. I had to keep Mattie safe, safe from me.

"Kill yourself!"

Both my sisters were still in the guesthouse, and when I went back inside Glennie was the first one I saw. She gave me a puzzled look. What had we forgotten?

"I can't stop thinking about killing myself," I blurted out, tears flooding my eyes. I sobbed, grief and terror winding themselves around me.

Glenn stepped forward and wrapped her arms around me. She guided me to a bench on the guesthouse veranda and called Tina. I felt like a child again as I explained that I couldn't think about anything but suicide.

Do they believe me? Is this just another attempt by Jessie to get attention?

I couldn't look them in the eyes. I was Jessie the fuckup.

"Kill yourself!"

Glenn spotted Mattie returning from the main house. She told her that we were not leaving yet. Mattie saw me crying and came over.

"It's all right, Mama," she told me, placing her hands on my shoulders. I cried even harder. "I'm sorry, Mouse; I'm so sorry," I told her.

For a moment, I considered telling them about the Creature. But I was too afraid—not afraid of how they would react but afraid of how the Creature would react. I didn't want it to get angrier than it already was.

"Kill yourself!"

It was Mom who suggested that I check myself into McLean Hospital. If the doctors there had helped Calen, then they could help me. Glenn offered to go with me to the hospital so I wouldn't be alone. Mattie would move in with my friend Suzy Nixon while I was away.

All I had to do was hang on for a few days while Mom and Glenn made all the arrangements. I felt grateful. But the Creature wasn't happy. He kept up his chanting, taunting me.

The flight from Bozeman to Boston three days later seemed to last forever. The Creature was still spinning, still ordering me to kill myself.

Where does he get his energy?

Glenn had gone ahead and met me at the airport. We were repeating the same drive that I had taken when I'd brought Calen here. As we approached the Pavilion, I remembered how Calen had gone through a series of physical tests and interviews. *Should I tell them about the Creature? Would the Creature be angry if I did? Would they understand?*

Glennie reached across the seat and took my hand.

"I'm here for you," she said reassuringly. "It's going to get better."

How does she know, when I certainly don't?

I saw a flash of what appeared to be sadness in Glennie's bright eyes. She'd been so busy living her own complicated life. Did she feel guilty? Why hadn't she realized how sick I was? She had always loved me, had always felt obligated to protect me, but what did she really know about my life in Montana—my five husbands, my drinking, my mercurial mood swings, and my suicidal depressions? In many ways, I was a stranger to her, even though we were linked by blood, genes, and sisterly love.

"Are you ready?" Glennie asked me.

The Creature answered: *"Kill yourself!"*

I opened the car door, and Glennie and I walked into the Pavilion.

CHAPTER THIRTY

Glennie helped me settle into my room at the Pavilion, where I would be staying while doctors evaluated me. My bedroom was comfortable, like one you'd find in a bed-and-breakfast, but the mattress was very hard. Glennie also surprised me with a gift of several outfits that she'd bought for me. The new clothes were lovely, but receiving them made me feel sad. I was fifty years old, and my older sister was still taking care of me.

I felt ashamed. What I was feeling went beyond my embarrassment about depending on Glennie and being in a mental hospital. I was ashamed because my own brain was failing me. The Creature was causing me to second-guess every decision I made. I was a wreck, struggling to piece together the remnants of my old self-image.

Glennie surprised me with another present—a leather-bound journal. She'd inscribed the first page: *For my beloved sister for her thoughts . . . big and small . . . boring and dynamic . . . light and dark. I love you. G.*

I felt abandoned when she left. To steady my nerves, I went outside to the long, open veranda and sat in a chair where I could smoke, a thirty-year-old habit. Opening my journal, I wrote my first entry.

Day one: WIRED! Agitated, afraid. Thinking about a piece of glass I just saw on the ground. Perhaps some pain would center me.

Rising from the chair, I walked behind the building to where the sliver was still lying in the grass and picked it up. It was about two inches long and an inch wide; not big at all. I tucked it into my pocket, closed my journal, and went inside.

Day three: 9:00 p.m. Jumped up out of a sound sleep still dressed. The Creature woke me. It was screaming. It occurs to me that Mattie's voice silences the Creature better than any other. I spoke with her at 2:00 p.m. this afternoon on the phone. The Creature just reminded me about the glass. I wish Mattie were here.

All day, except when I spoke to her, my thoughts have been about death. I want to walk. I want to lie down. I want to stay up but need to sleep. Want to read but don't want to risk either sleeping or being quiet reading because that's when the Creature talks to me.

My first week in the hospital was filled with tests. I had my blood drawn and was physically poked and prodded and verbally grilled by my three doctors, whom I dubbed the Three Musketeers. My primary doc was Dr. Alexander Vuckovic, the ultimate top dog at the Pavilion because he is its medical director. He'd graduated from Notre Dame and Harvard, where one of his specialties had been psychopharmacology—figuring out which medication would free me from the Creature and my erratic mood swings.

Dr. Vuckovic had a few distinguished gray hairs near his ears mixed with his otherwise black hair. I guessed he was about my age but looked youthful because he is a runner. From our first meeting, I felt comfortable with him, although I wasn't ready yet to tell him about the Creature or the piece of glass I was hiding.

Day four: I felt good this morning when thinking about my kids, but at 4:30 p.m. I felt sad, scared.

My thoughts: trying to figure out how to die without hurting kids. I tested the sharpness of my tweezers and saw how far I could get my veins to protrude pinching them. The Creature is mumbling, mumbling.

I put the blinds down in my room so no one could see me. Just want to be alone. Don't want to be here. But don't want to be home feeling like this. Where is a safe place for me?

3:36 a.m. Just woke up scared. I believed the Creature was in my bathroom. Turned on lights, left my door open after waking up the night nurse, who told me to return to my room.

I soon settled into a routine and found that I felt comfortable at the hospital. Everyone around me was crazy, too, and that was incredibly liberating! I could just be myself without any pretenses.

I began hanging out with a young man, Jeff, who liked to stay up late, just as I did. We would watch television and laugh hysterically. It was our mania, and our manic moods seemed to be in sync. Maybe mania is like when a group of women live together and all of them start having their periods at the same time. When I mentioned I was staying up late to one of the Three Musketeers, he said, "You do realize, Jessie, don't you, that getting only two hours of sleep at night isn't normal?"

I replied, "But I'd rather be up at night than during the day."

"Why do you prefer the night?" he asked.

"That's when it's quiet and I can draw and write," I replied. "Both are more important than sleeping."

Day five: Dr. Vuckovic has discovered if he sees me at nine in the morning, I am groggy and don't lie to him so well. I may tell him about the piece of glass I have hidden but not about the Creature.

I went to get my blood drawn. I don't understand people who find blood ghoulish. Bloodletting is the essence of pain flowing away from us. There seems no better way.

When I wasn't being tested, I attended classes about mental illness and medication. The doctors told me they were going to wean me off some of my meds and start me on others. Within days, I felt as if I were coming down with the flu, but the nurse told me it was because I was being taken off Lexapro, my antidepressant. I didn't believe the nurse, because I was certain it was the flu. I felt so exhausted, but after a while I began to feel better. It was a reminder that my body was being held hostage by my brain.

4-13-04: I woke up quite happily, with a shit-eating grin plastered on my face, until a girl I don't know asked me how long I've been here and I went blank. I felt panic and suspected she was a spy. She's evil. Paul came over next, but I thought he was Jeff. Maybe they are related to the Creature. Now Paul is gone, and I feel relief all the way down to my bones because it takes so much effort to "chat." Many brunettes here. Why? Are they spies?

I'm outside smoking, and someone's Prius just sits in the lot, a replica of Glennie's, making me sad. Same color, too. I need to read or watch TV to escape this panic or whatever it is.

Black ink slowly sliding down, covering the sparking glass.

Fell asleep while reading at about 10:00 a.m. Slept until 6:00 p.m. Woke at 6:15 and went to see Dr. Vuckovic. Fell asleep again after that until 9 something. Must be the meds. Woke around 10:30 p.m., called Mattie and Calen.

Glennie called to say she'll come up this weekend. Can't wait. Want to shower now. It's midnight but the shower is scary. The exit light outside my room seems to turn on and off at random. I wonder what it is out there. Will I be able to live without my shadows? Joan, the third Musketeer and house manager at the Pavilion, made me give her my piece of glass. I had decided the glass couldn't hurt me so I was sharpening it a bit by rubbing it against a rock, and she saw me. I don't like not having it. I don't like thinking I can't escape this horror when I need to.

Mood: a small roller coaster. Thoughts: happy, panic, sad missing Calen, Mattie, Sander, and dogs. Energy: restless, high, and low.

4-14-04: 1:04 a.m. Went out for a smoke, exhilarating at first, wind blowing, a loud drip from the gutter, puddles of moonlight gleaming orange off the wet asphalt. Wanted to jump, run, yell, and then three lights caught my eye. I think they're lit windows from the old trailer down the abandoned road near the hospital. My heart jumps, and fear floods through me. I can see the trailer, where a curtain is pulled back, slightly, as if someone is staring at me from the dark interior. I stub out my smoke, return to my room; fear still in my veins. I hope it passes soon.

I picked up my cell phone and just saw 1:11 a.m.—a power number—and was very happy to see the bright lights, but then the lights went out and the number vanished. The exit sign outside my room just went out, too. Another sign? An evil one? I don't know why *it would go out so quickly on the heels of 1:11 except that maybe it wants me to exit, as the exit sign was blinking and pointing to the door before it went out.*

It's 4:03 a.m. now. I need to go to sleep.

Woke at 7:30 a.m. and hit snooze until 8:00 a.m. John drove me to Dr. Klepser's office for a physical . . . I took 10 mgs of Valium to help me get through an MRI, and I did it! Can still feel my high, but now it's annoying because it seems like it's under a coating of peanut butter.

I finally told Dr. Vuckovic about the Creature, and not long after that he informed me of his diagnosis. He said that I had bipolar I disorder with psychotic features and a tendency to a mixed state. The "psychotic features" tag was new to me. Figuring out exactly what was wrong with me had been difficult, but that's true about everyone who has a mental illness. There are no blood tests or so-called biomarkers that can indicate the presence of mental illness. Instead, psychiatrists make a diagnosis based on "clusters of symptoms." They compare the symptoms you describe and the symptoms they observe with the canonical symptoms of bipolar disorder or schizophrenia and figure out where your symptoms fit best. My symptom clusters included erratic mood swings and the Creature.

I asked what "psychotic features" meant, and Dr. Vuckovic explained that, in addition to mood swings, a person with bipolar disorder can often hear or see things that aren't real. In other words, the Creature.

Apparently, Dr. Vuckovic didn't believe the Creature was real. Of course, the Creature wasn't in his brain, was it?

Dr. Vuckovic said the most dangerous time for me was when I was in what's called a mixed state. Generally, whenever I became depressed, I felt so exhausted and hopeless that I didn't want to do anything. Nothing. During a mixed state, a person can feel sad but also extremely energized, and that's why it's so dangerous. The bottom line is that when I was in a mixed state I actually had enough energy to kill myself.

Dr. Vuckovic began giving me two new medications: Geodon, an antipsychotic, and Neurontin, an antianxiety drug. He also gave me another antidepressant to replace the Lexapro and good old lithium, which was the only mood-stabilizer drug that I knew of that actually helped prevent suicide.

4-19-04: I am at war with the Creature. It was still this morning until I walked past a column of people: the woman out front looked into my eyes and said, "AB2." I nodded to her, although I don't know what that meant.

The Creature stirred as I asked myself what AB2 must mean. I turned back toward the Pavilion and spotted a plastic name tag caught in a bush. As I was picking up the name tag, I told the Creature to shut up in a loud whisper. I noticed Gretchen sitting close by and was overcome with embarrassment because the Creature told me that she'd heard me and she thought I was telling her to shut up and therefore the Creature didn't have to.

Did she hear me?

I went inside and asked Donna—I can't really remember her name because I don't like her—to come speak to me because of what happened. She told me to go ask Gretchen if she had heard me tell the Creature to shut up.

The Creature began taunting me and suggested that the AB2 woman had put a curse on me. I went outside, but Gretchen was gone. I do think Marianne is evil—I can't remember what happened next except I was making toast in the kitchen (I had told someone I would) and I started shaking harder and hyperventilating. I began hitting the back of my head, on the left side, with my hand to silence the Creature, who was screaming at me, but it didn't work so I kept hitting myself and I told Marianne and asked her for help.

I told her about AB2, too, and the curse and Gretchen. She calmed me down and gave me a Neurontin and my Geodon fifteen minutes early and said the weekend visit by Glennie might have overstimulated me. I don't agree and am worried the Creature will never be quiet . . . I realized the Creature lives in my brain near my right sphenoid sinus that almost killed me way back in 1985. Maybe he was trying to kill me then. Maybe he took over after I overdosed on amphetamines that caused intense pain when I tried to kill myself. Maybe the Creature is Brad, who could be dead. If he's not dead, maybe he wants me to die.

One afternoon, I went outside to smoke. I liked smoking. Someone said smoking—the nicotine—breaks down the medication and makes it act faster. I don't know. I began thinking about James, and I felt his presence. I felt he wanted me to kill myself so we could be together again.

After two weeks, Dr. Vuckovic sent me from the Pavilion to a women's house, where I was assigned a cramped upstairs room. I could hear the other women in the room beneath mine laughing and talking. I panicked, packed my suitcase, went downstairs, and reached over the half door into the medication room, where I grabbed a bag of meds that were in a white bag and newly brought over from the Pavilion. The woman in the meds room tried to stop me, but I was quick. I ran from the building. I was planning to hop on a bus whose route came by McLean, but I didn't have a destination in mind. I would look for somewhere peaceful where I could take all my meds—commit suicide—and be done with this particular life.

Before I could get outside, the house's director stepped in front me and ordered me to stop. She was no-nonsense: she demanded to know why I was fleeing and within an hour had arranged for me to go back to the Pavilion.

I stayed there a week before being sent to Waverley House, an older three-story Victorian house on the edge of the hospital campus. I liked it much better there.

I also had something to look forward to. My children were coming to see me.

Mattie had been angry when Calen was at McLean's Appleton House because I'd refused to let her visit him. I thought that seeing how sick some of the patients at the hospital were would be too frightening for her. But she was older now—and besides, I was eager to see her and my boys.

May 3, sometime early in the morning, at Waverley House. I'm anticipating my three kids' visit, but I had a horrible nightmare about my mother's dogs attacking me—her Bouviers!!

When I awoke, I felt the Creature stirring for the first time in a long while since I've been taking my new meds. I felt him roll, saw his eyes, and looked away. I will never describe his eyes—too terrifying and would give him more power. I never, ever, ever will. What did the Creature say? I can't remember now. I have no memory, not long-term, short-term, or even 30 seconds ago. It must be the meds.

I'm hanging in here . . . I have survived 50 years . . . but at this moment, staying here another week seems like torture. I want to go home, or at least to Glennie's. I feel like a freak to the outside world, more than before I arrived, because now I have been to a mental hospital and that will forever be part of my history. It will follow me everywhere.

Jessie Close, mental patient.

I read a passage in a book about mental illness. I am underlining it for my family. How do you explain . . . what's going on inside us? This passage referred to how important it is to treat the mentally ill as people first . . . What the authors of this book don't get is that—in my experience, anyway—when you've lived on the edge your entire life, it's actually comforting and fun to be in the company of others like yourself. The torture being here is not in living with others who are mentally ill, it's the physical inconveniences. I think a hotel would be less expensive and a hell of a lot cleaner and more comfortable.

My mood changed on the morning when my children were scheduled to arrive. I was frightened about what they might think. How they might be disappointed in me. I gave each of them hugs and broke into a huge smile when they appeared. The four of us went outside and sat at a picnic table to talk. After a while, Calen announced he was going to Appleton House to see some of the residents there whom he still knew. Sander didn't talk much. Mattie chatted nonstop. I asked her how she was doing living with Noah, her dad. When I'd first gone into the hospital, Mattie had stayed with Suzy Nixon, but Noah had insisted that he was going to take care of his daughter. I'd agreed to let him and his girlfriend move into my house so Mattie could stay in her own room. Mattie and Noah seemed to be developing a better relationship. A silver lining, perhaps?

After a half hour, I began to feel uncomfortable, because talking to my own children required more work from me than talking to the other residents of Waverley House. At that moment, I realized it was dangerous for someone to stay in a hospital for a long time. You feel safe, and before long you are lulled into thinking that you can't survive if you ever have to leave such a regulated environment.

May 6: Implements of suicide should be made available to the general public. We should make it easy. I think this planet heaves a sigh of relief every time a human leaves it.

May 16: Not writing every day now. Feeling aggressive, too much energy, want it to stop. Can't enjoy anything, picture taking handfuls of pills or drinking booze to stop the pushing and rushing inside of me. Yesterday I woke up with a headache, the left side of my head, where the Creature lives—had a sharp pain behind my right eye and I was scared a migraine was coming on. My agitation was HUGE— I wanted to kill something, smash something, to release the tension. Then I switched, became teary, depressed, but still couldn't relax. I got angry when a staff member asked me what I was upset about. I yelled at her . . . I switched, like it always happens, a few minutes later. I took a Neurontin to help me calm down. It did take the edge off. I picture my dead body, my family around it, as a deterrent. This is what's called rapid-cycling—no shit!

May 17: I awoke feeling great, but soon felt dark again, aware that my life has been a joke, all except my babies. I see no way out. Inside my head, where no one can see, my moods and thoughts are spinning, changing every minute.

May 18: I spoke with a young man who lives here. He happened to be sitting outside at the picnic table when I came out feeling despair. I told him how I'm losing my life with this medical "cure." I don't know how to balance creativity and art with stability and medication. He told me that maybe my children will become my art, that they are my gift to the world. I sobbed and sobbed at such a beautiful thought coming from a suffering young man. I must learn how to have creativity without lapses or relapses. The meds even me out but drain me of creativity of thought.

May 21: The evening of the 19th found me laughing almost hysterically, yelling, in a mood where I would have punched someone out if they'd spoken to me negatively. The next morning, I was so heavy I couldn't get out of bed. My mood was low, discouraged, the kind of mood that would keep me in bed all day if I was home. My vision had spots in it, still does. The day was an enormous effort to get through. It was difficult to walk and talk. The evening didn't see any change. I was so agitated I could hardly stand it. My body was humming, lights were too bright, noises too loud. There was something in the basement that scared me. I called Calen, who calmed me down a bit. The Creature was in hiding. Thank God! I was scared the Creature would team up with the bad presence in the basement. They were alike. Then there would have been two of them. I sat outside for smokes with other inmates and ended up laughing genuinely, not hysterically. Glennie invited me to see her, and I will take a train down.

I always felt calmness when I was with my sister. There was centeredness about her—that Yankee rock-solidness. My sense of family was now rooted in my own children, but my past sense of family was rooted in her, my mother, and my siblings. Not my father. I loved being with my sister because I felt safe with her.

May 24: On the train heading back to the hospital from Glennie's. Noise from the people around me is REALLY getting on my nerves: points out how quiet I am on the outside of myself, how loud I am inside. It's all too much. This train was delayed for an hour.

I didn't think I'd make it. I thought I would have to take a cab because I was so agitated. I took a Neurontin, walked outside in the sunshine, and when I came back into the station I sat as far away from people as I could.

Then a black woman wearing red and pulling a red bag sat next to me. It was a sign that I would be all right. Standing on the platform, not with the woman wearing red, was torture. The platform across from us was filled with people. I felt relieved when their train came along and blocked me from seeing them.

The platform on my side was very full. I was incredibly relieved when the train showed up, grateful that the car I stepped into was upholstered in red. God keeps showing me red, even out the train window.

I fell asleep, woke with a stiff neck, but calmer. I still smile and feel comforted when I see red or see 11:11 or 1:11 or any of the power numbers. I like knowing God is with me.

I'm very tempted to walk off the train somewhere other than Boston. I think the feeling would be one of freedom and adventure. No one watching. I want to be rid of the feeling that I'm being watched. I took another Neurontin because my thoughts were racing, uncomfortable. I saw red, and it really helped.

My behavior was appropriate to waiting for a train. No one could see my agitation. No one knew I was one of them—the mentally ill who walk among them. Every day.

I am back in Boston now. Heading back to the hospital, where people will watch me again and will know that I'm different.

CHAPTER THIRTY-ONE

Part of me wanted to go home. Another part wanted to live forever in the hospital, where I felt safe and could have the people who love me come visit. The part that wanted to return home won. I missed my children. Although I was still having suicidal thoughts, I decided to keep them to myself. I wanted Dr. Vuckovic to discharge me. I'd spent five weeks at McLean by the time he decided it was okay for me to leave. However, he felt I was fragile and didn't want to risk having me relapse in faraway Montana. The two of us met with Glennie, and she agreed to let me move in with her for two weeks before heading home.

I was excited to see my sister and Woofie, the white terrier mix that I had brought with me back east. Having a dog with me helped calm my nerves, and Woofie had been a perfect angel on the flight from Montana. Glennie owned two white terrier mixes, too, so I knew that she wouldn't mind boarding Woofie, although my dog did get us both in trouble for chewing the cord of Glennie's kitchen phone in half. My mom also had a white terrier, and so did my dad. All of them were from the same breeder, a woman in McAllister. That's why we called them McAllister dogs.

Glennie was busy when I moved into her house, so I kept occupied playing with Woofie and taking photographs. My sister had just finished shooting a film called *The Chumscrubber*, in which she portrayed a mother whose son had committed suicide, an irony that wasn't lost on either of us.

On May 30, 2004, I wrote in my diary that I felt fine when I first woke up. The Geodon, my antipsychotic, had silenced the Creature. I still knew it was there, but it had gone into hibernation. My Wyoming friend

Betsey Greenwood was back east on business, so she took the train from New York to visit me for the day. Glennie invited both of us to a neighborhood barbecue that she was hosting down the road. At one point, Betsey agreed to walk me back to Glenn's house because I was so out of it from my medications. Rather than going to bed, I spent twenty minutes searching the room for "a little gift," courtesy of Woofie. I could smell it but couldn't find it, which I noted in my diary.

It's the end of the day, and I feel overwhelmed and keep having suicidal thoughts. I know where there is a swimming pool just down the lane, and I could take an overdose and go there and drown. It isn't the Creature telling me to do it. Rather, it is a vision that keeps replaying over and over in my mind. I keep seeing myself dead, and I look free. I took a Neurontin, which helped, and then I took my bedtime meds, which helped even more. By the time bedtime rolled around, I was almost happy, except that I was having an olfactory hallucination. All I could smell was dog crap. Everything smelled like it. Why does my mind torture me this way?

Glennie invited me to accompany her to a screening in Manhattan of *The Stepford Wives*, which was about to open nationally. Before the screening, there was a party in an expensive restaurant. I didn't notice the restaurant's name, but the interior was a maze of screens covered in black fabric, and it was *noisy*. After a few minutes, I couldn't take it. I bolted for the exit but couldn't find it. I felt trapped amid those screens, but finally spotted a door and burst outside, gasping for air. I needed a cigarette and found a stoop where I could sit and smoke. I allowed myself to look up at all the tall buildings, and as I was doing that, I spotted David Shaw, Glenn's future husband, coming toward me. He'd left the party, too, and sat on the lower step of the stoop near me without saying a word. Maybe he didn't know what to say. Maybe he knew there was no need to say anything. Just having him there calmed me, and I felt grateful for his compassion. After a while, the rest of the partygoers came outside, and we walked to the theater. By the time we got there, I couldn't wait to get back to Glennie's country house that night.

After spending two weeks at Glenn's, I boarded a flight to Denver with Woofie in my arms. Calen was waiting at the airport baggage claim. He'd driven to Boulder to visit his brother at college and had decided to pick me up at the Denver airport. It was a ten-hour drive to Bozeman, but neither of us was dreading it. I wanted to be with him, and I could tell something was bothering him. I also wanted to talk to him about something that was bothering me.

What am I supposed to do now?

Doctors had given Calen a long list of instructions when he'd been discharged. They'd told him that he needed to stick to a daily schedule, which included getting plenty of sleep. Mania and depression often seep in when you get tired. The doctors had suggested that he walk away from other people the moment he began feeling overwhelmed. I'd seen him abruptly leave the room while my father was in midsentence. Dad had hurried over to tell me, thinking he'd said something wrong. I'd assured him that Calen had simply been following doctors' orders.

I'd left the hospital with my own list of dos and don'ts. I'd also been given Dr. Vuckovic's private telephone number so that I could check in with him once a week. But there were questions that doctors couldn't answer about returning home from a mental hospital—questions that only someone who had already walked in those shoes could tell me.

"Was coming home scary for you?" I asked as we were exiting the airport's parking lot in his truck. The Rocky Mountains rose before us, and I could still see snow on their peaks, even though it was nearly summer.

He thought before answering and said, "Yeah, Ma. It still is at times."

Calen lit a cigarette, and I bummed one. For a while, we traveled in silence, enjoying the open road, smoking and being together.

"What's bothering you?" I asked.

"It's Katie," he replied, referring to his girlfriend.

He said Katie had accused me of faking my mental illness to get attention. She'd said I'd checked myself into McLean because Calen had been there. I was a copycat.

I felt as if someone had punched me in the stomach. *Why would Katie attack me?* Even worse, did my own family, friends, and others who knew me in Bozeman think I was faking it? My already fragile confidence began to crumble. What is it about mental illnesses that makes people suspect you're faking it to get sympathy? If I had been diagnosed with breast cancer and gone into a hospital, no one would have thought I was simply trying to get attention. I would have been greeted when I got home by well-wishers, cards, flowers, and a refrigerator crammed with home-cooked meals wrapped in aluminum foil. Instead, I was going to be met with skepticism and disgust. I imagined the whispers that would be mouthed behind my back: *"Why doesn't Jessie just snap out of this and pull herself up by her bootstraps? I've been depressed, and I didn't need to go to a hospital because of it."*

"Do you believe I'm faking it?" I asked.

"No, Ma," he said. "What Katie said was stupid."

As we drove north, Calen told me that his relationship with Katie was in trouble. All relationships are tough. Throw two people with mental illnesses together, and it becomes a formidable challenge. Add a third, and we became quite the trio.

The closer we got to Bozeman, the more anxious I started to feel. But as soon as we pulled into the driveway at my house and I saw Mattie, all thoughts of Katie disappeared. I gave my little girl a big hug. Noah and his girlfriend had already packed their bags and were ready to leave, but I wanted to thank them for moving into my house so that Mattie could stay in her own bedroom while I was in the hospital. I put my arms around Noah for a hug and spontaneously began to cry. He pulled away. I was stunned and felt rejected. He clearly didn't want me hugging him. At first, I thought it was because his girlfriend was there, but after thinking about it I decided it was something else. I was one of those "crazy" people now, because I had been in a mental asylum. That hurt.

Mattie quickly filled me in on everything that she was doing while helping me unpack. She was a teen excited about life. I was almost fifty-one, feeling beaten and weary because of life.

That night, a girlfriend stopped by and we spent more than an hour sitting in the kitchen talking. During that entire time, all she did was talk about herself. I'd been gone for seven weeks, but she hadn't asked me one question about what had happened at McLean. It was the elephant in the room. I realized that this was how things would be. Awkward.

Because of my medication, the Creature remained dormant, but I still found myself being tormented by frightening thoughts and imagined fears. I became convinced that an evil spirit lived in our basement. It was real to me, and I refused to go down there.

Another night, as I started to go upstairs for a shower, I suddenly froze. Something evil was waiting for me upstairs. I instantly retreated and telephoned Glennie, breaking into tears as soon as she answered. She reassured me that it was okay, there was nothing upstairs waiting to pounce. She began coaxing me up the staircase, one foot in front of the next, while talking to me on the phone.

Getting well was not an overnight process.

I felt better on Geodon than I ever had and was confident I would eventually be able to live a "normal" life. But that's not what happened. I began feeling exhausted. When I became feverish, I thought I might be getting the flu, but I couldn't sit still or bear to lie in bed. The muscles in my arms and legs began cramping.

The Neurontin that I was taking to control anxiety didn't help. When my hands developed a Parkinson's-like tremble, I made an appointment with my family doctor, and she decided to run a series of tests, including a creatine phosphokinase (CPK) test to see whether my muscles were leaking creatine into my bloodstream. A CPK test helps doctors discover whether muscle tissue is being attacked or damaged.

As soon as my doctor read the results, she slapped me into the Bozeman hospital. Normal CPK values range from ten to 120 micrograms per liter. Mine were at seventeen thousand per liter! I had developed neuroleptic malignant syndrome (NMS), a life-threatening neurological disorder that was being caused by Geodon. My muscles were literally coming apart. The medicine that was helping me feel normal was also killing me.

My family doctor called Dr. Vuckovic, and he immediately took me off Geodon. I couldn't stop crying in the hospital. Why was getting well so difficult? Because of my raging CPK count, I wasn't weaned off Geodon. Dr. Vuckovic had to order me to stop it cold turkey, and that night in the hospital was one of the most horrific nights of my life. I'd only suffered shaky hands and afternoon nausea when I'd stopped drinking alcohol. Stopping Geodon made up for it.

I became physically ill, but the most terrifying reaction came after I finally drifted off to sleep. A monster, with blood dripping off his huge fangs, appeared at my bedside, glaring down at me, jarring me awake. My entire body was shaking. The monsters hiding in my basement were running free in my head.

I once read a quote by US Supreme Court justice Anthony M. Kennedy, who wrote in a legal opinion: "It must be remembered that for the person with severe mental illness who has no treatment, the most dreaded of confinements can be the imprisonment inflicted by his own mind, which shuts reality out and subjects him to the torment of voices and images beyond our powers to describe."

What I saw that night is beyond my powers to describe. From then on, I tried to sleep with my eyes open, because I was afraid to close them.

Alarmed by my poor physical health, Dr. Vuckovic asked me to return to McLean for a tune-up. I felt like a failure: physically ill and mentally drained. I knew I couldn't make the trip east on my own. Although Mark and I had separated, he offered to take me. He told my friend Liza that he still loved me. I was too ill to resist, and I still loved Mark, too. I'd come to believe that love isn't something that only happens when you live together; in fact, not living together seems to renew stale love.

Our flight back east was a blur, although I remember hanging onto Mark's arm as we moved through crowds at the Denver airport. It was as if I were lost in a netherworld. At any second, I could turn a corner and see reality, only to have it wash away seconds later. Monsters.

McLean Hospital had a room with two beds ready and allowed Mark to stay in the room with me. Love renewed itself; he was my husband, after all. We made love, cuddled, slept in one of the beds. Dr. Vuckovic spoke to Mark as though he were my husband; I'm not sure what they talked about, but Mark was sympathetic to my plight.

Dr. Vuckovic replaced the Geodon with clozapine, a different antipsychotic medication. I began feeling better but was concerned about getting sick again. Everyone reacts differently to antipsychotics. What might kill one person saves another. Seven days after checking in, I was discharged. My new drug was working.

Mark got me back to Bozeman, and we talked about whether the two of us should make another try at saving our marriage. He began coming over, mostly to make love, but that didn't last.

Having gotten me through one of the worst periods of my life, Mark had simply had enough. My moods still ran me, and he saw that. Even though I wanted to be with him, I also realized that having a man in my life was a complication that I couldn't handle. I needed to focus on my health, and that meant staying away from men and booze. I began attending AA again.

Calen and Katie also broke up. I'd liked her when she'd first arrived because I thought she was good for Calen, but it was time for her to leave.

My mother told me that the tenants renting my old farmhouse on the edge of Bozeman were moving out. It was where I'd raised my boys and written my novel. After Tom and I divorced in 1989, my mother and Glennie had purchased the farmhouse from us and brought in renters. I loved that house and asked if Mattie and I could move into it. Mom said yes, but Mattie didn't want to move. I had uprooted my daughter from one house to another ever since she was a baby, and she wanted to continue living in downtown Bozeman until she graduated from high school.

I decided to bribe her with what had become the coin of the realm in the Close family—a dog. Mattie had asked me for a Chihuahua puppy, so I agreed to get one if she moved with me into the farmhouse. We picked out a Chihuahua-Yorkie mix from the classifieds. Our new addition was named Cinder-Ellie. I got the better end of the deal; Mattie was in school all day while I was at home with Cinder-Ellie, and our new pet became my constant companion. Somehow, her name evolved into Snitz.

Mattie and I settled into the farmhouse. Tom had converted a chicken house behind it into a one-bedroom apartment, so Calen moved in there to be nearer to us.

I was getting better, but I began rubbing my skin again, picking at it until a bloody scab developed. Dr. Vuckovic asked whether I was also cutting myself.

I said, "I don't do that!"

I was insulted, but he explained that rubbing my skin raw and cutting myself are forms of self-mutilation. Dr. Vuckovic suspected comorbidity— more than one illness. It was possible that I had a "cluster B personality disorder"—most likely borderline personality disorder—as well as bipolar I disorder with psychotic features.

Geez. Wasn't one diagnosis enough? I looked up "borderline personality disorder" and noted that two symptoms of the condition are impulsiveness and an intense fear of abandonment.

Dr. Vuckovic then threw me a curveball. He said my rubbing and picking might not be related to borderline personality disorder at all. It could be stemming from trichotillomania, which usually manifests itself in hair pulling.

What was he telling me? That I had three illnesses?

I began to relax when I remembered what one of his colleagues at the hospital had told me. He'd drawn a line on a board and written the words *mental illnesses* underneath it. That line represented hundreds of different disorders, many of which bled into each other. It was a stew pot. My brain was somewhere on that line.

Apparently realizing how hopeless this all sounded, the good doctor reminded me that I was doing remarkably well. I was able to live on my own and function at a high level. It was time for me not only to understand my limitations but also to take charge of my life. It was time for me to control my illnesses—whatever they were or however many there were—and stop letting them control me.

CHAPTER THIRTY-TWO

I was sober now and stable, but I missed the old me, the wild, manic me, who enjoyed drinking in bars and driving too fast down the highway, causing the car to jump from the road into an open sky. I was in mourning, at least in the beginning, for my old self. I also mourned the loss of Calen as he had been before he became sick. Calen had been a bright spirit, charming and energetic, hard to pin down. Everyone loved Calen; he had been the leader of the pack and the charmer of teachers and friends. Who was he now? Who was I?

With each day that passed, I mourned less and less. I slowly realized that Calen and I were the way we were meant to be. I accepted the fact that I had a severe mental illness and that it would always be part of my life because it was part of me. The medications helped control my moods. The pills caused the Creature to remain in hibernation. I wished like hell the pills would kill him, but I could still feel him there and knew he always would be present. Thankfully, his terrifying eyes were closed.

There was no medicine that could protect me from the everyday realities of life, however. There would be days when I would feel sad, just as everyone else does. There would be days when I would feel happy, just as everyone else does. What made my days different was that I had to be on guard for red flags that could warn me that I was about to slip into a manic spell or slide into a bottomless depression. I couldn't risk either one. I couldn't risk waking the Creature. I had finally arrived at a place where I took no chances with my medication. I knew I had to take it no matter what, no matter how good I felt. I had plenty of evidence of what would happen if I stopped.

I had always been a night person. I understood that the word *lunatic* is heavy with stigma, yet I liked that word. I liked how it sounded rolling from my tongue. I'd read that it came from the old French word *lunatique*, which is from the Latin word *luna*, meaning moon. The ancients used to believe that the moon causes intermittent insanity in some people. Perhaps it does.

I have always felt a pull from the moon. I have stood outside on warm summer Montana nights and stared at that glowing orb and felt its influence over me. Even in winter, I could feel the full moon before seeing it creep from behind the snow clouds.

I was drawn to the night for its promise of solitude, for its lack of confusion. It's possible to feel the quiet at night. But my therapist had told me that I could no longer stay up late at night. I'd promised him that I would turn off the light at 1:00 a.m., and I kept that promise. I would switch it off and then switch it back on. Technically, I wasn't lying, but I was manipulating my environment, and for a while I thought I was being clever.

When I finally realized that staying up late every night put my mental stability at risk, I began taking my medication at 7:00 p.m. and going to bed at ten. It wasn't easy, but I was changing habits. I began to learn to write in the mornings and afternoons.

Recovery comes in baby steps, and when Tom invited me to have dinner at his house with his wife, Kathleen, a woman I genuinely liked, I felt anxious. I still loved Tom and probably always would, but I'd given up any thought of our ever being together. I wasn't anxious about being jealous because he had moved on. I was anxious about being in any social situation, even with people I knew well. I still had feelings of inadequacy and failure, not because I had done anything wrong but because of my broken brain. They call it self-stigma!

Tom invited me because Calen had a new girlfriend, and he wanted all of us to meet her. One of Calen's previous girlfriends had introduced them. She was already there when I arrived at Tom's house. Megan MacNichol was tall, strawberry blond, and cute. I liked it when we shook hands, because she had a confident grip. During dinner, I learned that Megan had her own recovery story.

Four years earlier, on March 12, 2002, Megan had been a carefree twenty-year-old Montana State University student driving home for spring break. Her best friend, Rebecca, was with her, along with Megan's yellow lab, Baker.

It was snowing hard, and the girls got caught in a Montana white-out while driving on a two-way road. Snow was blowing so hard and so thick that it became nearly impossible to see. Megan had slowed her car to fifteen miles per hour when a truck burst through the white sheet, coming right at her. It was a semitrailer going sixty miles per hour. Megan didn't have time to react. It slammed into her car, completely crushing the driver's side, pinning Megan inside. Neither Rebecca nor Baker was harmed, but Meagan was bleeding and pinned behind the steering wheel.

Six hours passed before a rescue team cut her loose. It was a miracle she survived. From her waist down she was cut and bruised. Her legs were shattered, but the worst damage was her traumatic brain injury. She was unconscious.

Scans showed that parts of her frontal lobe had been so severely injured that doctors warned her parents she might have a completely different personality when she regained consciousness. She might have little or no memory of the collision or her past. But when she opened her eyes, she was the same person she had been.

Megan went through dozens of painful surgeries and endless hours of grueling physical therapy. She had to relearn basics, such as how to swallow and walk. She fully recovered physically, but her TBI had permanently altered her brain, leaving her with limited short-term memory. She had to keep her daily routine written on a whiteboard so she could remember the rudimentary steps she had to follow each day, such as dressing herself, taking her medicine, and feeding her dog.

When I left dinner that night, she said, "I have trouble remembering names, but I will remember yours, Jessie."

I almost cried.

My children were moving on with their lives. Sander had finished college, and Mattie was graduating from Bozeman High School. Seeing her walk across the stage wearing her cap and gown made me cry. I'd been unstable and drunk much of Mattie's childhood. Yet Mattie had matured into a thoughtful and beautiful young woman who was wise beyond her years. I think she had coped so well partly because she always knew, no matter what I had said or done, that I loved her.

All relationships become journeys. I had made peace with myself and accepted my mental illness. I still needed to make peace with someone else: my father.

I'd always felt like an inconvenience to him. With therapy, I'd realized that my feelings of insecurity and abandonment were deeply rooted in my father's decision to go traipsing off to Africa, leaving all us children behind to be raised by MRA nannies. He had put my mother into the impossible position of having to choose between being with him and being with us. There was a gulf between Dad and me, and even as an adult my conversations with him were always uneasy.

I blamed him, in part, for my inability to sustain a stable relationship with a man. Parents are role models, and my father had been an absentee dad because of his own wants and needs. I felt strongly that his wants and needs had not included me.

Had my father remained a distant figure, it might have been easier for me to accept his coldness. But after my father and mother settled in Big Piney, Dad had become a fabulous grandfather. He'd been eager to entertain his grandchildren, to take my boys fishing, and regale Mattie with stories about his adventures in Africa. He showed each of my children the love and attention that he had been completely unable to give my siblings and me.

It was time for me to confront him and to put my anger and resentment to rest. I decided to do it when he came to visit me in Bozeman.

Like most of us, my father didn't like being criticized. His introspection was done in private, and as soon as I started talking about MRA and how I'd felt abandoned, he let out an irritated sigh, like a child waiting for a school bell to ring so that he could run outside for recess.

He believed he'd already acknowledged his "uselessness" by admitting in his autobiography that he'd felt more comfortable in a Zaire operating room or traveling with President Mobutu than being with us children. He'd published his mea culpa, writing:

Only years later did I realize that simply being there for your own children is more important than solving their problems. It takes time and hard work to become a doctor; fatherhood, I learned so late, requires at least equal, and often more, effort and perseverance.

Announcing in a book that you were a lousy dad is different from coming face-to-face with those you've hurt.

Dad sat quietly while I released my pent-up feelings. When I was done, he gave me a look and said, "Jess, how many times do I have to say I'm sorry? Do you want me to walk around on my knees and say 'I'm sorry' over and over until my knees are bloody?"

"Won't you just say you're sorry without being all dramatic?" I demanded.

"Okay, I'm sorry, and this isn't the first time I've said that, either, I know that."

I realized at that moment that I had to forgive him. There was no point in remaining hurt. He was who he was. It was as simple as that. A few days later, Dad sent me a note. It had always been easier for him to write about his feelings than to speak about them. He said that he was proud of my children and of me. He said he loved me.

Perhaps because I was by then a parent and realized how I had harmed my own children because of my weaknesses, that note melted any coldness in my heart toward him.

My father needed cataract surgery, and afterward he developed a staph infection in that eye. It was incredibly painful and also required him to wear a black eye patch to cover his now blind eye. In his early eighties, despite the pain and his failing health, he continued to make house calls around Big Piney, but only to the elderly and dying. My dad loved being a small-town doc. He also loved buying things. He had to have the best of everything, whether it was snow blowers or Dunhill pipes.

On January 15, 2009, Dad fell out of his bed late one night. A young woman, Deanne, whom my parents had hired to cook and look after them when necessary, rushed into his room and helped him back under the covers. A few moments later, Deanne heard him go into his bathroom. Then she heard him yell, "Oh, my God!" and heard the sound of his body hitting the floor.

Those were his last words.

A colon and prostate cancer survivor, he was dead at age eighty-four from a massive heart attack. I comforted myself by knowing that he had gotten all three of the things he had wanted when it came to dying. He had wanted his dogs with him—check; he had wanted to die at home—check; and he wanted his death to come quickly—check. He was as lucky in death as he had been in his adventurous life.

The New York Times, the *Los Angeles Times*, *The Lancet*, and the London *Times*, as well as the local *Kemmerer Gazette*, which served Big Piney, published flattering obituaries. *The New York Times* described my father as "a man with a take-charge personality" who had played a crucial role in helping stop the spread of the deadly Ebola hemorrhagic fever in 1976, when it broke out in central Africa. My father had used his position as President Mobutu's personal physician to fly investigators from the US Center for Disease Control (as it was then called) into the epidemic's hot zone.

My dad had told us about an African priest who had wiped the bloody tears from a woman's face with his handkerchief while she was dying. He later used that same handkerchief to wipe his own face. That priest had died ten days later. My father had been there in the thick of the outbreak without any show of fear.

All of us gathered in Big Piney for Dad's funeral. We agreed this would not be a religious affair, although we did have one short prayer. Dad's experiences with MRA had turned him against organized religion, although he had started going to church later in life and frequently prayed with his patients.

All of us wanted to play a role in his memorial service, which we called "In Celebration of the Life Force That Is Doc." Glennie became our director, helping choose which role each of us would perform. Mom picked out a reading from *Winnie-the-Pooh* that she wanted to read because my dad loved that story and often would quip: "Silly old bear!" quoting Christopher Robin.

Two doctor friends were chosen to speak about his professional accomplishments. Sandy, along with Tina's son, Keir Campbell, gave eulogies. I joined Tina, Calen, Sander, Mattie, and Glenn's daughter,

Annie, in reading a poem entitled "The House by the Side of the Road." Our "adopted" brother, Tambu, flew in from his Sacramento home to participate too.

Glennie and Sander chronicled my father's life through family photos and his favorite music in a professional video that they later posted on the Internet. It's difficult for me to cry in public, but each time I watch the video alone on my computer I sob for him.

Among the most poignant words were those spoken by Keir, who said:

What are we to say of such a man? To him, too much introspection was "navel-gazing." A solid person was a "good egg." And his mantra before entering any fray was "Do your homework."

A complicated simple man. A technophile who opposed gadgetry in medicine. To him nothing could replace hands-on care.

He was a man of indomitable will, an indefatigable fighter of great integrity, empathy, and tenderness. He loved unconditionally the underdog.

When I think of him words come to mind like: endurance, persistence, optimism, self-discipline, and compassion.

To say he touched people's lives is an understatement. He inspired and motivated and changed lives. He saved lives. He rallied those around him to fight with and against what he saw as humanity's true enemies: sickness, oppression, apathy—and any kind of bullshit!

If we are to take anything from his full and wonderful life, it is to view the world with your eyes as open as possible. And when you encounter apathy, cruelty, sickness, and pain wrapped in a cloak of normalcy, complacency, or bureaucracy, do not step aside. Do not walk past. But stand and confront it. Oppose it. Attack it. With persistence and optimism, grit and heart.

During Dad's funeral, I scanned the crowd of about two hundred people. There were prominent doctors alongside Wyoming cowboys with mud on their boots. My father had fallen into the habit of not charging people who couldn't afford his services. Many of the sick whom he visited were grateful because they had no insurance and little money.

They repaid him with home-cooked pies, casseroles, and enduring friendship.

After the funeral, our family retreated to my folks' compound, where Glenn's husband, David, set off fireworks, lighting the sky with burning stars that burst and then faded.

I was happy that Dad and I had made our peace.

Life continued after my father's death, as it always does. I was not surprised when Calen announced that he had asked Megan to marry him. Both had tried to return to college but simply couldn't. My mom had built Calen a studio behind his remodeled chicken-house apartment. It was large enough for his woodworking tools, an airbrush booth, and a painting room. He began making furniture and continued painting.

Megan had been angry and bitter after her accident because she'd felt it had cheated her out of her future. She told me that she'd changed her mind after she got a job at Eagle Mount, a therapeutic program in Bozeman, where adults and children with physical disabilities can swim, ride horses, camp, fish, canoe, and take part in other Montana outdoor activities. Megan began to see herself as an "ambassador of hope" who could relate to kids with disabilities in ways that others couldn't because of her accident and brain injury. Both she and Calen found silver linings in their challenges.

They were married on September 4, 2011, at a historic site called Springhill Pavilion, a dance hall that dates back to before Montana was a state and was featured in the movie *The Horse Whisperer*, which seemed fitting because Megan worked as an equestrian therapist.

I made it through the wedding without becoming too anxious or feeling the need for a drink, even when they had their Champagne toast. I was becoming more and more comfortable with my emerging new and sober self, and now that Calen and Megan were married, Mattie was going to be leaving for college in Portland, Oregon, and Sander was settled in San Francisco, I decided it was time for me to go to the home where I had always felt the most secure—my Mouse House, by North Meadow Creek in McAllister.

I was about to start yet another new chapter in my life, one of sobriety, hope, and purpose.

CHAPTER THIRTY-THREE

Glennie was on the phone, asking if I would "out" myself.

My sister was following through on the desperate plea that I'd made a few years earlier, when Calen had suffered his mental breakdown. I'd begged her to do something about the stigma that Calen—and now I—faced.

As always, Glennie had gone about it in her own way and on her own schedule. Her research had eventually led her to Fountain House, a Manhattan peer-to-peer program whose roots date back to the 1940s, when a former patient at a state hospital and a hospital volunteer began meeting in a New York YMCA with other people who had been hospitalized for mental illness. They believed they were capable of helping each other and didn't have to depend on "the well" for their care. Initially, the group called itself WANA, an acronym for We Are Not Alone. Over time, that group became Fountain House and helped pioneer what's known as the "clubhouse" approach. Fountain House programs are governed by its members, all of whom have mental illnesses. In addition to providing housing, food, and educational and vocational programs, Fountain House also oversees a unique job-sharing program. Knowing that some members want to work but can't handle the strain of a full-time job, Fountain House pairs members who perform the same job during different hours. For example, four members might share a forty-hour-per-week job, each working as many hours as they can tolerate during a day. Fountain House gives people who are often viewed as outcasts a home in a supportive environment where their voices can be heard. It gives them dignity and purpose.

Glennie had learned about the Child and Adolescent Bipolar Foundation, too, and had met Garen and Shari Staglin, a California couple who'd founded the International Mental Health Research Organization after their son, Brandon, had become ill.

Having familiarized herself with the mental health landscape, Glenn decided to found a nonprofit organization to specifically target stigma and misunderstanding. She named it Bring Change 2 Mind. The hitch was, however, that she wouldn't do anything unless Calen and I were willing to get involved. I agreed, then Calen agreed. We really didn't know what we were getting into.

Glennie wanted to do something to help. After she telephoned Calen and me, she began to raise money to create a website and pay for the filming of a public service announcement that would be aired on network television.

Glennie planned to officially launch Bring Change 2 Mind in October of 2009, and she wanted us to participate.

"I want you to be part of the PSA—if you are willing," she said, explaining that the advertisement would be released on launch day. When she added that Ron Howard had agreed to direct the spot, I was doubly impressed.

"Are you kidding?" I replied. "I'll do whatever I can to help!"

Glennie arranged flights for Calen, Mattie, and me, as well as Snitz, who had become my service dog, accompanying me everywhere. We flew from Montana to New York, where we stayed at Glennie's house. Annie joined us. With the exception of Sander, this was clearly going to be a family affair.

Ron Howard was to shoot the PSA inside Grand Central Terminal's massive main concourse in midtown Manhattan. It is a beautiful, majestic place with an ornate 125-foot-high ceiling. When you look up from the lobby floor, you can see a sky that has been painted "backwards." The artist had wanted to show what God sees when he looks down at the constellations rather than what we see when we look up at them.

Glennie had hired a New York advertising agency called the Watsons to write a script. They'd entitled it "Change a Mind About Mental Illness." The PSA would begin with a commuter train pulling into the station and hundreds of passengers scurrying through the crowded lobby on their way to work. One by one, individuals dressed in white T-shirts would appear in the crowd. The first couple would be Shari Staglin and her son, Brandon, who had been a student at Dartmouth College in 1990 when he'd first become ill. Written in blue letters on Shari's T-shirt would be the word MOM. Brandon's T-shirt would bear the word SCHIZOPHRENIA.

Another couple in white T-shirts would appear next, coming down steps inside the station. Their shirts would read POST-TRAUMATIC STRESS DISORDER and BATTLE BUDDY. From there, the camera would pan to commuters exiting a train and a young couple wearing shirts that said BETTER HALF and DEPRESSION.

During the entire PSA, singer John Mayer's haunting song "Say" would be heard in the background, with its beautiful chorus, "Say what you need to say," being repeated over and over.

Glennie and I would appear in our white shirts about two-thirds through the PSA. Glenn's shirt would state SISTER. Mine would be printed with the word BIPOLAR.

I'd been on movie locations before to watch Glenn, but this was different because I was going to be in front of the camera. As we were waiting for our turn to be filmed, I became aware of the noise. Sounds were echoing inside the cavernous lobby. Calen heard them, too. Repetitive and loud noises make me anxious, and the throngs of people, the electricity of the crowd, the chatter and excitement and activity started to get on my nerves. I slowly backed away from the action and found a deep armchair, where I curled up with Snitz and calmed myself.

Glennie found me when it was time for us to be filmed. She shot me an encouraging smile. "You ready?"

My heart was pounding, but she seemed completely at ease, of course. She was in her element.

I think most people believe they can be actors, but I soon found that it is much more difficult than it appears. Our scene called for Glennie and me to walk toward the camera while a swarm of commuters hustled around us.

Everyone took their places, and the camera assistant snapped the clapperboard. I was so nervous that I wasn't certain whether Ron Howard yelled out "Action" or something else.

Glenn quickly breezed through her line: "One in six adults has a mental illness."

But I hesitated when it was my turn.

Ron stopped filming and told me to relax. We tried it again. Glenn nailed her line, and I got the first few words of mine out before going blank.

I felt like an idiot. No, more than that: I was an idiot! I had literally hundreds of people watching me, all knowing that I was an idiot. But Ron just smiled and assured me that actors forget their lines all the time. He was wearing a baseball cap and blue jeans, and that helped. He wasn't at all pretentious.

We tried another take and then another, but with each one I kept getting more and more frustrated. When I did remember my line, I either wasn't smiling or I looked terrified.

Taking out a marker, Ron wrote my lines on a piece of cardboard that he taped directly under the camera. Now all I had to do was read while walking forward.

Ron started filming as Glennie and I began. I heard Glenn say, "One in six Americans has a mental illness." Looking at the sheet on the camera, I said, "And we face the stigma that can be just as painful as the disease itself."

I'd done it! I felt great!

Ron asked me to do another take. He suggested I take a big breath and slow down when I spoke.

I was confident now. We did it again. This time he suggested I accentuate the words "and can be just as painful" for emphasis.

We did it again, and this time Ron was happy.

For me, the difficult part was over. Now I got to see my kids. Ron shot footage of Calen standing between Mattie and Annie with his arms around them while passengers slipped past in the lobby. Calen's shirt had the word SCHIZOPHRENIA marked on it. He'd actually been diagnosed with schizoaffective disorder, but we didn't think the public would care about such a subtle distinction in a very short scene. Naturally, Mattie's said SISTER and Annie's said COUSIN.

The PSA ended with Glenn putting her arm around my shoulder while giving me a loving look and saying, "Change a mind about mental illness and you can change a life."

In the final seconds of the PSA, the white T-shirts in the film changed colors so that each of us became just another face in the crowd. The message was clear to me: we are all people, those who have mental illnesses and those who do not. We are your mothers, fathers, brothers, sisters, friends, children, grandparents, neighborhoods. We are you.

On launch day, the major networks began airing the PSA, and Glennie and I did a media blitz. We appeared on *Good Morning America*, *The View*, and MSNBC's *Dr. Nancy*. Of course, Glennie was incredibly at ease during these interviews while I was nervous. This was all new to me. It was a long and exhausting day, but when it ended I felt incredibly grateful. Glennie had kept her promise to me. I'd told her that I would never expect another birthday or Christmas present if she did something to fight the stigma of mental illness. But she does still give me presents.

There was only one thing that bothered me when I watched the PSA. I was disappointed when I saw myself.

The only mirror I had inside my Mouse House was mounted at eye level and showed nothing below my face. I hadn't realized how much weight my medication had caused me to gain. I looked huge, especially compared to Glennie.

I'm not a vain person, but we all like to look our best, and historically I'd always been the knockout Close girl, the California beach-blond beauty. Of the three Close sisters, I had been the one who once had gotten an offer to pose nude for *Penthouse* magazine. But I was no longer the svelte vixen who had been able to seduce men with a smile. I decided I would begin exercising and eating more healthful foods. I was also determined to stop smoking.

When we returned home I thought about my weight and my mental health, and I realized that my appearance was a reflection of a conscious choice I was making. I was choosing clarity of mind over vanity. I was choosing to be chubby and mentally well rather than skinny and sick.

I put a photograph of my old self by my mirror. Yes, I had been thin when that snapshot had been taken. But I also had hollow eyes that seemed to scream in pain. The photo reminded me that there are more important things in life than your appearance, especially when your sanity is at risk.

Because Glennie had spent years dealing with the paparazzi and media, she had been worried about what might happen once I "outed" myself. There would be no turning back, and she had been correct. My phone had started ringing almost immediately after launch day. I heard from my girlfriends, who all complimented me. I also got a call from a director of a mental health group who asked if Calen and I would give a speech at a convention in Nevada. A few days later, another mental health group in Canada invited us to speak. Glennie and I began getting invitations, too, including one in Washington, DC, on Capitol Hill.

Pamela Harrington, our BC2M executive director, asked me if I would write a weekly blog for the Bring Change 2 Mind website.

I decided to be gut-wrenchingly honest when I spoke and when I wrote. I was going to slit open a vein—literally speaking. I wanted to be frank about myself, my problems, and my recovery, because honesty would be the only way I could help others.

Sitting at my computer, I began writing about my descent into madness and found myself typing these words:

Before I was properly diagnosed in 2004 and given the right medications, I left a flattened path of houses, cars, and husbands in my wake. I honestly don't know how many cars I've traded in. Once I learned about balloon payments I was all over it. Houses were more trouble to get ready, and inevitably, once they were cleaned up and ready for the marketplace, my mood would change and I'd want to stay. Unfortunately, the real-estate agents wouldn't see it that way. I moved Mattie and myself twelve times in eight years. Now I watch *House Hunters* on television.

But husbands were the most trouble. I went through five. (It's easier to keep count of husbands!) Three of them told me, "I just can't take this anymore," and two died many years after we divorced—James, a Vietnam vet, by suicide and Brad, a major druggie, by heart attack. So now that I've passed the husbands quota (and now that I don't get manic or drunk anymore) I live with only my dogs. Any correlation you may make is strictly your own!

There are some avocations you choose in life. There are some that choose you.

I would use whatever writing and speaking skills I had to fight the stigma of mental illness. Glennie had asked me to "out" myself, and I was determined to do it in as big a way as I could.

CHAPTER THIRTY-FOUR

My new sobriety and mental stability came with feelings of guilt and regret.

Looking back, I could see how bipolar disorder and alcoholism had caused chaos not only in my life but in my children's and husbands' lives as well.

Every morning when Calen and Sander had been young, I had promised myself that I would not scream at them when they were getting ready for school. But as I remember it, I screamed every single morning. Bipolar disorder is not a buzzword for "calm."

Because my boys went to boarding schools during their early teenage years, they had been shielded from the worst of my alcoholism. Little Mattie hadn't. When my boys had returned home during summer and holiday breaks, I'd set no boundaries. I smoked weed and drank with them and their friends. I'd been the cool mom, but in reality I'd been the mom who'd put my children in harm's way.

The only stability in their lives had come from their fathers.

I needed to repair the damage I had done, but I wasn't certain how. As fate would have it, an opportunity surfaced when I received a call from Gayle Johnson, an official at Sound Mental Health, a mental health services provider in Seattle, Washington. Gayle said her nonprofit group held a gala each year to showcase its treatment programs and raise money. She wanted to focus on the ways families had successfully dealt with mental illness, and she thought having my children and me onstage would draw a crowd.

Gayle was determined to show that people with mental illness have many faces—not just those you see homeless on the streets. Many of those faces look like me and you and our family members.

I agreed to speak to my children and ask if they were willing to participate in the gala with me. I assumed Calen would, because we had done speeches together, and I thought Mattie would, because she had appeared in the public service announcement. The only question was Sander—and he agreed to join us in Seattle.

The gala was being held in a downtown hotel ballroom, where there were seats at dinner tables for several hundred people. I trusted that whatever my children were going to say would be the truth and that I was ready for whatever would unfold—or so I told myself.

After dessert and several awards to local advocates were distributed, the four of us stepped onto a raised platform, where four chairs were set for us at a long table covered with a blue tablecloth. We took our seats, and I clutched my dog, Snitz, in my arms as a spotlight came on and blinded our eyes.

I had told Gayle that none of us wanted to give a long speech. Instead, I suggested that since family was the theme of the night, why not let the audience listen in on our family discussion? Each of us would speak for a few minutes, then we would question each other. It was risky because it was unscripted, but that is what we did.

Calen described his break with reality and what it felt like to be lost in a confusing and terrifying delusional world. At one point, he addressed the audience directly, asking them to be kind and supportive to someone who finds himself or herself in the midst of a mental breakdown. He emphasized that underneath the shell is a person of worth and value.

Sander spoke next:

The more sensitive a person is the more susceptible that individual is to mental illness. It seems like a sick joke that our universe plays on us as children that the more it allows a person to see the world's beauty and deep connectivity, the more difficult it becomes for that person to maintain good mental health. In our culture, we tend to treat those dealing with that trade-off with a fierce double standard. As long as they are sharing with us beautiful insights into humanity, we will love and cherish them as heroes, but if they fall into substance abuse, depression, psychosis, or any other form of mental illness, we tend to say, "It's not our problem." Classically, these individuals with mental illness are artists, musicians, writers, etc., but of course, they come in all sorts, unsung or not. These people tend to add value and meaning to our lives. At their best, they are the types who make us laugh and cry, to learn and to take risks and to love. They are brave, and it angers me that as a society, we abandon them when their skies darken.

I thought I was going to cry.

Mattie told the audience that she was five years old when she realized for the first time that her mommy was different from other mommies.

"My mother was standing in the kitchen after dinner, crying and doing dishes. I pulled my little purple stool to the kitchen sink and asked timidly why she was so upset. My mother sighed and said, 'I'm bipolar, little one.' That was my first introduction to an illness that would dominate much of my life. I knew something was wrong because of Mom's behavior, but my mother's illness was never talked about and in many cases never looked at inside our family."

Not everything that was said by my children was easy for me to hear. They told the audience that I "was not a constant" in their lives. I was undependable. I was not a role model. Some days, they would feel loved, and on others they would feel that I was distant and cold. This was difficult for them to understand, and it was hurtful to them as children. At times they had felt abandoned.

I didn't like hearing that, but I knew it was true.

Mattie and Sander spoke about how scary it had been when Calen had gotten sick, and Calen talked about how frightening it had been for him to feel so lost and alone.

It was deadly silent in the cavernous room while my children were speaking. No one was glancing at a cell phone or fidgeting in a chair.

Near the end of their comments, my children reached a unanimous conclusion. They said that the reason Calen and I had recovered was because we had gotten excellent care—and they were grateful that our family could afford it, because many can't—but just as important, we had come together as a family. Despite our faults—especially mine—we had clung together. If I hadn't been able to provide one of them with comfort when I was at my worst, one of their siblings had. We had walked through hell, but we'd done it together.

I was the last to speak, and I admitted my failures. I had always felt abandoned by my own father, and in my own way, during my sickest times, I had abandoned my children. "I honestly don't understand how it is that my three children have turned out so well," I said. "They are strong and wonderful, and all I can say is that you can still love when you are suffering, no matter what, and love them I do."

My voice caught in my throat. Speaking through my tears, I continued, "I love them more than anything in this universe."

Perhaps it was fitting that our family had a cathartic moment during such a public forum. Like strangers who bare their souls to each other on a long airplane flight, the four of us used our appearance onstage to discuss what had been so difficult for us to share privately.

I would be lying if I wrote that all the issues between us melted away that night. Some of the hurts are deep cuts. Those will take time. Perhaps those hurts will never fully heal. I understand, because it took me years to reconcile with my father.

After the spotlight was turned off and everyone had gone, I went to my room, and for the first time in years I felt good about my relationship with each of my children. Not only was I becoming whole again, so was my family.

CHAPTER THIRTY-FIVE

When I heard the news, I laughed.

Dr. Deborah Levy, the director of McLean Hospital's Psychology Research Laboratory, called to tell me there was a mouse scampering around in a laboratory that had been designed to replicate genes found inside Calen and me.

I am not only living in my Mouse House, I have also helped create a Close family mouse!

The story of how my family got our own genetically engineered mouse begins when Calen first arrived at McLean Hospital in 2002 and agreed to donate blood as part of a research project. During a genetic analysis of his blood years later, doctors discovered that one of his genes had an intriguing mutation. Instead of having two copies of certain genes, which was what most people had, Calen had four copies. More important, one of the genes with four copies was not just any gene. It was one that scientists suspected could play a role in mental disorders.

Dr. Levy had spent much of her career searching for genetic links that could help explain the origins of schizophrenia. Energetic and brilliant, she is not only a researcher but also an associate professor at Harvard Medical School. She called Calen and asked whether he would undergo more tests and whether he would give her his permission to contact other members of the Close family about donating a blood sample for her research. She was especially interested in my blood because I also had been diagnosed with a mental illness.

Everyone agreed to participate: my children, my siblings, Tom (Calen's father), and my parents (Dad was still alive at the time). When the genetic results were analyzed, they revealed two things. First, I was definitely the daughter of Bill and Bettine Close, which automatically disqualified me from appearing on one of those awful "guess who's the father" tabloid television shows.

Dr. Levy and her research team also discovered that Tom and eight members of the Close family had the correct number of genes, but Calen and I did not. We had the exact same mutation, which meant that I had passed it to him.

Dr. Levy said this discovery was important because one of the mutated genes is the gene that codes for an enzyme called glycine decarboxylase, or GLDC, which breaks down glycine. Having extra copies of this gene could cause glycine to break down faster than it does in other people's brains. Without enough glycine, an important brain receptor known as the NMDA receptor won't function normally. Neuroscientists believe that a malfunctioning NMDA receptor is associated with psychosis, especially schizophrenia.

Dr. Levy and her team assured me that our mutated gene could be a "smoking gun" when it comes to figuring out the underlying causes of our mental illnesses. This is because no one really understands the genetic underpinnings of serious mental illnesses. Doctors rely on clinical assessments of the symptoms they observe and have to decide if an individual has schizophrenia, a mood disorder such as bipolar disorder, a smattering of both—as in schizoaffective disorder—or severe depression.

Finding an intriguing errant gene could be the first step in understanding the biology of mental illness and, many researchers hope, eventually finding a cure.

Dr. Levy asked whether Calen and I would be willing to undergo additional tests if she could get funding for research from the National Institute of Mental Health. We said yes, and after several years and endless paperwork, Dr. Levy finally got the green light. Ten years after Calen first donated his blood at McLean, we were about to become guinea pigs.

Mattie and I were the first to go to McLean for a full week of tests, including brain-imaging scans (MRIs)—which I hated because of my claustrophobia—various cognitive tests, brain-wave tests (EEGs), clinical interviews, and movement disorder assessments. Both of us also had a plug of skin removed from our derrieres.

Dr. Levy sent a sample of our DNA to the laboratory of Dr. James Lupski at the Department of Molecular and Human Genetics at Baylor College of Medicine in Houston to be "sequenced." The skin cells from our butts were converted into neurons by Dr. Kristen Brennand, a stem cell biologist at the Icahn School of Medicine at New York's Mount Sinai Hospital, who is an expert at developing in vitro models of schizophrenia.

But of the many scientists working on Dr. Levy's research project, it was Dr. Uwe Rudolph, the director of the Laboratory of Genetic Neuropharmacology at McLean, who got the best assignment. He genetically engineered a mouse with the same gene mutations that had been found in Calen and me!

I call that mouse the Close family mouse.

After Mattie and I finished at McLean, Calen and Sander arrived for a week of tests at the hospital and went through the same procedures, including having skin samples taken from their butts. The reason Mattie and Sander were included was that we are all in the same family, yet Mattie and Sander didn't have our mutated genes.

After the doctors collected all the data from the four of us, we moved to the next stage of research. Every two weeks big boxes were mailed to Calen and me containing doses of liquid medicine prepared by McLean Hospital pharmacist Laura Godfrey. We were supposed to drink one dose after each meal at specific intervals for a total of six months. Some of the doses contained glycine powder with lemon flavoring. The other doses were a look-alike, taste-alike placebo. We didn't know which doses contained glycine and which were the placebos, but the first time we took glycine, Calen and I both became nauseated and vomited. This meant that we were getting too much glycine, so the amount was cut back until we had no side effects. Because this was a "blind" study, we weren't supposed to be able to tell the difference—but trust me: after you have vomited because of something you drank, you don't forget. Calen and I could both tell which drink contained the glycine, because it was the only time we had any side effects; that did not happen on the placebo, no matter how high the dose got. To be fair, we both got a lot better on glycine, and once the dose was adjusted we had no side effects. That made it worth it. The amazing thing is that we persevered. That is something we are very proud of. It turned out to be a good thing, because we got so much better on glycine. It was particularly hard for me, because I got glycine first, then I had to get through thirteen weeks waiting for the time when I knew I would get glycine again.

I was proud that both of us completed the first twelve weeks. After that came the six-week "open label" phase, during which the study was no longer blind and we were told that we were getting glycine. Dr. Levy and her team began increasing our glycine intake while giving us periodic blood tests and checking our weights. The results showed that our symptoms improved when we took glycine, but not when we took the placebo. Dr. Levy said this was significant because it demonstrated that our mutation was "medically actionable," which meant the deficiency caused by the mutant gene could be at least partially corrected by taking glycine.

Dr. Levy and other researchers have found mutated genes in individuals with mental illnesses, including those with schizophrenia, bipolar disorder, autism, epilepsy, attention-deficit/hyperactivity disorder, and intellectual disability. Sadly, she and others still have a long way to go before they understand the mysteries of our brains. This is just one reason it is so important to support biomedical research. There are so many individuals and families who would benefit from such an investment.

Although the clinical tests are finished, Calen and I are still being studied. With the support of NIMH, we are continuing to take glycine to see if it will enable us to cut down on the pharmacopoeia of meds that both of us are now taking. If it does, glycine (or something like it) in pill form may become available for others with similar mutations.

I'm really proud that my family has played a key role in helping scientists pinpoint a possible cause for severe mental illnesses, but I'm also happy that Dr. Levy got us involved for several reasons. The fact that my children, siblings, parents, and Tom immediately agreed to donate their blood and be tested says a lot about their characters. I've been frank in this book about my family's disputes and our different personalities. But when it came to helping Calen and me, and possibly others, they were "all in."

There's another personal reason why these tests mattered. When you have a mental illness and people are talking behind your back about how you are "crazy," when everything in the media suggests that persons with mental illnesses are dangerous and scary, and when you realize that sometimes you can't trust your own brain to interpret reality for you, you often feel as if it is all your fault, that somehow you are to blame and that you are responsible for your wild mood swings or for seeing things that aren't there or hearing sounds that no one else hears.

I've made mistakes in my life, and I am not trying to avoid taking responsibility for many of the foolish decisions I've made, but what Dr. Levy's research documents is that it isn't just all me. I have mutated genes that affect my brain, just as some people are born with a physical challenge. And despite our illnesses, Calen and I were able to make a unique contribution to medical science. If we had decided not to participate, no one would ever have known that our mutation was actionable and we would not have experienced the benefits of glycine.

Why some individuals develop a mental disorder and others don't remains a mystery. Uncle Seymour had one, so do I, and so does Calen. Other illnesses have been mysteries to us, but scientists have solved them. I hope someday we will not only find ways to help those of us who do have one but also find a cure. I hope that day comes soon.

CHAPTER THIRTY-SIX

I'm finally home after giving two speeches with Glennie and spending a week at McLean Hospital for more testing with Dr. Levy. Two weeks gone was too long, but I'm basking in the quiet once again. Last night, after finally getting home, I lit a fire in my woodstove, then walked outside my house in the dark and, with the creek as background music, reacquainted myself with the stars and the moon. The sweet, thick scent of smoke from the chimney wrapped around me. The huge snow-covered mountains looming above me glowed in the moonlight. I was home.

This past summer saw a new roof on my house. I can't help but think in metaphor—that the new roof represents me, a woman who went from being severely mentally ill to being capable of living life almost unhindered by my disorder. My old roof was growing lichen, and pieces of the dark green shingles blew off whenever a wind picked up, which is often. Now, with my new roof, I welcome and even challenge the wind.

I no longer have the constraints of living with a husband or children. My last husband, Mark, and I officially divorced ten years ago and we remain friends, and my three children are now gone from my home. I protect myself from alcoholism and bipolar disorder by—obviously— avoiding alcohol and taking my medications. But I'll always carry the shame of doing the things I did when I was drunk and unmedicated. I'll always question my diagnosis. I think questioning the validity of being mentally ill plagues everyone who's on the right meds and no longer feels symptoms. This questioning can lead to stopping medication unless you're very careful and compliant. Even after writing this book and reviewing everything that happened to me, as well as undergoing all the weeks of testing at McLean with Dr. Levy, I asked Mattie one night when I was feeling good if she thought I really was bipolar. She responded with, "Are you fucking kidding me?" So there's that!

I wouldn't mind being manic again for a day, manic without the ugly parts, but I never want to be depressed again. Losing mania because of fear of depression is a good thing. I don't know if I'd make it through another depression, and that scares me. I have so much to live for these days and have managed to carve out a really wonderful life for myself.

My dog pack is up to four after rescuing a rat terrier named Rosco. He is my problem child, having suffered three abandonments, but I love him and will stick by him. Snitz rules the roost as the alpha, and only, female. She is my heart's companion. She's tiny at seven pounds but forceful, loving, and stubborn. She accompanies me on many of the trips I take to speak. She sits on the various podiums and never puts up a fuss. Snitz seems to absorb the angst I carry when I'm out in the world. She is classified as my Emotional Support Service Dog and is allowed to travel on my lap everywhere. I am grateful for her.

My life has been filled with sadness and loss, but I don't concentrate on those things anymore—most of the time, anyway. I am alive. I have three wonderful children, I'm friends with my siblings and mother, and I have friends outside my family whom I cherish. What more could I ask?

I'm pleased to live alone, but there's more to it than that. I not only protect myself from my mood disorder by avoiding alcohol and taking my medication, I also respect my conscious decision to remain mateless. This really isn't much of a sacrifice, because I've had more relationships than most people have in three lifetimes. But I still look; I just don't touch. And I still feel great relief when I look around my home and see only my things. The specter of being involved with a man and destroying another relationship strikes fear in my heart.

I can only dream about what it would have been like to live my early years with treatment. I can pine and feel the grief that comes from losing so much of myself in this lifetime, but then I'm questioning what is. I'm questioning reality and my faith, refusing to see what's in front of my face. I'm grateful that we know so much more now and that people like Calen can get help early in their lives. I'm grateful to Glennie for her huge efforts to help end the stigma of mental illness, and I'm grateful to all the people with mental illnesses who have stood up to declare that they are ill in the face of such a stigma, both with and without the help of Bring Change 2 Mind.

But when all is said and done, it's been my mom, Moo, who has stuck by me, even in my absence. As a mother I know what it feels like to know that I did the wrong thing as far as my children are concerned. I know, as a mother myself, how she must have been tortured by our absence in her life with Pop but I also know now that during those times I was in her heart, 24-7. I have no doubt about that. When she was with me, I felt especially loved. She was a fun mom and a cozy mom, a mom who read to me and cuddled with me, who brought me trays with food when I was sick, and who loved to laugh with me. And she helped save Calen's and my lives with her unflinching generosity. Mom turned 90 this year. She's frail and wisp-like now but her eyes and Yankee chin still show her spark, her determination, her love. I believe that when we each get close to passing from this life it's the love we have nurtured in others that lights our way and makes our journey smooth. My mom will have a very smooth journey filled with extreme light. I love you, my Moo!

Resilience has allowed me to "put it all down," to put all to rest. The four stages of grief are Denial, Anger, Acceptance, and Advocacy.

Now, when the final page is written, I can close this book and continue advocating for the mentally ill. It is my heartfelt wish that all of you join me.

EPILOGUE
by Glenn Close

Jessie and I are in the wings of Roy Thomson Hall in Toronto, waiting to be introduced. We can hear the murmurings of the more than two thousand people who have come to hear us speak—the title of our talk is "Mental Illness: A Family Affair." Jessie has flown in from Montana, and I have flown in from Maine. It is April, often a difficult month for Jess—and for many who live with bipolar disorder—because it is a month of transitioning weather and light. While most of us glory in spring's rebirth, Jess and many like her battle the fearsome possibility of crippling depression.

Back at the hotel, Jessie had told me that she is not doing so well. It had been a struggle to leave her house, her dogs, and her tiny home-town and to make her way through several airports to Toronto. And she is hurting herself again—rubbing the skin on her arm until it bleeds. Even though she has fought to manage her illness for a good ten years, it can still be a daunting challenge. As we wait to walk onstage, I see that the fresh abrasion on her arm is hidden by a Band-Aid. In fact, both her arms are covered with white scars caused by similar self-inflicted wounds as well as by sores from a near-death reaction to a medication. Whenever I look at those scars, I am taken back to the little girl who stood in the hallway, hurting herself so many years ago.

In 2010, I cofounded Bring Change 2 Mind—the culmination of a journey I began when Jessie and Calen asked me to help do something to fight the stigma and misunderstanding surrounding mental illness. Before doing anything, I asked them if they would be willing to talk openly, on a national stage, about living with mental illness. Because it wasn't about me, the so-called celebrity, it was about them and our family together. Without hesitation, they said yes. They both admit now that they had no idea what they were getting into. Neither did I.

In the four years since Bring Change 2 Mind was launched, as the three of us have spoken across the country, I have witnessed a remarkable transformation in both Jessie and Calen. As they began to tell their stories, in speech after speech, on national television talk shows and in two public service announcements, they began to function better. They found their own voices, and they got stronger and more confident. We have since learned that all the research points to the fact that the most effective way to change people's attitudes about mental illness and their behavior around mentally ill people is for them to meet someone living with a mental illness and to hear that person's story. Becoming an advocate in order to help others can also result in significant recovery.

When Jessie told me in Toronto that she was struggling and hurting herself, my immediate reaction was, "Then tell them that. Let them know *exactly* where you are coming from. Start there." She blanched because she had never talked openly about hurting herself. It was a mortifying secret. I hoped that revealing her struggle and talking openly about it for altruistic reasons would help her heal. As we stood together in the wings, I didn't know if she could overcome her feelings of shame and distress, and it didn't matter. The truth is that she has been consistently brave, has done so much, and has come so far.

We are introduced and walk out onto the stage to a standing ovation. That is something new. Somehow, our message has preceded us. The word is getting out. Jessie leaves the stage and I begin:

"The real truth is that I'm here tonight as the warm-up act for my sister, Jessie. It is because of *her* that I am here."

I meant what I said. Jessie has grown into an extremely eloquent speaker. She is a natural. She is deeply moving in her authenticity and in her courage to speak about what makes so many feel isolated, full of shame and fear. It is her story that truly speaks to people. I went on to tell the audience about some of the characters in our family, setting the stage for Jessie. I also talked about how our family had no vocabulary for mental illness and at what cost, how vital it was for us to educate ourselves, and having the courage to start the conversation and provide support for our loved ones.

Jessie is very aware of the fact that she and Calen got help along the way, that our family happened to have the means to pay for stays at McLean Hospital and to help with ongoing support. The truth is that, no matter the circumstance, every family has its own particular quotient of pain. The question is, what do you do with it? Jessie and Calen are proof that, with help, those living with chronic mental illness *can* lead full and productive lives. Calen is seriously pursuing his art and is a married man. Jessie manages her world in a way that fulfills her and keeps her creative juices flowing. She is now a shamelessly doting grandmother.

That evening in Toronto, I end with a story told by Calen's wife, Megan. When she mentioned to her parents that a handsome young man had asked her out and that he had schizophrenia, they were horrified. When asked what had caused her parents to change their minds about Calen, Megan simply said, "They met him."

I turn and see Jessie waiting in the wings, smiling. Our eyes meet. Jess nods. She is ready. I turn back to the audience.

"Ladies and gentlemen...please meet...my sister...Jessie Close."

ACKNOWLEDGMENTS

I have a very long list of people to acknowledge; in fact, everyone in my life has made contributions to my life. But I must say the one who's been at my elbow throughout the writing of this memoir is Pete Earley, my cowriter, who came up with the idea in the first place and has taught me so much during the process of writing this book. My friends Nan, Bethany, Molly, Liza, Pam, Mike, Suzy, Dick, Leonna, and Kerry were always full of encouragement when I needed it, as were my three children, Calen, Sander, and Mattie, and my other three siblings, Tina, Sandy, and Tambu. A special thanks to Dr. Alexander Vuckovic for his dedication to keeping my demons at bay and to Dr. Deborah Levy who now knows me on a genomic level.

I'm thankful to Grand Central Publishing, and Deb Futter in particular, for believing in my story, to Dianne Choie, Grand Central assistant extraordinaire, and to David Vigliano, my literary agent, who found my story a home.

But the person who has had a huge influence on me my whole life, who has been instrumental in getting me well, and who not only personally stands up in defiance of the stigma of mental illness but also does something about it is Glennie—my sister, my friend, my advocate. Because of her cofounding BringChange2Mind.org, thousands have become aware of the stigma we put on ourselves when we're mentally ill and have been given the support we need to stand up tall. All together, thanks to Glennie, we have made headway into conquering the stigma and misunderstanding surrounding mental illness.

ABOUT THE AUTHOR

JESSIE CLOSE is an internationally recognized speaker, author, poet, and advocate for mental health reform. She lives with bipolar disorder in the foothills of the Tobacco Root Mountains outside Bozeman, Montana, with her Service Dog, Snitz, and three other dogs. She is the author of *The Warping of Al* (Harper & Row 1990), and she writes a regular blog for BringChange2Mind.org, an antistigma organization that her sister Glenn created at Jessie's request.

Jessie has received awards from the National Alliance on Mental Illness, the largest grassroots mental health organization in America with more than 600,000 members, and Mental Health America, the largest grassroots group of persons living with mental disorders. Along with her son Calen and sister Glenn, Jessie has also received the Jed Foundation Award, the McLean Award, and Research America's Isadore Rosenfeld Award for Impact on Public Opinion.

PETE EARLEY has penned thirteen books including four *New York Times* bestsellers. His book *Crazy: A Father's Search Through America's Mental Health Madness* was one of two finalists for the 2007 Pulitzer Prize in nonfiction. After fourteen years as a journalist, including six years at the *Washington Post*, Pete became a full-time author with a commitment to exposing stories about social issues. *Washingtonian* magazine described him as one of a few authors with "the power to introduce new ideas and give them currency" after he spent a full year inside a maximum security prison for his award winning book, *The Hot House*. When his adult son was diagnosed with a severe mental illness and arrested, Pete recounted his family's struggle in his book *Crazy* and became a tireless advocate for mental health reform, traveling to forty-eight states and multiple countries to deliver speeches about our troubled mental health system. A lifetime member of the National Alliance on Mental Illness, his book received every major writing award given by mental health advocacy groups. In addition to contributing articles to national publications, he writes an often-quoted blog about mental health.